ROUTLEDGE LIBRARY EDITIONS: RURAL HISTORY

Volume 8

ANTHROPOLOGICAL PERSPECTIVES ON RURAL MEXICO

ANTHROPOLOGICAL PERSPECTIVES ON RURAL MEXICO

CYNTHIA HEWITT DE ALCÁNTARA

LONDON AND NEW YORK

First published in 1984 by Routledge & Kegan Paul plc

This edition first published in 2018
by Routledge
2 Park Square, Milton Park, Abingdon, Oxon OX14 4RN

and by Routledge
711 Third Avenue, New York, NY 10017

Routledge is an imprint of the Taylor & Francis Group, an informa business

© 1982 and 1984 Cynthia Hewitt de Alcántara

All rights reserved. No part of this book may be reprinted or reproduced or utilised in any form or by any electronic, mechanical, or other means, now known or hereafter invented, including photocopying and recording, or in any information storage or retrieval system, without permission in writing from the publishers.

Trademark notice: Product or corporate names may be trademarks or registered trademarks, and are used only for identification and explanation without intent to infringe.

British Library Cataloguing in Publication Data
A catalogue record for this book is available from the British Library

ISBN: 978-1-138-89481-5 (Set)
ISBN: 978-1-315-11336-4 (Set) (ebk)
ISBN: 978-1-138-74372-4 (Volume 8) (hbk)
ISBN: 978-1-138-74375-5 (Volume 8) (pbk)
ISBN: 978-1-315-18161-5 (Volume 8) (ebk)

Publisher's Note
The publisher has gone to great lengths to ensure the quality of this reprint but points out that some imperfections in the original copies may be apparent.

Disclaimer
The publisher has made every effort to trace copyright holders and would welcome correspondence from those they have been unable to trace.

Anthropological perspectives on rural Mexico

Cynthia Hewitt de Alcántara

Routledge & Kegan Paul
London, Boston, Melbourne and Henley

First published in 1984
by Routledge and Kegan Paul plc
14 Leicester Square, London WC2H 7PH, England,
9 Park Street, Boston, Mass. 02108, USA,
464 St Kilda Road, Melbourne,
Victoria 3004, Australia and
Broadway House, Newtown Road,
Henley-on-Thames, Oxon RG9 1EN, England
Set in IBM Press Roman by
Hope Services, Abingdon, Oxon
and printed in Great Britain by
St. Edmundsbury Press Ltd, Bury St Edmunds, Suffolk
© Cynthia Hewitt de Alcántara 1982 and 1984
No part of this book may be reproduced in
any form without permission from the publisher,
except for the quotation of brief
passages in criticism

Library of Congress Cataloging in Publication Data

Hewitt de Alcántara, Cynthia.

Anthropological perspectives on rural Mexico.
(International library of anthropology)
Includes bibliographical references and index.
1. Ethnology — Mexico — History. 2. Sociology, Rural —
Mexico — History.   I. Title.   II. Series.
GN 309.3.M6H48   1984   306'.0972   83-21299

British Library CIP available

ISBN 0-7100-9923-1

*For Cynthia Parker Hewitt
and
John Pollock Barbour Hewitt
and their granddaughters
Rebecca and Adriana*

Contents

	Preface	ix
	Introduction	1
1	Particularism, Marxism and functionalism in Mexican anthropology, 1920–50	8
2	A dialogue on ethnic conflict: indigenismo and functionalism, 1950–70	42
3	Cultural ecology, Marxism and the development of a theory of the peasantry, 1950–70	70
4	Anthropology and the dependency paradigm in Mexico, 1960–75	97
5	Historical structuralism and the fate of the peasantry, 1970–80	131
6	Conclusions	178
	Notes	192
	Index	217

Preface

The work which follows, like the anthropological schools of thought with which it is concerned, has suffered a number of changes both in definition of subject matter and choice of methodology since it was first conceived in 1976. At the outset, it was to have been a discussion of changing levels of living and forms of livelihood in different regions of the Mexican countryside during the post-revolutionary period; and the raw material from which evaluation of change was to be drawn was nothing more nor less than the total body of available anthropological and sociological literature produced by observers of rural life from the 1920s onward. This conceptualization of the topic was ambitious, but did not seem methodologically impossible: at the suggestion of Rodolfo Stavenhagen, the better part of a year had already been invested in combing the libraries of Mexico City and Washington, DC for records of all studies, whether books, articles, or theses, concerned with rural Mexico; and the preliminary bibliography so gathered (and classified by geographical region) ran to almost a thousand entries. In addition, a first perusal of the material had already turned up a number of cases in which the same village, or region, had been studied and restudied over considerable periods of time by social scientists, and in which it should therefore be possible to count upon relatively reliable empirical data with which to sustain a discussion of local conditions varying in relation to the opportunities and constraints provided or imposed by the particular nature of insertion within a wider regional, national or international setting.

To carry this exercise a step further, very detailed notes were typed on two-row punched cards for ten of the cases characterized by substantial numbers of independent observations. Classified according to a comprehensive index of topics, information could then be retrieved through manipulating the border indexing system of the cards. Similarities with the Human Relations Area Files were not coincidental: at one point, the possibility of setting up some comparable bank of anthropological and sociological data on rural Mexico had indeed been considered.

The primary purpose of comparing information on levels of living and forms of livelihood in particular regions or villages over time was, at this early stage of the endeavor, to provide qualitative insights for planning. Such an interest was fostered concretely by the decision of the United Nations Research Institute for Social Development to deal sytematically (and cross-culturally) with construction of 'indicators of real progress at the local level,' setting out simultaneously from a re-examination and re-evaluation of instruments developed primarily for developed industrial societies by what had come to be called the 'social indicators movement,' on the one hand, and from field work (or analysis of field work) in Third World countries on the other. The original use which was therefore made of the body of indexed cards derived from studies and restudies of Mexican villages or regions during the post-revolutionary period was an attempted reconstruction of the course of change in ten cases, emphasizing not only broad socioeconomic trends but also the specific impact of those trends upon wellbeing.[1]

The discussion was made possible largely by the fact that by far the greatest part of all material related to the ten cases under consideration had been written by anthropologists working within a general framework of functionalism. Robert Redfield, Oscar Lewis, George Foster, Ralph Beals, Alfonso Villa Rojas, Sol Tax, Fernando Cámara, Edward Spicer, Charles Erasmus, Raymond Wilkie, Manuel Avila, and others who had participated in the studies upon which analysis was based, shared a theoretical understanding sufficiently similar to standardize certain basic categories of observation and to permit comparison of the factual content of each book without undue concern for variation in perception of reality. This is not to say, of course, that differences in emphasis did not exist; the argument which arose between Redfield and Lewis is so well known that it probably requires no further comment. Nevertheless, all authors were likely to cover much the same terrain in the course of their discussion, and in so doing to facilitate later extraction of comparable data which could be utilized to permit commentary upon the course of change.

The situation was drastically modified, however, when a much broader body of literature was consulted in an effort to extend the discussion of socioeconomic change in rural Mexico beyond the limits of the ten communities or regions originally considered in the UNRISD paper. It soon became obvious that much of the work which an empiricist might hope would provide information of a comparative nature

Preface

on the development of certain concrete phenomena over time, was in fact totally unsuited to that task. The passage of years between one anthropological or sociological observation and another marked not only the deepening of a process of change in the countryside, but also the evolution of theory; and the latter implied profound alteration of the very analytical categories through which scholarly observers understood reality. As a result, aspects of daily life given much importance in one treatment of a particular group or region might receive no mention at all in another. And one was then left with the basic question of whether the element observed in the first case had simply ceased to exist in the second, or whether its disappearance was rather an artefact of a changing anthropological or sociological imagination.

One answer to such a question might have been to assert the total relativity of all observation in the social sciences and thus to discard any possibility that the existing literature on the Mexican countryside could provide a coherent commentary on the course of change in the post-revolutionary period. A second was to suppose that evolution of anthropological theories guiding observation and analysis reflected real changes in the social universe of which the peasantry formed a part, and therefore was not irrelevant to an understanding of the changing livelihood patterns of the peasantry itself. It might, in other words, be necessary to elucidate the nature of peasant studies in Mexico before one could hope to contribute substantially to the modern history of the peasantry. Given the obvious interplay between the vision of rural life attained by social scientists and a consequent elaboration by nonpeasant groups of policy toward rural areas, this second argument seemed doubly interesting; for even if the changing theories elaborated by professional observers did not fully capture the varying circumstances of the Mexican peasantry, they did indeed influence the range of alternatives from which rural people ultimately had to choose in coping with pressures exerted by urban interests upon their livelihood.

Proceeding on the assumption, then, that one central element within any collective effort eventually to understand the changing situation of various rural groups would necessarily have to be an analysis of the evolution of non-peasant perception of critical aspects of rural life, the purpose of sifting through published literature on the Mexican countryside was redefined. Work was no longer oriented by interest in turning up comparable facts, as such, but rather by the hope of placing observations by students of the peasantry in categories which would permit comprehension of the epistemological structure within which their research had taken place. In so doing, the original goal of 'seeing' real patterns of change in the Mexican countryside was not abandoned; but it was recognized that the view would always be mediated through the eyes of non-peasants, whose particular urban experience and training, in interaction with the situation confronting them upon entering rural Mexico, determined the picture encountered thereafter by all later readers of their work.

Such a redefinition of research priorities required entrance into the realm of the sociology of knowledge — not by any stretch of the imagination a field in which this writer claims complete familiarity. At the same time, it required a commitment to embark upon a long-term investigation of the life histories of principal anthropological and sociological observers of rural Mexican society, for no one could pretend full understanding of the world view of the latter without a detailed consideration of the social and psychological forces shaping their choice (or perhaps it would be more exact to say their use) of paradigm. To guide this larger effort, the requirements of which amply transcended the possibilities of one person, however, it became immediately necessary to produce a preliminary 'history of ideas' — a kind of mental map with which to traverse the labyrinth of written observation on the Mexican countryside, permitting the tentative placement of key figures and works within schools, and a subsequent illustration of theoretical points at which those schools differed or converged. Without such a map, the lines of which could be corrected and the shading altered through discussion with others over the course of time, a common effort by social scientists to develop a deeper awareness of their own inherited ways of seeing peasant livelihood seemed virtually impossible.

The pages to come are therefore presented in the hope that they will provide part of the groundwork for a systematic analysis of peasant studies in Mexico. The *partial* nature of the contribution cannot be too greatly stressed: the reader is reminded that the effort is based almost entirely upon reference to published material, supplemented when possible by interviews or an exchange of written communications. It has not been informed by access to other sources, such as private correspondence or documentation in public and private archives, which would undoubtedly be of great value in gaining deeper insight into the social and political forces surrounding the practice of anthropology at different moments in the twentieth-century history of Mexico. And even within the universe of published anthropological literature, the election for discussion of certain authors or works, to the exclusion

Preface xiii

of others, has required the exercize of an element of arbitrary choice at once personal and inescapable.

To make the discussion feasible, in terms of space and disciplinary coherence, it has been limited to the general field of social anthropology; no systematic attempt has been made to deal with changing paradigms in history, rural sociology, or agronomy, although there can be no doubt that such an effort is necessary, and furthermore that it would provide a fascinating counterpoint to changes occurring within the terrain of anthropology. As peasant studies have become increasingly interdisciplinary, however, all boundaries between academic domains in fact have a tendency to blur. This phenomenon will be clearly visible in the final chapters of the book, where no understanding of prevailing anthropological paradigms could be reached without including reference to the contribution made by rural sociologists and economists to the intellectual heritage of anthropology.

It is a pleasure to acknowledge the invaluable support of Rodolfo Stavenhagen, who stood behind both the original project for UNRISD and subsequent financing for eighteen months (1977-8) by the Ford Foundation; Peter Cleaves, of the latter institution, whose patience though sorely tried was never lost; Raymond Buve, Benno Galjart and Adam Kuper of the Institute for Cultural and Social Studies of Leiden University, who saw the project through the Dutch university system and into the hands of Routledge & Kegan Paul. Indeed the real concern of Galjart for the development of the book had everything to do with its completion, and the interest of Kuper was most important in encouraging its ultimate revision for publication. Equally central to the entire endeavor was the constant support of Robert Wasserstrom, whose remarkable knowledge of the history of anthropology in Mexico was drawn upon any number of times. The presentation in print of Wasserstrom's reflections on the evolution of Mexican anthropology is an event to be awaited with great anticipation. The same might be said for the work of Robert Kemper, who disinterestedly offered this author much information gathered in the course of a parallel project on the social and intellectual heritage of anthropologists in Mexico.

A preliminary version of the manuscript was read and commented upon by Gonzalo Aguirre Beltrán, Lourdes Arizpe, Roger Bartra, Rodolfo Stavenhagen and Eric Wolf. Each gave generously of insights and criticism; none should be associated with the final interpretation presented herein.

The book stands, finally, as the product of dialogue with a singular

Mexican anthropologist, Sergio Alcántara Ferrer, whose concern for the future of the Mexican peasantry, as well as his conviction that anthropological knowledge must play an important part in making that future liveable, will hopefully be reflected in the chapters which follow.

Introduction

If the history of the social sciences can broadly be conceived as the continuing effort of human beings to understand themselves — their past, their present, their future — the specific history of social anthropology and rural sociology for long revolved around the special requirement of understanding 'others,' of taking up the striking elements of difference between the sociocultural organization of the scientists' own immediate world and those of other peoples or groups, and trying to describe or explain them. In the case of anthropology, this challenge was posed particularly during a process of colonial expansion, which exposed European and American students of man to a vast new field of human experience; in the case of rural sociology, during a concomitant process of internal capitalist development, which increasingly distinguished urban industrial centers from surrounding rural areas within Europe and America, and thus created the objective possibility of concern with 'rurality.'

Those who studied primitive, or peasant, or rural society were, then, by definition outsiders; they came to their subject matter imbued with the culture of an urban, and quite frequently a metropolitan, society. At the same time, they were the intellectual product of particular educational experiences, shaped within specific socioeconomic contexts, during concrete historical periods. They could not entirely escape the determination of relevant enquiry exercised by the social dynamics of their own time and place, nor would the product of their thought have found echo had they done so. It was their task, in each generation, to pick up the threads of discourse on the nature of 'ruralness' or 'primitiveness' and to propose in turn convincing answers to the recurrent questions posed by their own society: 'Who are those people still organizing their livelihood in ways outside our immediate experience?' 'What is their relation to us?' These were not questions, it should be added, which could ever be entirely devoid of political content, nor were the answers offered ever unlikely to contribute to shaping future relations between urban and rural (or metropolitan and colonial) societies, and in the process altering the reality with which future social scientists would some day have to deal.

When one attempts to characterize the evolution of anthropological and sociological thought concerned with the theme of rural 'otherness,' one is immediately presented with a series of shifting patterns, conformed by continuous drawing and redrawing of intellectual boundaries around areas of experience which, at particular moments and for particular groups of social scientists, seemed to offer the most promising field within which to search for fundamental elements of differentiation, and interaction, between rural and urban society. Boundaries have been fixed along a number of dimensions: geographical, cultural, topical. Observation may be limited (to take only a few examples) to a single community or neighborhood, or extended to the furthest reaches of the world capitalist system; it may center primarily around rural people exhibiting a common ethnic identity, or a common class; it may be guided by an overriding concern with ecology, psychology, relations of production or social organization. In the last analysis, it is the peculiar combination of decisions taken along all dimensions which constitutes the intellectual terrain of each investigation, both limiting its possibilities and defining its contributions to the common quest for knowledge of rural or nonurban industrial society.

Thomas Kuhn has called the mental maps which scientists apply to the infinite complexity of the human and physical universe their 'paradigms' or 'world views.'[1] The latter constitute, in effect, a kind of metaphysical belief that certain areas of nature, implying certain boundaries of attention and commitment, are particularly worthy of study; and they form the basis for specific research traditions, in which theory is elaborated and methodology reglemented to provide a recognized foundation for the practice of a particular discipline. When such a paradigm gains the virtually unanimous adherence of all practitioners in a field (and here Kuhn draws his historical examples largely from the natural sciences), it allows daily attention to very specific and precise forms of 'puzzle-solving' (occurring within paradigmatic boundaries assuring the eventual resolution of the puzzle) which have come to be associated with science as an ideal type of human enquiry. Scientists, whether individually or in groups, then take upon themselves the resolution of particular problems thrown up by the paradigm, displaying in the process ingenuity and perseverence, but not bringing into

Introduction

play any fundamental challenge to the basic suppositions of the paradigm itself. And this kind of 'normal science' continues until anomalies or absurdities recur with sufficient frequency to force growing consideration of alternative views, leading eventually to the acceptance of an alternative paradigm.

It is obvious that nearly unanimous acceptance of a single paradigm over a long period of time has never come to characterize most of the social sciences; and for that reason, the latter have at times been characterized by Kuhn himself as protosciences.[2] Nevertheless, as Margaret Masterman has convincingly argued in an extremely useful discussion of 'the meaning of paradigms,' there is no reason to conclude that 'multiple paradigm' disciplines are not proceding scientifically. As long as work is carried out within specified research traditions, drawing intellectual boundaries around particular areas of experience singled out for exclusive attention and reflection, then 'multiple-paradigm science [must be] full science, on Kuhn's own criteria.'[3]

It should be equally clear, however, that the continued existence of competing paradigms, within which each group of adherents sees the world in a fundamentally different way, creates tensions which, while perhaps embodying some of the valuable elements of all well-founded challenges, also diverts resources away from more profound testing of the intellectual limits of a single paradigm, toward defense of its broadest outlines from hostile criticism. The difficulties of competition are compounded by a fundamental inability of those carrying out research within any given tradition to communicate adequately with colleagues oriented by another. This is not a simple outgrowth of personal pride or whim. It is inherent in the nature of paradigmatic conflict. Kuhn and other philosophers (or historians) of science have repeatedly pointed out the 'linguistic center' of scientific activity — the inescapable need to transmit experience through recourse to words and concepts which can never be totally neutral. Scientists working within different paradigms are therefore continually subject to 'communications breakdowns,' in which any real understanding across traditions can only be reached through consciously translating one person's ideas into another's conceptual language, defining and redefining terms until one reaches a 'redistribution of objects among similarity sets' sufficiently precise to allow a meaningful exchange of ideas.[4]

Under such circumstances, it would be naive to suppose that one can make simultaneous inter-paradigmatic comparisons of validity, that any research tradition can be judged to 'correspond' more closely to the 'real world' than another at any given moment in time. Each paradigm looks at a somewhat separate part of reality, sees it in peculiar terms, and describes it in a particular theoretical language. As Kuhn so tellingly put it, the position of adherents of different research traditions is not unlike that of two subjects involved in a gestalt experiment: both look at a mass of dots and lines on a uniform background, but one organizes the markings into a rabbit and another into a man. To conclude that one better represented reality than another would be absurd.

What one can do, however, and what in fact seems most regularly to account for the decline of some research traditions and the eventual appearance of others, is to judge each paradigm on its own terms — not in relation to its competitors, but according to its own internal consistency and utility. It is undoubtedly true, as a number of historians of science have illustrated, that adherents of any research tradition will make extraordinary efforts to explain away an anomaly or absurdity within their own paradigmatic boundaries without stepping outside them; but it is equally true that there are certain challenges to explanatory or predictive power which no paradigm can leave unmet and survive. If a research tradition repeatedly demonstrates incapacity to overcome such shortcomings, it must be abandoned.

Particularly in the social sciences, the likelihood that any paradigm will be confronted in relatively short time with challenges beyond its capacity to meet is enormously increased by the continuously changing nature of its subject matter. Research traditions governing work in chemistry or physics or astronomy may break down when pushed to explain phenomena outside their traditional boundaries of concern; but the natural elements with which they deal do not generally engage in irrevocable departures from a normal state. Human beings, on the other hand, make extremely unstable research material. Thus while a philosopher of science primarily concerned with the study of the natural world may comment that 'finding a new theory for given facts is like finding a new production for a well-known play',[5] a counterpart in the social sciences would have to disagree: given facts are constantly changing, and the script of the play can never be taken for granted beforehand.

When evaluating the adequacy of various research traditions in the social sciences *over time*, one is therefore constantly faced with a question largely irrelevant to students of the physical sciences: did a particular paradigm gain importance during a given period because in fact it was concerned with significant aspects of contemporary social relations,

Introduction 5

afterward so altered that the paradigm lost credibility? Is there, in other words, an 'historical moment' for a sociological paradigm, determined not simply by the sociocultural environment shaping the outlook of the investigator in his own immediate society — discussed above — but also by the objective social situation with which he is confronted in the field? The question is obviously of particular relevance in the case of the kind of perceived social separation between the world of the researcher and that of his subjects which arose during the early period of anthropological and sociological investigation of 'otherness.'

Upon the answer to this query rests the judgment which a later student of rural life must make concerning the adequacy with which social scientists working within earlier paradigms represented the situation of the people whom they studied. Are their portrayals relatively faithful reflections of the forces shaping the quality of human interaction at the time and in the place where observation occurred? Or was the influence of a previously shaped world view too insistent to permit social scientists to 'see' clearly? Have now superseded paradigms been rejected because they were in themselves unable to provide an adequate framework for analysing existing social facts, or because evolving social facts escaped their boundaries?

Not surprisingly, there would seem to be evidence in the following pages with which to answer both parts of the latter question affirmatively. And to the extent that such is the case, it becomes especially important to understand well the critical areas of rural livelihood which each superseded paradigm failed to explain; for these failures provide vital clues in reconstructing the course of social change in the countryside. At the same time, one must remain constantly alert to the possibility that the conclusions of researchers working within different paradigms were affected, through chance or design, not only by the intellectual boundaries of their own research traditions, and the temporal boundaries of an historical moment, but also by the particular socio-economic and ecological characteristics of the setting within which observation took place. Until the intellectual and pecuniary resources of the social sciences permit systematic comparative effort, guided by a single research tradition, to deal with regional differentiation in the countryside, and thus to gain for the first time an overall understanding of the range of variation within which livelihood options may be elaborated, there is always the real possibility that competing paradigms are based in part upon the observation of qualitatively different situations, even within a single historical period. The dots and lines in the gestalt experiment are then not the same at all, and there is additional reason to doubt that meaningful comparison — or communication — between adherents of different paradigms can ever be effected.

These preliminary remarks are perhaps sufficient to indicate the kinds of problems which will be encountered in the subsequent discussion of how paradigmatic boundaries have been drawn in postrevolutionary anthropological studies of the Mexican countryside. For purposes of analysis, the latter have been grouped into seven broad categories, representing seven distinguishable ways of looking at rural life, and of attempting to deal with the single fundamental topic of differentiation and interaction between countryside and city. Of the seven, three are clearly incompatible among themselves: *ethnographic particularism*, which pretended to find no generalizable patterns of social change or interaction, but only to describe culture traits; *functionalism*, which insisted upon analysing social interaction and change in terms of balanced reciprocity, employing an analogy of society as an integrated human organism, and eschewing historical research in favor of synchronic studies largely carried out at the local level; and *historical sturcturalism*, which inverted the importance granted by functionalism to local synchronic events, replacing the latter with a constant emphasis on macrostructural analysis over long periods of time, and looking most persistently at unbalanced reciprocity, maintained through mechanisms of domination and repression. Within historical structuralism, however, three further research traditions developed along lines which also brought them into frequent conflict: *cultural ecology*, *orthodox and revisionist (circulationist) Marxism*. A fourth, *dependentismo*, originally made an independent contribution to the theoretical arsenal of historical structuralism, and was later increasingly absorbed *ad hoc* into the structure of debate of the first three. The coherent anthropological component of dependentismo shared large areas of agreement with cultural ecology, and in fact became little distinguishable from the latter (except for a lesser interest in details of ecological adaptation) by the end of the period under discussion. Finally, *indigenismo* represented a peculiar half-way house between functionalism and historical structuralism, beset by internal contradictions and eventually impelled by political necessity toward the former of the two world views.

An effort has been made to place discussion of differing schools of thought along a continuum which runs from greatest concern with the ethnographic study of local culture, at one extreme, to greatest concern with the analysis of power at the other. Such has in fact been the

Introduction

general tendency underlying the anthropological treatment of the Mexican countryside during the postrevolutionary period; and as the reader advances from earlier chapters to later ones, he or she should be aware of this changing emphasis. Nevertheless, debate has never been as neatly compartmentalized as one might like to have it for the purpose of textbook-like presentation. Most particularly during the immediate postrevolutionary years, there was great variety in ways of explaining central elements of rural life; and even afterward, proponents of one view coexisted with those of another, despite a tendency toward progressive adherence by newer members of the profession to later explanatory frameworks. The entire period of time under consideration in the book is, after all, only six decades: more than enough time for development of an extraordinary richness of anthropological interpretation, but hardly enough to warrant the mechanical disappearance of one school at the moment another began to make headway.

The following chapters should therefore be read in relation to each other, not as single commentaries on isolated, or entirely independent, rigidly sequential paradigms. This is particularly true of Chapters II, III and IV, which deal with schools simultaneously under elaboration during the 1950s and 1960s. It is one of the primary purposes of the exercise to illustrate the cumulative, and dialectical, nature of the elaboration of anthropological theory; and the fact that lines must be drawn, and labels affixed, in order to make comparison possible should never be taken to imply a total disjuncture.

1 Particularism, Marxism and functionalism in Mexican anthropology, 1920–50

At the turn of the twentieth century, as indeed in a number of preceding periods, the necessity to understand the nature of agrarian life loomed large on the agenda of Mexican intellectuals. The nation as a whole was caught up in a process of extremely rapid, and brutal, modernization promoted under the dictatorship of Porfirio Diaz; and both the liberals who saw in rural 'backwardness' a basic impediment to progress, and the socialists who impugned contemporary depredations of capitalist agricultural entrepreneurs for causing unbearable suffering among rural people were determined to get to the heart of the 'rural question.' How should the countryside be organized in order to contribute to national development? What was there in the current arrangement which impeded a more rational and equitable use of the physical and human resources of rural areas?

These questions implied, for all observers of the period, an important preoccupation with culture, mistakenly conceived at the time in terms of race. Perhaps the single most visible characteristic of much of the rural population of Mexico was its ethnic differentiation, promoted and maintained over centuries of colonial domination through the artifice of a racially justified caste system in which 'Indians' were separated from mestizos or creoles. The legacy of prejudice left by such a system had not been eradicated, even among the most enlightened, at the turn of the century; and it was therefore virtually inevitable that intellectuals should be consistently concerned with 'Indianness' as they discussed what began to be seen as the 'great national problems' of Mexico.[1]

Such a preoccupation was magnified immeasurably by the outbreak of the Mexican Revolution in 1910, for agrarian unrest lay at the heart of the conflict. Rural people rebelled against the impositions of the Porfirian order and for a brief period experimented with their own locally devised forms of organization. Their opportunity to determine the parameters of local livelihood was, however, short-lived; by 1917, they were once again subject to the authority of a national state, now in the hands of a fragile coalition of revolutionaries of varied political persuasions. Intellectuals who had long debated the merits of new forms of rural community were placed in a position to advocate policy, and a period of noteworthy social experimentation began. There was, to be sure, little agreement at the time concerning the details of necessary land redistribution or rural development programs. But there was virtually unanimous agreement that the 'Indian' population of the countryside had to be integrated as quickly as possible into the wider national society, both as an instrument for promoting social justice and a bulwark for future national unity.

The newly created discipline of anthropology quite obviously had something of relevance to say concerning that issue. During the gradual formation of a separate area of anthropological concern within the social sciences of the late nineteenth century, anthropologists had begun to counterpose the concept of culture to that of race, and to challenge the prevailing supposition that some peoples or races were inherently inferior to others. Most particularly under the influence of Franz Boas, even the idea that there was likely to be a process of unilinear evolution from simpler to more advanced forms of cultural elaboration was questioned, and in its place was inserted a strong adherence to relativism. Each culture was to be considered on its own terms, its principal characteristics recorded and analysed. But there was to be no normative judgment of its value when compared with others, for Boas doubted that the social sciences, at their contemporary state of development, were capacitated to reach valid conclusions concerning the probable course of evolution of human society.

This was the point of view which underlay the kind of anthropology introduced in Mexico with the founding, under Boas's direction, of the Escuela de Arqueología y Etnografía Americana in 1909. Its denial of the validity of racial stereotyping was to provide an important counterweight to prevailing prejudices among intellectuals, and its dedication to the careful searching out and recording of even the most isolated human cultures was to contribute fundamentally to the post-revolutionary scientific reconnaissance of Mexican rural areas. But the decided relativism of Boasian ethnographic theory could make very little headway against the tide of liberal faith in progress which sustained the intellectual inheritors of the revolution. The latter had been fought, they were convinced, to sweep away the 'backwardness' of the past; and a significant part of that backwardness was to be found in 'Indian' communities. Therefore the ethnographic knowledge produced by early anthropologists, even when not specifically intended to serve the ends of national integration, was nevertheless to be inextricably interwoven with the practice of 'applied' development work. A science as close to the concerns of daily livelihood as anthropology could not be maintained outside the mainstream of debate on the future of indigenous peoples in postrevolutionary society, all pretensions of analytical detachment notwithstanding.

Manuel Gamio and the liberal reinterpretation of ethnographic particularism: incorporation and indigenismo

There can be no better example of the peculiar mutation suffered by Boasian particularism under the impact of a liberal faith in progress, associated with revolution, than the work of Manuel Gamio, generally taken to represent the inauguration of the modern practice of anthropology in Mexico. During the last days of the Porfiriato, Gamio was a student of Franz Boas at Columbia University, and he was therefore thoroughly trained to study the culture of 'primitive' peoples in a static and nonhistorical framework. Human settlements isolated from any contact with surrounding modern society were the privileged setting of the Boasian paradigm, and the entire range of nonbiologically determined activity the legitimate object of observation. Ethnographers were to describe the complexities of livelihood as they saw them, neither questioning their past development nor speculating concerning their likely future course.

Such a theoretical prescription left the understanding of possible patterns of interaction between 'primitives' and 'nonprimitives,' as well as the probable nature of culture change, entirely undiscussed; and in a rural setting devastated by seven years of civil strife, this could only be a wholly untenable omission. Therefore when Gamio was placed at the head of the Direction of Anthropology of the Ministry of Agriculture of the first revolutionary government in 1917, he appended to his ethnographic training the prevailing liberal interpretation of human development, forming in the process a theoretical synthesis more akin to the unilinear evolutionism of pre-Boasian schools than to the tradition of his own generation at Columbia.

Put briefly, Gamio's theory was based on the assumption that the glory of Mexico's indigenous cultures lay entirely in the precolonial past. Contemporary differences in culture among the country's 'small nations,' as he liked to call them, were on the other hand simply stumbling blocks in the way of national unity. They represented a degeneration of preconquest customs, which if allowed to continue without fusion into the 'progressive' mainstream of mestizo culture would doom a large part of the inhabitants of Mexico to ever-declining levels of living and eventual extinction. The purpose of ethnographic field work was therefore less to preserve cultural idiosyncrasies than to understand them in order to hasten their disappearance.[2]

Gamio set as the first task of his Direction of Anthropology the systematic study of indigenous groups thought to be representative of seventeen regions into which the country was to be divided. In this respect, he was the precursor of work on delimiting 'culture areas' in Mexico which was to continue for a number of decades. So little was known at the time about the location and characteristics of various indigenous cultures that Gamio's department could base its regions only on state boundaries: each region contained one or more states, within which certain broad ethnic similarities were supposed to exist. In fact, however, during the eight years in which the Direction of Anthropology functioned, it proved possible to carry out a large study of only one area within one region: that of Teotihuacan, within the 'Central Mesa' states surrounding the Federal District.

Teotihuacan was chosen for reasons having to do at least as much with its preconquest past as with its miserable contemporary plight. It had once been the center of a flourishing Indian state, the physical remains of which included monumental buildings grouped around a complex of pyramids. But in 1917, its population was made up of both Indian and Spanish-speaking laborers, surviving at infrasubsistence levels on the proceeds of occasional work for seven large landowners, who dedicated 90 per cent of the agricultural land of the region to commercial crops entirely consumed in the Federal District. It was Gamio's plan to work simultaneously in archeology and ethnology, reconstructing the famous ruins of Teotihuacan while investigating the culture of its modern inhabitants, and at the same time beginning programs designed to better living conditions among families of workers employed on the archeological site. This integration of archeology, anthropology and community development was to appear again and again in the design of projects carried out by other institutions in the Mexican countryside in the decades following the 1920s. It deployed the academic and practical resources of anthropology in the widest possible way, and constituted a justly famous pioneering venture.[3]

Unfortunately, however, the quality of both the ethnographic study and the practical contributions made to improving the level of living of landless families was undermined by the way in which Gamio and his team drew the intellectual boundaries of their enquiry. Trained to study 'folklore,' and caught up in the heady ethnocentrism of a revolution which promised to sweep away all injustice through creating a 'modern' Mexico, they tended to fault 'folkloric' world views, and exclusion from the national socio-economic system, for the 'backwardness' of indigenous people. It was not that they did not see the injury caused by the hacienda system which dominated the valley; in fact, they repeatedly petitioned for agrarian reform as part of community development efforts. But the paradigm within which they worked did not allow them to relate the development of large landholdings, the course of socioeconomic change at the national level, and the culture of rural people within a single conceptual framework.

The picture of rural life painted in *La Poblacion del Valle de Teotihuacan*, published in 1922, is uniformly negative. The people wear 'anti-esthetic and unhygienic' clothing, live in 'unhealthy' huts, produce 'degenerated' pottery; they are malnourished and sickly. Their lack of access to basic livelihood resources had most obviously reduced them to the most exiguous levels of existence. For Gamio, however, the crux of their problem lay in the realm of culture, in their 'archaic life which flows on in the midst of artifices and superstitions,' and which must be altered through 'incorporation into contemporary civilization' in the future.[4] The 'folk culture' which Redfield was at that moment preparing to immortalize as a viable adaptation of small, relatively self-sufficient groups to their environment (in the non-hacienda setting of Tepoztlan) appeared in a partially degenerated, 'folkloric' form to be completely unviable in Teotihuacan.

The community development program which grew out of Gamio's work in Teotihuacan was, not surprisingly, heavily oriented toward changing the local culture through education. Primary schools were introduced for the purpose of teaching Mexican and world history, as well as to reinforce the use of the Spanish language; local curers were confronted with competition from modern medical personnel; and the consumption of traditional alcoholic beverages was tenaciously combated. At the same time, an effort was made to widen the productive base of a virtually landless population through the introduction of beekeeping and the importation of the Talavera pottery technique from Puebla. Always guided by the premise that better living conditions depended upon reorganization directed by enlightened outsiders, this program could have little real impact upon livelihood until local people themselves were able to join together to break the monopoly of the hacienda system over vital productive resources. It did serve, however, as the opening experiment in an official program of induced culture change which was to figure prominently in public policy toward indigenous areas for a number of decades to come.

'Indigenismo,' as this policy came to be called, rested on the conviction that the indigenous groups of Mexico were culturally distinct from the rest of the nation and therefore required special study before particular ways of attacking their livelihood problems could be worked out and put into effect. Whether the end result of 'indigenismo' was to be the complete incorporation of these separate cultures into the dominant mestizo culture, or the preservation of some elements of indigenous culture felt to be particularly valuable, was to become an element of debate (in which, clearly, Gamio was at this stage of his intellectual development to be found near the pole of complete incorporation). All indigenistas stood together, however, in their insistence that general programs of rural modernization could not be applied to the countryside indiscriminately, without adaptation to the reality of a number of specific indigenous cultures.

Such a point of view was challenged by groups of intellectuals equally as interested as the indigenistas in bettering the livelihood conditions of rural Mexicans, but inclined to feel that treating indigenous groups separately would only increase their low status in national society. For men like José Vasconcelos, who became Minister of Education in 1921, it seemed indispensable to provide all rural families in the nation with certain basic elements of national culture (or perhaps it would be better to say of Western culture); whether these families spoke indigenous languages or practiced peculiar religions made no difference in the program. They were Mexicans, and furthermore they were citizens of the world.[5] Under a banner of this kind Gamio's Department of Anthropology was dismantled in 1925, as was the Department of Indian Culture within the Ministry of Education. For a decade thereafter, a wide-ranging program of rural education and modernization was carried out in mestizo and Indian regions alike, without benefit of the organized participation of anthropologists in policy-making.

Moisés Sáenz: a precursor of anti-incorporationist indigenismo

One of the principal architects of the remarkable effort made to utilize education as a tool of community development during the 1920s and early 1930s was Moisés Sáenz, like Gamio a graduate of Columbia University. Sáenz was not an anthropologist by training; he received a doctorate in philosophy for his work in the field of education. Yet his contact with Boas and, to a much more significant degree, with John Dewey (who held a chair at Columbia during the early part of the century) predisposed him to look at the culture of rural Mexicans with a critical eye. After writing his thesis on the application of the principles of Dewey's 'action school' to the livelihood problems of the Mexican countryside, he returned to his country to assume the post of Director of Education in the state of Guanajuato, roughly at the same time Gamio was promoting the establishment of his Direction of Anthropology in the Ministry of Agriculture.[6]

By 1925, Sáenz had become Vice Minister of Public Education, charged precisely with the integrated program of rural community development which had made Gamio's separate anthropological effort temporarily irrelevant. Rural schools in all communities were to become laboratories for experimentation in socioeconomic change, and rural teachers were to serve the interests of the whole population, rather than limiting their contribution to the traditional field of formal instruction. They were assisted in this task by mobile Cultural Missions, containing teams of specialists in fields deemed useful for community development: doctors, nurses, veterinarians, home economists, carpenters, musicians and others. The purpose of the program, carried out with a dedication which encouraged numerous observers to qualify it as the best product of the Mexican revolution,[7] was to raise levels of living in the countryside and to incorporate rural people into the mainstream of national culture and society. It was assumed, as Gamio had assumed, that physical and sociocultural isolation were the reasons for rural 'backwardness,' and that education was the proper tool for ameliorating the most pressing problems of rural people. But it was not at first deemed necessary to divide the rural population into separate cultural categories.

The constant visits made by Moisés Sáenz to rural areas where the programs of the Ministry of Education were under way, however, as well as insights gained during a long trip through the predominantly Indian regions of much of Central and South America, soon made him doubt the soundness of a single approach to community development, and eventually led him to question certain aspects of the 'incorporationist' bias which underlay his own (as well as Gamio's and Vasconcelos's) work. Within the course of a few years, around the turn of the 1930s, Sáenz became an indigenista, appreciating the cultural differences which made it necessary to take the special situation of indigenous groups into account when designing policy; and as the decade advanced, one could see in his work the suggestion of a new kind of indigenismo: that which defended cultural plurality within the Mexican countryside and rejected complete incorporation as a policy goal.

The immediate experience which perhaps contributed most to confirming Sáenz's conversion to indigenismo was his stay, during six months in 1932, in the small Tarascan village of Carapan. He went to Carapan, with a team of assistants, in order to look firsthand at the problems of education in an indigenous setting; and what he found was the most complete rejection of induced culture change. The rural school was, in such a village, a total failure. 'As far as change goes,' he concluded in his report on the project (published in 1936), 'I'd bet more on the road than the rural school to bring it about.'[8] One Tarascan villager after another informed the outsiders that they liked their community the way it was, and that they wanted help from no one.

Problems of health, literacy and agricultural productivity nevertheless seemed real enough to Sáenz. He therefore cast about for a policy formula which would improve material livelihood within a pluricultural setting. This led him to propose the founding of a high-level Autonomous Department of Indian Affairs, which would coordinate the development efforts of all public agencies working in indigenous areas and adapt them to the particular requirements of each group. By the time this Department was established in 1936, however, Sáenz no longer determined the course of rural development programs in Mexico. His conversion to indigenismo made it difficult to remain in the Ministry of Education; and he entered the Mexican diplomatic service for a short time before being designated first director of the Interamerican Indian Institute in 1940.

In the collected essays of Moisés Sáenz, written during the late 1920s and early 1930s and published in 1939, one sees fragments of thought which were later to reappear continually in the work of indigenistas more concerned with the material, or socioeconomic, than with the cultural roots of livelihood problems in indigenous communities. These fragments were not yet presented within a coherent explanatory framework; they were still only partial revisions of the prevailing paradigm, which had given primordial importance to the negative effects of Indian 'isolation.' Thus Sáenz saw exploitation in indigenous communities, and called it so: 'This indigenous world is one... of miserable people, terrorized and exploited.'[9] But he did not specify the nature of the exploitation, nor did he clearly relate it to the form of incorporation undergone during centuries by Indian groups. He continued to link 'isolation' and 'exploitation' in a rather incongruous way: 'throughout the country the Indians are criminally abandoned by the ruling classes, and subjected to the most iniquitous exploitation.'[10]

At the same time, Sáenz was more aware than many other contemporaries of the positive aspects of indigenous life. His essays contain many references to elements of culture which should be respected by the larger society, indigenous government being one of the most important: 'perhaps it will be possible to establish a kind of "indirect government" through which the Indian can effectively preserve his own organization while articulating it with that of the rest of the country.' This was part of a larger concern 'not to incorporate the Indian, but to integrate Mexico,' through the building of a 'great nation [of pluralistic cultures] linked together in a just and efficacious economic system.'[11] Such a concern was to receive considerable political support during the presidency of Lázaro Cárdenas, from 1934 to 1940.

A Marxist defense of cultural pluralism: Lombardo Toledano and Chávez Orozco

The idea that the roots of livelihood problems in the Mexican countryside lay in unjust economic relations rather than 'backward' systems of belief, and that local cultures should in fact be respected and preserved, formed a basic element in the work of Vicente Lombardo Toledano and Luis Chávez Orozco, who drew upon Marxism to analyse the structural elements of misery in indigenous communities and to demand the kind of agrarian reform program in fact undertaken by the Cárdenas government. They insisted that land, credit and technical assistance were indispensable prerequisites for raising the level of living of rural people. At the same time, they argued against earlier incorporationist biases in Mexican educational policy and championed the right of indigenous groups to maintain their own languages and customs.

This defense of local autonomy, it should be noted, was not a stance necessarily implied by Marxism. Other Mexican Marxists of the period were adamant in their belief that village autonomy stood in the way of a rapid advance toward the dictatorship of the proletariat; and in fact, it is difficult to argue that their logic was faulty. The indigenismo of Marxists like Lombardo grew less out of nineteenth-century social thought than out of the twentieth-century Leninist experiment with 'national self-determination' for Russian minorities. And in the end, even that revision of Marxist thought played less of a role in the Indian policy of Lombardo Toledano than the reality of Mexican politics and society with which he was confronted. When it became clear, in the course of the 1930s, that only a strong and united Mexican nation could deal successfully with the international pressures unleashed by Cárdenas's support of agrarian reform and the expropriation of the petroleum industry, Lombardo and others of his conviction abandoned the idea that each ethnic group could be a separate nation-within-a-nation, and championed instead 'maximum political rights ... within the framework of the current national system.'[12] This goal implied, in operational terms, the redrawing of state and municipal boundaries so that each ethnic group would coincide with a political unit, as well as respect on the part of national authorities for regional and local officials elected autonomously.

Once the necessity to strengthen internal cohesion in the face of external pressure had been recognized, local self-government in rural areas was not separated, ideologically or practically, from broadening participation in national political affairs. The greater part of Lombardo Toledano's adult life was spent as a labor leader, including a period from 1936 to 1948 in which he played a decisive role, within the Confederation of Mexican Workers, in molding the policy of the national government toward the working class, both urban and rural. It was he, and his followers, who provided the kind of grass-roots organization of the rural proletariat on the large foreign landholdings of the richest agricultural areas of the country required to support agrarian reform during the 1930s. And in the newly formed mestizo *ejidos*, or agrarian communities, constituted following the expropriation of those capitalist holdings, an erstwhile proletariat was given a new form of community self-government designed to increase local decision-making authority at the same time that it allowed integration into a hierarchy of regional and national pressure groups. The principle was not fundamentally different, in theory, for indigenous communities.

The resources with which the Cárdenas government could support the kind of policies proposed by Lombardo, Chávez Orozco and others for the ethnic minorities of rural Mexico were limited indeed. Nevertheless, the Autonomous Department of Indian Affairs, proposed by Sáenz, was established in 1936 and Chávez Orozco placed at its head. The broader programs for the socioeconomic development of the countryside in general, including agrarian reform and rural education, were channeled through that department when destined for indigenous areas. A noteworthy effort was simultaneously made by department personnel to inform and organize members of various ethnic groups through the calling of Indian Congresses, intended not only to incorporate new groups into the national political process, but also to reinforce ethnic identity.

To reach indigenous people, it was necessary to find ways to communicate. In the immediate postrevolutionary past, that way had been almost exclusively through promoting the teaching of the Spanish language in Indian communities, in the hope that Spanish would eventually replace Indian languages in the daily life of the people. But under Chávez Orozco, a shift in emphasis occurred: Spanish was no longer to be imposed as the dominant idiom in daily life, but rather was to serve as a second language, complementary to − and not in conflict with − the traditional languages of Indian communities. Such a position was supported by new currents in American linguistic theory, which held that literacy could best be achieved through learning a native tongue, and that attempts simultaneously to impose a new language and new reading or writing skills were doomed to failure. Therefore teaching personnel were trained, to the extent that limited temporal and economic resources allowed, to conduct the first steps of elementary education in Indian languages, and then to teach Spanish to indigenous pupils as the latter themselves became aware of their need to use it for concrete purposes. The specialized services of a newly formed Summer Language Institute, financed by American Protestant missionaries and directed by William Townsend, were enlisted to this end.[13] Nevertheless, it was the opinion of one well-qualified observer of the period that at the local level in most rural areas, 'the postulate of incorporating the Indian into civilization and its corollary, direct teaching of Spanish, never ceased to form part of the mentality of the rural schoolteacher.'[14] Inertia in the field of education, as in land tenure and agrarian social relations, was not to be quickly overcome.

The work of indigenistas like Lombardo and Chávez Orozco was, then, quite clearly predicated upon the conviction that socioeconomic change was of primary importance in raising levels of living in the

Particularism, Marxism and functionalism, 1920-50   19

countryside, that such change could only be brought about to any meaningful degree through the political organization of Indian groups, and that the maintenance of ethnic identity could constitute a positive, rather than a negative, element in the organization of rural people. Theirs was thus a third, distinct, variation on the theme of incorporation as it was being progressively developed in Mexico: while Gamio supported the relatively complete socioeconomic and cultural integration of indigenous groups into national life and Sáenz championed a rather marked rural isolation (or 'reinforcing rural consciousness,' as he called it), Lombardo advocated rapid economic development of the countryside (including the promotion of rural industry in order to further proletarian consciousness) at the same time that he fought to foster cultural pluralism. Within the political arena of Mexico in the 1920s and 1930s, these three positions correspond to liberalism, populism and socialism.

Redfield and structural-functionalism: a theoretical justification for the study of 'folk' communities

The anti-incorporationist indigenismo of the Cárdenas period, associated not with academic anthropology but with practical development work, gained support for its defense of cultural pluralism from a growing number of Mexican and American anthropologists who were engaged, from the 1920s onward, in a somewhat uncoordinated effort to obtain a clearer picture of the nature and extent of indigenous regions in Mexico. This work, first proposed by Gamio (and like his own, generally associated with the tradition of ethnographic particularism) grew out of a broader trend in European and American anthropology of the early twentieth century toward mapping the 'cultural areas' which were to serve as the scientific universe from which students of men could draw empirical material. It continued throughout the 1920s and 1930s, as men like Wigberto Jiménez Moreno, Roberto Weitlaner, Juan Comas, Carlos Basauri, Lucio Mendieta y Núñez, Miguel Othón de Mendizábal, Alfonso Fabila, Alfonso Villa Rojas and Ralph Beals roamed over the Mexican countryside, encountering different linguistic groups and recording as much as possible about the way of life of each in monographs with titles like *Los Indios de México*, *The Tepehuán*, *The Seri*, *The Cahita*. These groups were in the beginning considered 'native,' or 'primitive,' and thus fit subjects for an anthropological science which restricted its field of study strictly to human groups minimally contaminated by contact with the modern world.

Simultaneously, however, it became necessary to confront the fact that a very large part of the Mexican countryside was inhabited by people who combined an indigenous heritage with a long history of contact with European culture, first at the time of the Spanish Conquest and later through intermittent dealings with mestizo Mexicans. These people often continued to speak Indian languages, but their culture contained such disparate European elements as the plow, the long dress or Catholic saints. They were obviously not 'primitives,' nor were they 'modern.' They stood somewhere in between the two poles, living a kind of life which Gamio had seen in Teotihuacan in 1918 and characterized as 'degenerated.' It fell to Robert Redfield to provide a more scientific conceptual framework for the study of such cases: the 'folk culture,' first presented in *Tepoztlán: A Mexican Village*, published in 1930, and elaborated more fully in *Chan Kom*, written with Alfonso Villa Rojas and published in 1934.

In order to understand the significance of Redfield's work, not only for Mexican and American cultural anthropology as it was practiced during the coming decades but also for Mexican Indian policy, one must keep in mind that the ideas he presented in *Tepoztlán* and *Chan Kom* accomplished several things at once. They established the right of anthropologists to study 'folk' communities, which although not entirely isolated from modern society nevertheless were characterized by a coherent way of life clearly distinguishable from city life; and they lent support, among anthropologists, to a new way of looking at culture itself.

The definition of culture utilized by all anthropologists working in Mexico from the time of Gamio onward was basically that proposed by Tylor in 1857: that body of learned social behavior which differentiated men from animals, and one group of isolated human beings from another. To document the particular content of any given culture, a catalogue was drawn up of all the discrete ways in which inhabitants went about their daily lives: what they ate, how they dressed, where they lived, how they worked, what they said and thought, how they grew up, married and died. The relationship between each cultural 'trait' and all others was not particularly clear, nor was there any good reason why a specific element should have taken one form and not another.

This rather unsystematic way of looking at culture began to be challenged during the 1920s by Kroeber, in the United States, and by

Malinowski and Radcliffe-Brown in England. All were concerned to find 'patterns and processes,' as Kroeber entitled certain chapters of his famous overview of the discipline of anthropology, published in 1923.[15] And all were influenced by Emile Durkheim's insistence that society was not simply a collection of social facts, but a single integrated entity, composed of men but outside and above them, shaping their behavior in ways which they could only nominally control. For anthropologists like Kroeber, Malinowski, and Radcliffe-Brown, Durkheim's autonomous 'society' became an autonomous 'culture'; and for Radcliffe-Brown, in particular, that culture was made up of parts which fit together in a smoothly functioning whole, the purpose of which was to maintain existing relations among groups (the social structure). This was the beginning of structural-functionalism, a paradigm with which Redfield quickly became associated.[16]

If structural-functionalism had the virtue of encouraging analysis of the interrelationship among all parts of a culture, it also had the vice (from the standpoint of later critics) of promoting a particularly static picture of social interaction. An explicit analogy was made between cultures and biological organisms, clearly bounded off from the outside environment and maintained through the harmonious interaction of internal elements. The whole and its parts were to be studied in themselves, at one moment in time, rather than having recourse to the kind of historical analysis which members of the school considered unscientific, given the paucity of written materials within primitive societies.

Both the vices and the virtues of structural-functionalism were present to some extent in the work of Redfield. In a masterful treatment of the culture of Chan Kom, he presented what must surely remain one of the most compelling arguments ever made for the success with which a small, relatively isolated, illiterate peasant community could meet the physical, social and psychological requirements of daily life, without recourse to any of the trappings of modernity considered by the apostles of incorporation so essential to wellbeing. He was aided in this endeavor by the fact that Chan Kom was, by chance, a rather prosperous community, formed by refugees who had escaped the most disruptive effects of the hacienda system in Yucatan and who – up until quite recently – have impressed a stream of visitors as particularly well organized and pleasant. The bias toward harmony inherent in Redfield's paradigm therefore was reinforced, it would seem, by an objectively harmonious social situation.[17]

The stress which Redfield and his pupils placed on the 'functionality' of folk cultures provided strong support to that branch of Mexican indigenismo which sought to defend cultural pluralism. It also tended, however, to encourage a certain blindness among subsequent students of peasant society to the real dilemmas confronted by rural people not living in well-endowed and well-governed, self-sufficient communities. The problem was quite clearly one of boundaries, both geographical and temporal. By drawing the lines of relevant enquiry at the level of the isolated rural community, and around the present or recent past, a very great part of the likely area of conflict which might have become clear through investigating the relations of the community with the wider society over a long period of time was obliterated. Following the structural-functionalist model, the work of Mexican and American cultural anthropologists after Redfield was increasingly to be reduced to 'community studies,' in which the functionality of local cultural elements was stressed at all costs.[18]

Functionalist theories of culture change: acculturation and the folk-urban continuum

Although in fact most community studies carried out in subsequent decades proved to be isolated endeavors to understand contemporary life in a single human settlement, it is obvious that Redfield at no time saw the study of a single rural community as an exercise devoid of relevance for theories of sociocultural change. On the contrary, he was, from his first visit to Tepoztlán, vitally concerned to understand the way in which primitive or folk cultures responded to prolonged contact with other, technologically more advanced, cultures — whether the latter be colonial Spanish or modern urban industrial. His interest in the first kind of contact situation, that between primitive Indian societies and Spanish settlers, during the Conquest and colony, was of course inherent in his definition of the folk society. Like a number of other anthropologists of the 1920s and 1930s, he dealt with this question not through reference to colonial archives or other forms of direct historical investigation, but through pointing out those elements in the contemporary culture of Tepoztlán which were of obvious European origin and illustrating the way in which they had been adapted to Tepoztecan life. To this completed process of adaptation, he gave the name 'acculturation.'[19]

To the ongoing process of contact between folk and urban cultures, which was to form the background for his lasting contribution to sociological and anthropological theory, Redfield first assigned the term 'diffusion.'[20] Within a few years, however, he and a number of his colleagues had agreed upon the utility of using the word 'acculturation' to characterize all 'those phenomena which result when groups of individuals having different cultures come into continuous firsthand contact, with subsequent changes in the original cultural patterns of either or both groups.'[21] Acculturation was to be distinguished from diffusion precisely by the continuous and inescapable nature of the contact, often between groups with unequal degrees of power, and by the possibility that the content of either or both cultures might be fundamentally modified in the course of interaction, forming an entirely new synthesis rather than merely leading to the passive adoption of a 'diffused' trait.

Surprisingly, the study of acculturation, which now seems such an obvious element in the study of any group, was not immediately accepted as a valid concern for the discipline of anthropology. Although the realities of the colonial situation in Africa, and the progressive incorporation of Indian groups into national society in the United States, increasingly impelled utilization of the concept in both British and American field work in the 1930s, a considerable part of the anthropological profession was only slowly convinced that its province could include a study of any group 'who participate in civilized life.' Ralph Beals reported that a motion made at the 1936 meeting of the American Anthropological Association to affirm that 'papers in the field of acculturation lie within the interests of anthropology, and that, at the Editor's discretion, they not be discriminated against in the American Anthropologist,' was not passed, but tabled for further consideration.[22] Many participants felt that such studies belonged exclusively to the realm of sociology.

In fact, the broad theoretical orientation of Redfield, and the school of Mexican and American anthropologists soon to be formed around his work, could be traced quite clearly back to nineteenth-century social thinkers, who provided the classical groundwork for both sociology and anthropology, before the social sciences were divided into narrowly defined, separate disciplines. Just as Maine had been concerned with the difference between societies based upon status and contract, Tönnies with the movement from community to society, and Durkheim with the difference between mechanical and organic solidarity, so Redfield dealt with the transition from folk to secular societies. All were ideal types, intended to promote the scientific study of the process of social change. But while the typologies of Redfield's predecessors were drawn from the study of history, his own were the product of a carefully constructed comparison of neighboring contemporary settlements, exposed in varying degrees to the influence of urban society.

The Yucatán Project, which provided the setting for Redfield's now famous synchronic study of sociocultural change in the Mexican countryside, began in the latter 1920s under the auspices of the Carnegie Foundation. Like Gamio's investigation at Teotihuacan, it was designed from the beginning to combine archeology, social anthropology and applied anthropology, and to include the participation of medical doctors, plant scientists, nutritionists and other natural scientists who could supplement the anthropologists' limited knowledge of the physical world. During the early stages of the endeavor, Sylvanus Morley (then in charge of the group) made the acquaintance of a young schoolteacher working in the Maya community of Chan Kom, not far from the ruins of Chichen Itzá where the project had its headquarters. That schoolteacher was Alfonso Villa Rojas, destined with the passage of time to become, through his own remarkable effort at self-instruction as well as his association with the Carnegie team and posterior education at the University of Chicago, one of the leading figures in Mexican anthropology. It was the presence of Villa Rojas in Chan Kom which prompted Morley to suggest the village as a field site to Redfield, and the latter to accept the suggestion in 1930, when Villa Rojas formally became his ethnographic collaborator.[23]

By 1931, Redfield was living sporadically in Chan Kom, where he relied upon Villa Rojas's knowledge of Maya to supplement his own interviews with Spanish-speaking informants. As his knowledge of the region grew, a program of investigation was mapped out which included field work in four communities, forming a supposed continuum from the most isolated and primitive (the Maya settlement of Tusik), through less isolated but still rural (the 'folk' village of Chan Kom), to the town of Dzitas and the city of Mérida. Each would be the subject of a separate study, clarifying the nature of local culture (conceived as a functional whole) and the extent of contact with urban life. The results of the four studies would then be compared to provide grounds for generalization on the nature of the acculturative process.

It is clear from a reading of Redfield's early work that the broad outline of his conclusions on the transition from folk to urban culture had been sketched before the Yucatán project,[24] and that the latter served more to provide illustrative material than to generate new hypotheses. Nevertheless, the final academic product of the Yucatán experience, *The Folk Culture of Yucatán*, published in 1941, brought together Redfield's thoughts in a powerful synthesis which marked the midpoint on a path toward the eventual construction of a general theory of civilization, worked out during the coming decade. Briefly, Redfield held the single most important element in the process of change occurring throughout the Mexican countryside (and by extension, within all primitive or peasant regions) to be the breakdown in isolation which followed upon increasing urban contact. Small rural communities, in which behavior had long been determined by virtually unanimous agreement on the principal elements of right conduct, stipulated in local 'tradition' and reinforced by strong sacred sanction of deviation, were more and more subject to the disorganizing effects of contact with a 'great tradition' which challenged local values. Alternative forms of behavior were consequently introduced: a man could forget traditional obligations to kin and community, and to village deities. He could think in terms of individual gain, including the appropriation of private property from a formerly communal fund of resources. He could refuse to participate in traditional celebrations, and thus withdraw a contribution which he might formerly have made to the general wellbeing through the distribution of goods and the pleasing of exigent gods. He could cease to recognize the traditional hierarchy of authority within the village, once based primarily upon age and quality of service to the community, but in an urban framework more likely to be based upon wealth, education and ties to modern political groupings. He could practice a new occupation or join a new church.

For Redfield, all these changes, consequent upon increasing contact with urban culture, could be summarized under three general headings: individualization, secularization and disorganization. The third was by far the most fundamental of the processes, and in fact included the other two, for it referred to the way in which the meaning attached to all elements in a culture became fragmented and inoperative as a unifying force — in functionalist terms, the way in which the parts of the whole ceased to fit together in harmony and began to enter into conflict. The integration of maize agriculture and folk religion might, for example, be annulled, as maize became a product for sale rather than a sacred element of sustenance. The authority of local government might no longer be reinforced by widespread unwritten agreement on norms of right conduct. It was possible, Redfield thought, for the cultural whole to be 'reorganized' along new lines, creating a community integrated according to principles more in harmony with the requirements of outside contact. But it was perhaps even more likely that community, in the sense of meaningful interdependence among neighbors, could not be maintained or reconstructed, and that one would find it necessary to write 'a natural history of disintegration of small rural communities in the course of the development of civilization.'[25]

To test his fully developed theory of culture change, and to add a diachronic element to earlier synchronic comparison, Redfield returned to Chan Kom in 1948, fifteen years after completing his first study there. Despite some material changes, and a shift from 'acceptance of traditional ways to a zeal for progress and reform,' there was no significant sign of cultural disorganization. Redfield attributed this underlying stability to the fact that new aspirations had not yet undermined the fundamental unity of village 'ethos,' or world view. Members of the community were still in sufficient agreement on the meaning of life, and of local institutions, to preserve a holistic cultural pattern. Chan Kom had not yet become a mere appendage of a wider sociocultural system.[26]

At the heart of all Redfield's work on acculturation, then, there was clearly an overriding interest in the mental, rather than the material, elements of culture change: his primary concern was to understand what life meant to individual members of peasant communities, towns or cities, and how that personal meaning was related to a broader 'collective mentality' which shaped the organization of particular cultural wholes.[27] This concern was passed on to a number of students and colleagues in anthropology, who made an analysis of 'world view' an important part of their ethnographical field work.[28] It was also taken up with interest by sociologists of the structural-functionalist school who, following Talcott Parsons, were engaged from the late 1940s onward in an effort to categorize social systems according to their value orientations. Redfield's work therefore foreshadowed in some respects the 'modernization' studies which dealt so tenaciously during the 1960s with the question of how aspirations and values change during the transition from 'tradition' to 'modernity.'

A number of the assumptions underlying the folk-urban continuum, in particular, were soon to be challenged by Redfield's colleagues within the school of functionalist cultural anthropology, as well as by others more closely linked to cultural ecology and Marxism. The former, including Oscar Lewis, George Foster and Ralph Beals, objected to the implication that homogeneity, integration and a sacred tradition were variables which depended upon isolation from urban culture; on the contrary, they pointed out, such variables were entirely independent of the rural-urban dimension. There were sacred urban communities and rural secular ones. And in addition, folk societies were historically not isolated at all; they lived in symbiosis with the city and their past, as their present, was filled with conflict stemming from constant internal adjustment to the demands made by the wider economic and political system of the nation. To these criticisms, anthropologists less influenced by structural functionalism were to add a mistrust of Redfield's particular emphasis on the mental or psychological elements in culture and to urge that more importance be given to the role of economic and environmental factors in determining the course of change. Redfield consistently responded by stressing the heuristic value of his ideal types: they were intended not to describe real communities, but to provide a standard for judging the kind of cultural integration present in any human group. And they were based in the last instance upon 'ethos' or world view because while the physical environment could set limits beyond which men could not venture, it could not determine the particular use which those same men would make of the resources at their disposal. Only a mental organization of reality could explain the latter.[29]

Redfield, Gamio and applied anthropology in Mexico

In the 1930s, these debates were still a decade or more in the future. For the moment, a solid institutional framework for the professional practice of anthropology was being built in Mexico around the methodology and theory provided by Redfield, Tax and their associates, on the one hand, and Gamio and his group on the other. In 1937, Alfonso Caso (an archeologist associated with the Chicago school of Redfield) presided over the founding of the Mexican Anthropological Society. In 1939, one of Gamio's assistants during the Teotihuacan project, Lucio Mendieta y Núñez, took over the direction of the Institute for Social Studies of the National University and reoriented its work toward rural sociology, initiating a number of monographs on Indian regions. The same year saw the founding of a Department of Anthropology within the National Polytechnic Institute, absorbed in 1942 into the newly formed National School of Anthropology. And in 1940, an Interamerican Indian Institute (III), with headquarters in Mexico City, was founded by delegates from a number of Latin American countries meeting in Pátzcuaro. The purpose of the institute was, in large measure, to forge links among those concerned with the 'Indian problem' throughout the hemisphere, so that programs could be supported which would raise levels of living in indigenous areas while defending cultural plurality. The importance of the recent Mexican experience in this field was made patent by the election of Moisés Sáenz as first director of the institute; and following his untimely death shortly after assuming the post, by the naming of Manuel Gamio as his successor.[30]

The way in which ethnographic particularists like Gamio were accustomed to look at rural reality lent itself more easily to the practical tasks of indigenismo than that of structural functionalism, although anthropologists of the latter school were present from the beginning among the ranks of indigenistas. The crux of the difficulty for structural functionalists lay in how to change some aspects of Indian cultures while preserving others: how to raise levels of living without destroying 'Indianness.' For Gamio, this was not a theoretical problem. The culture of any given group could be separated into 'traits,' some of which could be considered useful, beautiful, or otherwise positive, and therefore worthy of support or preservation by development agencies, while others considered harmful could be eradicated. For anthropologists like Redfield, Tax and Villa Rojas, on the other hand, this way of approaching culture change was anathema. Cultures were complex wholes, and a change in any part of that whole implied profound alteration in all the rest. What position could they take, then, toward applied anthropology?

The answer to the question is to be found in the pages of *América Indígena*, the newly founded journal of the III, which during the early 1940s printed a running debate between the 'anthropologists' of Redfield's group and the 'indigenistas' of the III. The former held consistently that the future of Indian communities was assimilation into the wider national culture, in a process not so much desirable as inevitable. Applied anthropology could – and should – serve to make the process as painless as possible, and to defend the values of local people as far as possible. But this would have to be more of a defensive than an offensive operation. As Redfield put it in a letter to the editor of *América Indígena* in 1943,

It seems to me at least arguable that in the long run . . . the trend of change for native groups is in the direction of assimilation to ways of the dominant group. The value and virtue of [indigenismo] lies in the imagination and practical success attending your efforts to mitigate the disorganizing effects of this trend and to help the native peoples retain something of their own life.[31]

There was no guarantee that the quality of life, understood broadly as encompassing all socioeconomic and cultural elements and not simply material wellbeing, would improve with incorporation, just as there was no guarantee that a 'core of positive Indian traits' would survive material modernization. Given such doubts, Redfield, Tax, and their followers ideally preferred to dedicate their own energies to the scientific study of culture, which they hoped would contribute to an eventual improvement in the human condition, and to leave applied anthropology to others.[32]

Problems of formalism in functionalist applied anthropology

To avoid the constraints which a strict application of the holistic paradigm imposed upon applied work, many anthropologists within the functionalist school, working in Mexico in the 1940s, adopted the position that while cultures were indeed complex wholes, some parts of the whole were more closely related to each other, or to a central cultural 'core,' than others. Therefore, it was possible, through field work among a given group, to determine what aspects of life could be changed — or were the easiest to change — and which would be difficult to alter or would imply an unhealthy degree of disorganization. Such an approach was being taken at the time by Julian Steward, in the United States, and Bronislaw Malinowski in Europe. In Mexico, the work of Ralph Beals can serve to illustrate the way the paradigm was used.

Beals, who shared with Julian Steward a background of training within the California school of anthropology associated with Kroeber, lived among the Yaqui and Mayo of Sonora in 1930-2, and among the Mixe of Oaxaca in 1933. His early studies were not far removed from a very academic ethnographic particularism, their primary purpose being to seek 'aboriginal survivals.' Nevertheless, Beals was already tangentially concerned with how to remedy livelihood problems of indigenous groups; and the opportunity fully to combine scientific analysis with applied anthropology presented itself in 1939, when Daniel Rubín de la Borbolla (the director of the Department of Anthropology of the National Polytechnic Institute) suggested collaboration in the founding of a project intended to piece together a picture of the past, present and future of the Tarascan Indians of west-central Mexico. In its interdisciplinary nature, the program was to follow the model of the Carnegie Foundation's Yucatán Project, just completed. Practical consideration of the possibility of raising levels of living was to be given special importance.[33]

In three monographs published during the 1940s, Beals and his colleagues looked at the culture of the Tarascan community of Cherán, with a view toward contributing both to a better understanding of a generic entity, the Indian community, and to providing 'an adequate basis for intelligent administration.'[34] Two of the publications were dedicated entirely to practical questions.[35] The third, *Cherán: A Sierra Tarascan Village*,[36] was a functionalist community study which analysed the life of the village in what had become, by that time, the classic anthropological format. Agricultural resources and techniques, implements and calendars were presented in great detail; religion, healing and folk beliefs were described; the life cycle was reviewed; and the interrelation of all elements of the culture was emphasized in an attempt to come to a conclusion concerning what it meant to be a villager of Cherán.

From this overview, Beals attempted to draw conclusions of use for applied anthropology, not − as in the case of his analysis of housing or diet − on the level of detailed consideration of how to meet material needs, but through a discussion of the cultural background of livelihood. Like a number of others working within similar theoretical frameworks, he felt that his analysis provided grounds for concluding that the people of Cherán were amenable to any material change which would raise their level of living without disturbing the core of customs ('los costumbres') which defined their most intimate nature. The latter included behavior centering around the family, religion and community service. Beals was therefore true to the (applied) functionalist paradigm of the period, which placed the spiritual life or values of rural people at the center of attention and saw changes in the technicoeconomic aspects of culture as somewhat peripheral to the central design for living.

Absolutely lacking in Beals's account, as in many others of the period, was any attention to the political requisites of the kind of economic change proposed for raising levels of living. Such an omission sprang from the rigidly formal definition of 'economic' and 'political' realms within the prevailing paradigm, and their consequently unrealistic separation. It sprang as well from a continuing limitation on discerning meaningful relationships beyond the boundaries of the community or *municipio* under study, which proved particularly troublesome for functionalism when turned to practical, applied analysis. The economics of village life was seen as nothing more than a series of local self-provisioning exercises, unrelated to the play of power, within or without the community; and when so depicted, it was entirely amenable to modification through the introduction of elements which disturbed neither political balance nor the cultural 'core' of local life.

An interpretation of this kind was particularly ill-fitted to reality in the Tarascan region, for the latter was, in the 1940s, far from being one of the more physically or socially remote areas of Mexico. Even Cherán, which Beals characterizes as 'one of the most isolated of the mountain Tarascan towns,' contained families a 'majority' of whose members had either 'been in the United States or [had] relatives living in the United States.' By 1940, Beals continued, 'there were individuals whose livelihood had been seriously affected by the outbreak of war and who furthermore were quite aware of their relationship to outside markets.'[37] Yet nothing more is said of these individuals, nor indeed of any other way in which the process of exchange between members of the community and the outside world affected local livelihood.

The formalism and isolation with which economics was treated found a parallel in the field of politics. The political process was generally presented as an exercise in formal administration, and only tangentially as the interplay of interpersonal relations escaping those boundaries. The impression was therefore given that politics was an entirely local affair, and devoid of serious conflict among socioeconomic strata. That this could not really have been the case in Cherán is suggested by Beals's own passing remark that the community contained well-defined socioeconomic groups, including a significant contingent of landless laborers who were paid in cash for their work and who complained of low wages. It is also suggested by the historical work of other scholars in the Tarascan region, who have noted the prevalence of *caciquismo* from the time of the revolution onward and classified Tarascan villages as among the most conflict-ridden in the nation.[38] If applied anthropology were seriously to contribute to raising levels of living in the countryside, it would have been imperative to confront the phenomenon of *caciquismo* on an intellectual plane, and to understand it. Functionalism could not, however, provide the conceptual tools with which to do so.[39]

Wartime concern with the psychological requisites of national unity: George Foster and the 'image of limited good'

By minimizing the disruptive effects of contact with an urban culture (through supposedly protecting the cultural 'core' of folk communities), and ignoring questions of unequal power entirely, it was posible, then, for anthropologists like Beals to take a very sanguine view of modernization, which was reduced to simple material betterment. In this scheme, the 'nation' came to play a particularly benevolent part, for it was the repository of needed techniques and products. Such a conviction was in all probability not unrelated to the wider ethos of a wartime culture, for during the 1940s anthropologists in Mexico, as in many other parts of the world, were engaged in official programs to strengthen bonds of solidarity within somewhat disaggregated, pluricultural nation states (or colonies, as the case might be). Just as Marxists like Lombardo Toledano had seen the need to integrate the nation in the face of hostile pressure from the United States during the 1930s, so functionalist anthropologists were drawn into efforts to make Mexico a satisfactory place for all its citizens, as it became a (partially unconvinced) member of the Allied camp in the following decade.

Part of this effort was directed by the newly founded Institute of Social Anthropology of the Smithsonian Institution, headed by Julian Steward, which channelled wartime funds for technical and scientific cooperation into a number of projects throughout the hemisphere. When Beals's and Rubín de la Borbolla's Tarascan Project ran into financial difficulties, for example, its ethnological component was salvaged by the Institute, which sent George Foster and Donald Brand to Mexico in 1944 to teach in the National School of Anthropology, and to carry out field work in Michoacán (in 1945-6) with students from various Latin American countries and the United States. This prolongation of the Tarascan Project provided material for the publication of two studies by cultural geographers,[40] and one ethnography which stands in the history of Mexican anthropology as the first attempt by a member of the functionalist school to challenge Redfield's extremely positive evaluation of the system of values characteristic of 'folk' societies.[41] In so doing, the ground rules of functionalist applied anthropology underwent a significant change, for if the 'folk' world view were inherently negative, it was no longer necessary to find a way to protect it during the course of modernization. On the contrary, public policy could come full circle, and return to an emphasis on the kind of modernizing education associated with Gamio's first efforts.

The setting for this inversion of prevailing anthropological belief was Tzintzuntzan, a mestizo village on Lake Pátzcuaro studied by George Foster during 1945 and 1946. While observing the patterns of interpersonal behavior of Tzintzuntzeños, Foster was struck by their incongruence with the prevalent 'assumption that [collectivism] is the dominating characteristic of rural peoples.' On the contrary, he was impressed

> not with collectivistic but rather with the strong tradition of individualistic attitudes... Land is owned privately, and rights to it jealously guarded... There is no social mechanism whereby the poor and less favored are helped, and little pity for those who experience personal or financial catastrophes. Cooperative work in the fields, found among some of the more isolated Indian groups, is unknown; the custom of the *faena*, labor dedicated to the community, is grudgingly observed. Only through the mechanism of *compadrazgo*, and through joint participation in Church functions, is mutual help and service to others evidenced.[42]

In general, Foster found 'mistrust, suspicion, and fear ... the common reactions to new persons or situations,' and 'individual and group lethargy' the most likely approach to work.[43]

Why should this be the case? The paradigm which shaped Foster's analysis in the 1940s precluded looking in any detail at elements of power, exercised by groups with similar interests either within the community or outside it. He might have concluded, however, following Redfield, that Tzintzuntzan was in the throes of cultural disorganization, accompanying contact with urban society. (It was manifestly no longer Tarascan, although it had once been the center of the Tarascan Empire.) This Foster clearly did not wish to do. Rather he explained the prevalence of mistrust, suspicion and fear as an outcome of the fact that 'the possibility of real material success is so limited by ecological and economic factors that few persons ever can expect to get far ahead ... Since one's own life is so much a series of frustrations one takes pleasure in noting the difficulties of neighbors ...' And the only way to overcome these material barriers to more satisfactory interpersonal relations was to use the wider resources of the nation, to construct a 'much more thoroughly integrated economic and social system.'[44]

By the time Foster returned to Tzintzuntzan in 1959, to conduct a restudy of the village, his first impressions of disharmony had been incorporated into a concept which he called the 'image of limited good' — a world view made rational during four centuries of colonial domination but increasingly dysfunctional within the context of a benevolently modernizing nation state. Basically, Tzintzuntzeños (like members of other folk communities with similarly limited resources) were seen to orient their behavior according to the conviction that local goods were finite, like the proverbial inelastic pie, and that a larger share for one family inevitably implied a smaller share for all the rest. Although this view of the world originally sprang from enforced political impotence and economic deprivation, it had taken on a life of its own, far more troublesome for community development than either of its original causes. Psychological factors had replaced economic or political ones as the principal stumbling blocks in the way of raising levels of living and increasing the general wellbeing of rural people. Until the former were dealt with through 'instilling new values,' peasants would 'remain problems.'[45]

Whether the 'problem' was really the peasants themselves, or whether it was in fact the way in which they were inserted in the wider society, was soon to become a question for intense debate within the anthropological profession, as was the related disagreement revolving around whether to deal first with material privation or local values ('limited goods' or the 'limited good').[46] In the field of practical policy, Foster's emphasis on the need to 'instill new values' and to strengthen interaction between local and national systems nevertheless proved congruent with the turn effectively taken by Mexican development programs after Cárdenas. Most efforts to provide programs specially adapted to the peculiar needs of rural, or indigenous, areas were abandoned, and the earlier emphasis on cultural pluralism exchanged for an equally decided support of cultural uniformity.[47]

At the same time, Foster's concern with negative elements in the supposedly generic world view associated with 'folk' society established him at the forefront of a second current within the group of anthropologists devoting increasing attention to 'culture and personality' in the Mexican countryside after 1940. While Redfield's associates continued to draw attention to the positive aspects of the peasant world view, students working under Foster's direction, or associated with his department at Berkeley, began to produce a growing number of studies stressing psychologically explained elements of conflict in rural communities.[48] The conclusions of each group were based upon equally impressionistic research methods, and were equally open to the charge of subjectivism levelled on a broader plane against the 'culture and personality' school as a whole. It was perhaps relevant to the differences among the two that the group upholding the Redfieldian picture tended to restrict its work to Indian communities, while that supporting Foster carried out studies almost entirely in mestizo villages. They were, then, to a certain extent conducting an argument about two uncomparable cases.

Oscar Lewis's challenge to Redfield: social and psychological dimensions of conflict in Tepoztlán

A similar incomparability of field situations could not be adduced in the case of the challenge levelled at Redfieldian structural-functionalism by Oscar Lewis, surely one of the best known members of the 'culture and personality' school working in Mexico. Lewis first entered the country in 1943, as part of a wartime program of scientific cooperation much like the one in which Foster was concurrently participating. The Interamerican Indian Institute and the United States Bureau of Indian Affairs jointly sponsored a project 'to provide government agencies working in rural areas with a better understanding of the psychology and needs of the people,' and Lewis was appointed field representative of the Bureau. With the advice of a number of Mexican anthropologists, including Gamio, Rubin de la Borbolla, and Julio de la Fuente, it was decided to conduct a study in Tepoztlán, which not only was typical of many 'folk' communities of the central highlands, but had also been studied fifteen years earlier by Redfield. Redfield's work was to provide the ethnological base upon which Lewis and his Mexican students could build an investigation of personality.[49]

In fact, the situation Lewis found in Tepoztlán after settling in and beginning interviews was so fundamentally different from what he had been led to believe by Redfield's book that it became necessary to carry out an entirely new community study, and in so doing, to challenge not only Redfield's theory of folk culture, but also his methodology and some of his ethnographic data. A precedent was thereby set for restudies of a single community by different anthropologists (breaking an unwritten rule that a community once studied by anyone 'belonged' to him and should be restudied by him alone), and for admitting that the picture painted by any anthropologist observer was likely to contain subjective elements making 'scientific description' a definitely relative matter.[50] In this endeavor, it must be noted, Redfield collaborated fully.

Lewis broadened Redfield's analysis in two ways. First, he placed Tepoztlán within a modern historical context, treating it not as a rather isolated 'folk' society but as a community of people intimately involved in the life of the nation. To accomplish this, Lewis not only interviewed Tepoztecans (in traditional anthropological fashion), but also consulted national and local archives, the records of government agencies, newspapers, and other sources too often reserved for historians. And second, he carried out the program of psychological testing and detailed observation of selected families which had been the original purpose of his stay, utilizing a large team of assistants and the latest diagnostic devices, including the Rohrschach and TAT tests. He thus both ascended above the community level on which Redfield had worked, and descended below it, achieving a picture of 'life in a Mexican village' unrivalled in anthropological or sociological literature up to that time.

When Lewis broke the boundaries associated with earlier functionalist community studies, he found conflict — not just material privation, noted by applied anthropologists from Gamio to Beals, nor the conflict between high aspirations and limited real resources which produced frustration in Foster's Tzintzuntzan, nor conflict between urban and rural values according to Redfield, but conflict among social groups acting within changing historical circumstances. This conflict he saw primarily in terms of politics. Lewis was particularly unhappy with the formalistic way in which Redfield and other functionalists had limited themselves to a cursory investigation of the administrative institutions of particular communities. By turning to a historical analysis of the political process, he was able to point to a long history of rule by caciques, followed by a more recent manipulation of loyalties through networks of relationships leading directly to the state governor. 'The municipio,' he concluded, was 'no more than an administrative dependency of the governor.'[51] And within the village, political conflict was rife. In fact, 'the year that Redfield was [in Tepoztlan], political schisms culminated in open violence bordering on civil war, and it was this situation which finally resulted in Redfield's leaving the village.'[52]

Nevertheless, political conflict is never meaningfully related in Lewis's account to economic differentiation. The extremely detailed censuses carried out by members of the project showed that 81 per cent of all families in Tepoztlán had less than 'a minimum for decent subsistence' in 1943, while 4.4 per cent constituted an upper stratum with from five to twenty times the resources of the average poor family. The latter group controlled 25 per cent of all land, 'including some of the best land.' There was, in addition, 'a trend toward the concentration of wealth, especially in land,' and 'little upward mobility [was] possible.'[53] Yet Lewis repeatedly insisted that no 'single group control[led] sufficient capital or labor to achieve wealth by its use or exploitation,' and that the continued availability of communal lands for the poor prevented the formation of social classes. Politics was apparently a purely personalistic confrontation, unrelated to a deeper competition for the control of scarce economic resources.[54]

It would seem that while Lewis was able to escape formalism in his study of politics, and to trace informal networks of political dependence which tied Tepoztlán to a wider regional and national system, he could not extend that new outlook to his treatment of economics. Like Foster, Beals, and other contemporaries interested in applied anthropology, his material on the way different groups of Tepoztecans went about securing a livelihood is extremely detailed; but it is also contained within the same conceptual categories utilized in any other community study of the period. Lewis's treatment of 'industry and trade' is especially relevant here. Despite the fact that 'most Tepoztecan produce [was] sold outside the village, primarily in Cuernavaca,' to a variety of intermediaries, and that 'many poor people complain[ed] that they [had] to go to Cuernavaca to purchase corn because none [was] available locally,'[55] Lewis provided no information at all on the mechanisms of exchange involved, nor on their effects. He was aware of the fact that Tepoztlán, as the 'center' of its surrounding hinterland, 'dominated' 'the periphery' of villages smaller than itself 'politically, economically, and socially';[56] yet this intriguing (and from the standpoint of later theoretical developments, prophetic) statement is not taken up further, nor is the concept ever extended into the field of Tepoztlán's economic relations with its 'center.'

In the last analysis, it was the broader interaction of Tepoztecan culture with elements of national culture which preoccupied Lewis throughout the ethnographic section of his book, just as the phenomenon had preoccupied Redfield; and much of what Lewis found to have changed in Tepoztlán during the period 1928-43, interestingly enough, confirmed Redfield's predictions. Cooperative labor was declining; the authority of elders and parents lessening; the sacred elements of agricultural practice disappearing. 'On the whole,' Lewis wrote in his concluding chapter, 'many of our findings for Tepoztlán might be interpreted as confirming Redfield's more general findings for Yucatán, particularly in regard to the trend toward secularization and individualization, perhaps less so in regard to disorganization.'[57] Lewis remained unconvinced of the inevitability of the relationship between those three variables and urban contact; and in a later study of migrants to Mexico City, he made a case for the increasing cohesion and improved interpersonal relations of some rural families in an urban context.[58] Nevertheless he was clearly impressed by the positive aspects of traditional social organization in Tepoztlán, and, like Redfield, concerned that the kind of culture change then under way would not do much to improve the quality of village life.[59]

On the psychocultural level (which occupied the second half of Lewis's book), he attempted to counterbalance the 'Rousseauian quality' of Redfield's picture, 'which glossed lightly over evidence of violence, disruption, cruelty, ... and maladjustment,'[60] by emphasizing the negative traits of the typical Tepoztecan world view. His picture was therefore comparable, at first glance, to that which Foster painted of Tzintzuntzan during the same period. 'Successful persons [were] popular targets of criticism, envy, and malicious gossip.'[61] 'There [was] a readiness to view people as potentially dangerous, and the most characteristic initial reaction to others [was] suspicion and distrust.'[62] The Tepoztecan was 'an individualist with faith in his own power alone and with reluctance to seek or give economic aid, to borrow or lend, or to cooperate with others in public and private enterprises.'[63] Such a personality complex, Lewis added, was 'not neurotic,' but 'rooted in the hard realities of Tepoztecan economic and social life.'[64] Personality was therefore in a certain sense dependent upon culture, and like the latter it tended to change more slowly than rapidly modernizing social and economic structures. It came to constitute an impediment to adaptation over the short run, as Foster noted in his second Tzintzuntzan study and Lewis implied in his concept of the 'culture of poverty,' developed in the 1950s.[65]

Despite the similar orientation of Foster's and Lewis's early work, however, there were significant differences in the implications of their concepts of peasant world views and the way those world views reflected wider socioeconomic and cultural patterns. Foster never doubted that the 'image of limited good' (an essentially peasant phenomenon) was an anachronism within the setting of a modern, 'progressive' capitalist state. Lewis, on the other hand, drew from his long discussions with peasants and urban slum dwellers the eventual lesson that their behavior was intimately related to patterns of exploitation having much to do with the nature of the contemporary capitalist system. The 'culture of poverty' was therefore a syndrome especially associated with situations in which the disorganizing effects of modernization were most strongly felt: in which there were wage labor, high rates of under and unemployment, a conspicious consumption ethic, and failure to provide adequate forms of social, political, and economic organization for a low-income population.⁶⁶ This was not the prevailing condition in Tepoztlán, nor in other peasant villages still characterized by relatively strong 'traditional' forms of organization; and indeed, Lewis is careful to point out in his biography of a Tepoztecan leader, *Pedro Martínez*, that Martínez did not live in a 'culture of poverty.'⁶⁷ The latter was rather to be found in proletarianized peasant communities or in the urban slums which were to constitute the setting for Lewis's later field work. Tepoztecans were poor, individualistic, and often engaged in conflict; but they and their culture were not disorganized, and it was this Redfieldian variable which ultimately saved them from the 'emptiness' of those who lived in the culture of poverty.⁶⁸

Symptoms of crisis in the functionalist paradigm: the Viking Fund Seminar

The concern with conflict, whether in the psychocultural or the historical-political realm, which began to appear in the work of anthropologists like Foster and Lewis in the 1940s, was symptomatic of strain within the predominant functionalist paradigm, as it was applied to an ever-broader range of rural situations and proved increasingly inadequate to deal with them all. Eloquent testimony of this strain was provided in 1949, when the Viking Fund (later to become the Wenner-Gren Foundation) brought together many of the principal anthropological figures of the period for a week-long seminar at which they were to compare their field experiences and attempt to reach some general conclusions on 'the culture of Mesoamerica.'⁶⁹ With considerable frequency, generalizations presented by one participant were not congruent with the field experience of another. Mestizo Tzintzuntzan was simply not comparable, in many respects, with the Tzotziles of highland Chiapas, nor with the peculiar situation prevailing in lowland plantation areas, brought repeatedly into the discussion by the only rural sociologist attending the seminar, Nathan Whetten.

True to the intellectual boundaries of cultural anthropology at that moment, participants opted for comparing disparate situations by placing them along a continuum of acculturation, ranging from 'most Indian' to 'most mestizo or ladino.' The Lacandones of Chiapas were established as the point of comparison, for having retained the greatest proportion of pre-Columbian traits (in language, technology, social organization, and religion), and other Mesoamerican groups rated against them. Implicit in the continuum was the folk-urban dimension, for a ladino was clearly most integrated into the wider national culture.[70]

Members of the seminar thus succeeded in making some order out of their differing experiences by adhering strictly to descriptive criteria of culture, but it was not a very satisfying accomplishment. Saying *where* certain groups stood on the Index of Acculturation did little to explain *how* or *why* each case exhibited peculiar economic, political or social arrangements. Degree of urban contact was not a sufficient explanatory variable, because groups with similar degrees of contact obviously had very different qualitative experiences. Throughout the discussion, queries concerning concrete historical sequences arose again and again; and in order to answer such questions, it became necessary to place given communities within wider regional and national contexts. Oscar Lewis was not present at the seminar, but his contemporary critique of 'ideological localism' found an echo among many of the anthropologists who were.

A particularly bothersome question for participants, it might be added, was that of how to define an Indian, or an indigenous culture. The extreme case of the Lacandones, who were virtually a primitive tribe, might be easy to establish. But for all the numberless rural communities which stood further along the acculturation continuum, how could one determine which was Indian and which was not? This had indeed long been a question of considerable practical import for official development programs: was a particular community or region 'Indian' enough to merit the expenditure of funds specifically marked for indigenous areas? Gamio simply answered by inserting questions concerning supposedly indigenous traits within the national census of 1940 and drawing his conclusions accordingly.[71] Caso and others within the Bureau of Indian Affairs (converted in 1948 into the National Indian Institute) reviewed all alternative definitions and concluded that 'Indianness' was a subjective feeling and that an Indian community was any group of people who felt themselves to be so.[72] But by the late 1940s, neither of these approaches seemed adequate to most who confronted the enigma of 'Indianness.' A new explanation of the phenomenon was imperative; and in the search for it, a first partial turn toward elaboration of an historical, structuralist view of ethnicity was soon to be taken.

2 A dialogue on ethnic conflict: indigenismo and functionalism, 1950-70

During the 1950s, a growing number of anthropologists working in Mexico stepped outside the geographical confines of the isolated rural community and the temporal confines of the functionalist present. They began to see not so much what separated rural people from the wider socioeconomic system as what integrated them; not so much the characteristic features of disparity as those of domination. That this turn of events was intimately related to the changing nature of life in the Mexican countryside could hardly be denied: in Mexico as in most of the rest of the world, rural areas were rapidly being integrated into new kinds of socioeconomic and political arrangements congruent with the development of modernizing nation states. But alteration in the way anthropologists defined their subject matter was equally related to a conscious effort on the part of many formed in the functionalist or particularist tradition in Europe, the United States, and Mexico to look beyond the original limits of their professional concern in hopes of explaining long-recurring phenomena for which no adequate explanation had yet been found. They were, in other words, confronted with the necessity of paradigmatic revision, not immediately implying a brusque abandonment of earlier paradigms, but increasingly incorporating new elements which over the long run produced a structure of ideas ever further removed from the tenets associated with the normal practice of their discipline in previous decades.

The urgency of this revision was perhaps particularly clear to indigenistas, who had a professional obligation to work on the borderline of interaction between peoples of remarkably different cultures. Up to the 1950s, the range of anthropological explanation which they could bring to bear on their situation was indeed rather narrow: neither functionalist nor particularist theory could provide a convincing definition of 'Indianness,' nor explain why cultural differences were so extraordinarily marked in the Mexican countryside. Yet answers to these questions were required if the practice of applied anthropology were to report any but the most superficial of contributions to the integration of a Mexican nation.

The kind of micro-level research on culture consistently associated with previous anthropological work had made an important contribution to descriptive ethnography and, especially in the work of functionalists, had mapped out a way of looking at the disorganization and reorganization of rural cultures upon contact with urban ones. But it had nothing to say concerning the structural roots of ethnic identity, and at bottom, that was the point upon which community development efforts floundered. It was one thing to introduce modern techniques or services into an isolated village in the hope of raising levels of living without distorting a valuable 'cultural core,' as applied functionalist anthropologists were wont to advise in the 1940s and beyond; or simply to leave local people to work out their own adjustment to change, with recourse to benign outside assistance, if required, as more academically inclined functionalists preferred to suggest. But the doctors, teachers, and community development workers who constituted the second generation of Mexican indigenistas, active in the countryside from the 1930s onward, came face to face with what they saw as culturally rooted *resistance* to material change, and that resistance was in turn related to the way in which local people had experienced a concrete historical process of exploitation at the hands of outsiders. Therefore postwar indigenistas began to work out a way of understanding local cultures which required modifying the intellectual boundaries of structural-functionalism through inclusion of close attention to the historically determined causes of conflict between inhabitants of isolated rural settlements and neighboring urban groups.

There was a significant element of Marxism in this revision, for it will be remembered that Mexican indigenismo first developed in a maelstrom of postrevolutionary work in the countryside which was closely associated with socialist ideals. Yet despite the incorporation of Marxist concepts, second generation indigenistas remained sufficiently within the boundaries of the 'culturalist' world view characteristic of functionalism to permit continuing and close collaboration between members of the two schools, culminating during the 1960s in agreement upon a synthetic interpretation of ethnic identity in which indigenista insistence upon the importance of exploitative historical experience had been widely accepted by functionalists, but functionalist insistence upon the priority of mental over material elements in the determination of human behaviour had at the same time reinforced the tendency of indigenistas to concentrate upon induced cultural change as the single most critical aspect of applied development work. The content of this dialogue will be the subject of the following pages.

Center and periphery enter the functionalist and indigenista vocabulary: Malinowski and de la Fuente in the Oaxaca market

Although structural functionalism tended from its inception to restrict anthropological observation to cultural phenomena at the level of an isolable local community, such a narrow delineation of intellectual boundaries had never been entirely feasible within indigenismo. In part because of its applied nature, in part because of long-standing association with the tradition of anthropological particularism, indigenismo from the time of Gamio onward had been consistently characterized by an underlying concern with the delineation of culture areas, and thus by extension with the definition of regions. What had not been accomplished within the 'culturalist' framework of indigenismo in the prewar period, however, was the construction of a theoretical link between Indians and non-Indians living in close geographical proximity. It was one thing to look at the livelihood of all Nahua groups whose villages could be identified within a given segment of a map of the Mexican nation, but quite another to consider how they might materially interact with rural or urban mestizo neighbors, interspersed between one Nahua-speaking village and another, in a manner more complex than that suggested by prevailing functionalist notions of culture contact and acculturation. Interestingly enough, the first steps toward dealing with such a question — and in the process emphasizing the role of non-Indians in determining significant material elements of Indian livelihood — were taken at the turn of the 1940s during the course of an improbable collaboration between an outstanding, and conservative, European functionalist who specifically dissociated his approach from that of the Chicago school, and a radical young indigenista who was to have long professional ties to Chicago.

In 1940, Bronislaw Malinowski arrived in Mexico City, drawn by an interest in comparing contemporary processes of social change in the Mexican countryside with those he had briefly studied a few years earlier under the aegis of colonial administration in Africa. After preliminary discussions with representatives of the National Institute of Anthropology and History (INAH), and a reconaissance trip to the city of Oaxaca, Malinowski decided to study the marketing system of the Valley of Oaxaca, which drew the inhabitants of Indian and peasant villages within a wide radius of the mestizo city into a process of regular interaction and exchange recalling, for the anthropologist observer, an 'ephemeral, dramatic museum of the moment.'[1] The phenomenon met all the requirements of Malinowski's particular functionalist paradigm: in a single institution one could encounter intertwined the threads of an entire culture, which could be painstakingly unwound in order to examine the relationship of the parts to the whole. At the same time, the market constituted a fundamental element in the complex of human behavior associated with securing a livelihood, which Malinowski had placed at the heart of his theoretical scheme. While Radcliffe-Brown and the structural functionalist school considered all aspects of culture ultimately related to the maintenance of the existing social structure, Malinowski carefully differentiated his approach through referring always to the function of elements of culture in satisfying 'individual biopsychological needs.' That this was not, at bottom, in any sense a materialist position has been demonstrated by Marvin Harris.[2] Nevertheless, it implied studying primitive or peasant economics in great detail.

Malinowski's Mexican counterpart for the Oaxaca project was Julio de la Fuente, a textbook illustrator for the public schools and an ardent indigenista whose concern for the welfare of the poor had led him to organize workers in New York during the 1920s and to publish newspapers for the agrarian cause in Veracruz during the early 1930s.[3] De la Fuente was at that time a Marxist; but he became disenchanted with Marxism in the 1930s and found in recently published works by Redfield and Gamio the incentive to take up a systematic study of the discipline of anthropology, at that time entirely outside the field of Marxism. The extent to which he absorbed Redfield's view of rural change is illustrated in de la Fuente's first full-length monograph, *Yalálag*, published in 1949, which constituted a strict functionalist analysis of secularization, individualization and disorganization within a Zapotec village of Oaxaca.[4] The extent to which he also believed in indigenismo was to be proven in coming years through decades of association with indigenista institutions.

De la Fuente's excellent papers on ethnic relations and education, presented at the Interamerican Indian Conference in Pátzcuaro in 1940, brought him to the attention of Alfonso Caso, head of the INAH, who recommended him highly to Malinowski.[5] The ensuing period of joint field work was, by all accounts, not lacking in friction. But the result was noteworthy: the combination of Malinowski's concern with tracing the boundaries of systems, and de la Fuente's practical knowledge of the web of rural communities surrounding the Oaxaca Valley, produced an effort to understand 'the unity of the center and its surrounding region... as well as the economic dependence of neighboring districts upon the Valley.'[6] The final report of the project, *La économia de un sistema de mercados en México*, stands in consequence as the earliest example in the literature of the utilization of the concept of a socio-economic region, defined not in terms of culture traits or political boundaries, but in terms of networks of relations surrounding livelihood in interdependent urban and rural settings.

Once this has been said, however, it must immediately be added that the report dealt only sketchily with the topic defined as central to the study: the 'influence which the market [exercised over] the wellbeing of the Indians, the peasants, and the townspeople, as well as [over] their style of life and that of vested interests such as the commercial agents of the district.'[7] In part, that was because Malinowski died before he could do more than set down preliminary thoughts on the project; and in part, it was because Malinowski insisted upon seeing the market as satisfying everyone's needs: the needs of the poor for small quantities of goods, exchanged for home-produced goods; the needs of the local authorities for tax revenues; the needs of the large intermediaries for cheap staples in volume. The fact that the needs of each group were in conflict was mentioned, as were the words 'exploitation, economic pressure, extortion, and direct misrepresentation.'[8] But beyond the promise that a full-length treatment of the dealings of wholesale maize buyers would be forthcoming, there was no further treatment of the mechanisms of conflict, or the impact of unequal exchange upon the level of living of market participants.

Julio de la Fuente on the role of ethnic stereotypes in maintaining patterns of regional domination: 'Indianness' as an invention of mestizos

At the time of his collaboration with Malinowski, Julio de la Fuente had already begun to study the topic which was to receive much of his attention during the coming decades and which provided his principal contribution to postwar indigenista theory and practice. That topic was interethnic relations. Until the mid-1940s, the overriding concern of those who dealt with the question had centered around the reconciliation of elements of Indian and non-Indian culture (in the case of particularism and functionalism) or around handling a kind of conflict which pitted all Indians, as a class, against all mestizos (as the process was understood by Marxist indigenistas of the Cárdenas period). Neither of these approaches satisfied de la Fuente entirely. As he observed interethnic relations during innumerable stays in the towns and villages of predominantly Indian areas, he found cultural differences to form the primary defense of many separate local groups which considered themselves threatened by outsiders. In many cases, both the threatened and the threateners were 'Indian,' according to the criteria of a mestizo observer. In the opinion of local people themselves, however, there was no such thing as an Indian. There were 'people who live here with us,' or (at times) 'countrymen' from surrounding villages speaking the same language. In some areas, there was also a consciousness of pertaining to a historically and geographically defined cultural grouping, such as the Zapotecs or the Mixtecs or the Tarascans. But the term 'Indian' was simply an epithet coined by 'castellanos' and was not universally understood, by those with whom de la Fuente talked, to mean anything more than that.[9]

The Indian/non-Indian dichotomy thus became valid only as it was utilized by mestizos to ascribe an inferior status to a large group of rural people among whom there was much cultural diversity. It was, in other words, a concept based upon the need to place all those who were ethnically different from mestizos in a structurally disadvantageous position, and as such it served as an instrument of domination. In accordance with the opinion of others who were simultaneously involved in an effort to understand the structural implications of interethnic (Indian/non-Indian) relations in Mesoamerica,[10] de la Fuente eventually characterized forms of interaction among the two groups in most areas of Mexico as 'quasi-caste' relations, although he pointed out cases in which 'quasi-class' relations could also be said to exist.[11]

The 'dual society' which de la Fuente saw as a result of his research on interethnic relations had definite geographical boundaries, not corresponding to those of the nation. Ethnic groups categorized as 'Indian' and maintained in a position of caste-like inferiority to mestizos experienced domination within the specific socioeconomic context of backward, relatively isolated regions, containing mestizo groups not yet fully integrated into modern Mexican economy and society.

The peculiar position of the latter, both in relation to the Indians and to the wider national system, constituted a fundamental impediment to the disappearance of caste relations; for mestizos based their own livelihood upon control over the Indians, rather than upon participation in a modern capitalist system. They were cultural and economic brokers between a fragmented and disorganized mass of ethnically distinct villages, on the one hand, and the national system on the other.

Given this evaluation of reality in certain strongly Indian areas, de la Fuente proceeded to suggest, at the Second Interamerican Indian Congress of Cuzco in 1949, that 'integration, before it could be national, would have to be regional.'[12] Indigenismo could not continue to carry out policies designed to build economic and cultural bridges between scattered Indian communities and national society without taking measures to deal with the decisive structure of regional mestizo mediation which imposed the fundamental characteristics of caste upon ethnic minorities. Regional development, offering new alternatives to mestizos and Indians, was imperative.

Pilot projects for the study of regional integration

This point of view came to be sustained as well by Gonzalo Aguirre Beltrán, a friend and colleague of de la Fuente who was both a medical doctor and an outstanding ethnohistorian, originally specializing in the scrutiny of African roots of Mexican rural culture.[13] After returning from a year's study with Melville Herskovits and Irving Hallowell at Northwestern University in 1945-6, Aguirre was named director of the Bureau of Indian Affairs; and with de la Fuente as his assistant director, he attempted to put incipient concern with 'regional integration' to the test by proposing the establishment of a regional development office in Tantoyuca, Veracruz. The project had barely been suggested when both were removed from their posts, but the setback proved to be only temporary. Postwar efforts to promote economic growth in Mexico were at any rate being organized with some regularity around the concept of regional development, in direct recognition of the success of efforts like the TVA in the United States; and within a few years after the transformation of the Bureau of Indian Affairs into the National Indian Institute in 1948, it had become clear that any future effort to oversee government programs in Indian areas would have to take place at the regional level.[14]

An early example of the need for regional studies could be discerned in 1949, when the federal government commissioned the National Indian Institute to carry out an evaluation of the impact of massive irrigation projects on the Indian population of four river basins. Within the following year, Aguirre Beltrán, Alfonso Villa Rojas, Moisés T. de la Peña, and Francisco Plancarte directed teams of investigators who produced now classic studies of the socioeconomic conditions prevailing among the Tarascans, Mazatecs and Tarahumara at the turn of the decade.[15] These volumes are extremely useful for students of rural livelihood; but it must be noted that there is little in their format, except the extension of the territory involved, to distinguish them in theoretical terms from the great majority of studies carried out by particularists and structural-functionalists in the past. With the exception of Plancarte's work on the Tarahumara, they deal only minimally with the problems of different kinds of mestizos within each region;[16] and they do not come to grips with the nature of relations between Indians and non-Indians, supposed in the theoretical work of de la Fuente and Aguirre Beltrán to lie at the heart of the need for a regional focus. As Aguirre was the first to admit, the river basins proved to be 'research units too large and complex to be handled by one investigator and his small group of collaborators'; the 'extension and complexity of the area' simply encouraged the investigators to 'lose sight of the [principal] mechanisms of their internal functioning.'[17]

At the close of this project, the director of the INI, Alfonso Caso, was convinced that the boundaries within which his new institution worked could not continue to be determined simply on the basis of the momentary needs of other government agencies. The programs of the Institute had to correspond to areas which had a real scientific and practical relation to the tasks of indigenismo. Therefore it was necessary to set up a pilot project, on the order of that proposed for Tantoyuca, where studies of the mechanisms of regional integration and domination could be carried out, and various strategies for promoting regional development designed and tested.

The area selected for this experiment was the Chiapas highlands, which both de la Fuente and Aguirre Beltrán knew well, and which offered the added advantage of having served as an ethnological field site for students of Tax and Redfield throughout the 1940s. It was at the same time one of the most remote, the most predominantly Indian, and the best studied regions of rural Mexico. And it was presided over by a notoriously retrograde mestizo elite centered in the city of San Cristóbal de las Casas. From 1951 to 1953, Aguirre Beltrán observed interethnic relations in this sociogeographic space at close range, as director of the first Regional Coordinating Center of the National Indian Institute. Then he left the post and returned to Mexico City, where he completed work on one book (*Formas de gobierno indigena*) and began several others,[18] all of which contributed to the delineation, in the course of the 1950s, of the finished indigenista paradigm of the postwar period.

The 'refuge regions' of Aguirre Beltrán: metropolis-satellite relations in isolated reducts of the colonial past

Aguirre Beltrán began, as Lewis and other American colleagues like Eric Wolf were doing at the same time, with an attempt to place the peculiar characteristics of rural social structure and culture in Mexico within a broad historical context. He therefore turned to the work of archeologists and ethnohistorians, as well as to the records of the Spanish Conquest; and he found in his studies ample evidence with which to refute the prevailing functionalist belief that peasant communities could be understood in temporal or spatial isolation. From pre-Conquest times, rural people had been integrated into a 'city-state system with a folk hinterland' which in periods of greatest cohesion made strong demands upon food cultivators, and in times of relative disintegration allowed them more freedom to pursue their own interests as members of self-provisioning households. The Spanish Conquest reinforced this historical tendency by placing rural communities under the authority of Spaniards located in 'seniorial cities,' and collecting tribute destined not for rural improvements but for urban development and export to Spain. Despite the egalitarian proclamations of both the independence movement at the beginning of the nineteenth century and the Mexican Revolution during the twentieth, neither succeeded entirely in destroying the pattern of metropolis-satellite relations which bound peasant producers to regional urban centers; and anthropologists therefore ignored this phenomenon of 'socioeconomic symbiosis' only at the risk of seriously distorting their vision of reality in the countryside.[19]

In this formulation of rural-urban interaction, Aguirre Beltrán was very much closer to the Marxist than to the functionalist view of Mexican history. Exchange between peasants and urban dwellers was not based fundamentally upon the principle of reciprocity or mutual gain, but rather upon that of domination. It was true that urban dwellers, in return for agricultural products, offered peasants 'a series of specialized services'; but those services were carefully maintained within the boundaries of the city in an effort to ensure that they could not be 'learned by dominated countrymen.' And in fact, on a more general level, Aguirre pointed out that

> the possibility that folk communities might be urbanized or modernized has always been limited, and is limited today, by the [interposition of] the economic and social interests of the city. The fact that the great mass of Indians have remained in a position of ancestral subordination, enjoying a strongly stabilized folk culture, has not only been desired by the city, but imposed by coercive means.[20]

'The city' of which Aguirre Beltrán spoke was, however, not intended to be a generic term applied to any urban area of the country. It was a prototype of the 'seniorial city' consolidated during the colonial period and not transformed, within certain backward and relatively isolated regions of Mexico, into the kind of modern urban center characteristic of postrevolutionary society in less isolated regions. It was still sustained, as in colonial times, by what it could extract (through unequal market relations and political extortion) from its rural hinterland, rather than having developed independent means of generating wealth through applying the fruits of modern technology and organizational capacity to the task of production.[21] And it therefore ensured its own survival only through constantly reinforcing the structural bases of domination over satellite communities held in a tributary position from the time of the Conquest.

One element in maintaining the dominant position of the seniorial city was, Aguirre Beltrán thought, the outright use of force. But a much subtler and more efficacious tool of conquest was the manipulation of ethnic identity in a way which ascribed to rural people with cultures different from those of the conquerors a permanently inferior status, and thereby legitimized their exploitation. This was the institution of caste relations between Indians and mestizos which de la Fuente analysed, and which Aguirre Beltrán also stressed in his own discussion of metropolis-satellite ties. Through reinforcing the real desire of members of rural communities to maintain their own way of life, mestizos of seniorial cities could collect tribute without admitting tributaries into the larger society, and therefore without granting the latter any option to participate in that society, even as an exploited class.

It was with the 'intercultural region' surrounding — and including —

backward seniorial cities, then, that postwar indigenismo should concern itself. The limits of the area which Aguirre Beltrán called a 'refuge region' in reference to its relative isolation from postrevolutionary national society, could be clearly determined by examining the pattern of interaction linking rural communities to neighboring urban centers. All communities bound by caste-like relations to a mestizo city, and therefore largely cut off from economic or social exchange with the broader system, obviously fell within the region. Groups engaged in freer exchange with a number of people not associated with a seniorial city, on the other hand, fell outside it. In practice, the structural differences between these two kinds of situations would be reflected in degrees of cultural idiosyncrasy or ethnic identity.

For Aguirre Beltrán, and for all anthropologists who began to think as he did (both within the applied tradition of indigenismo and outside it), the Indian thus ceased to be primarily a representative of pre-Conquest American culture and became instead an inhabitant of a relatively remote rural region, exploited for the benefit of urban counterparts in an anachronistic (colonial) way, not as part of a modern class structure, but rather as a member of a culturally defined caste to whom all posibility for advancement within the larger society had for centuries been absolutely denied.[22]

Theoretical and practical problems in the postwar indigenista paradigm

Up to this point, Aguirre Beltrán's analysis represented, then, a clear departure from the prevailing functionalist world view. But as soon as Aguirre shifted his attention from the regional to the national level, an underlying affinity with traditional applied functionalism became immediately apparent. Exploitation, which was only too visible within backward, isolated reducts of colonialism, disappeared entirely once the boundaries of those regions were crossed. Increasing interaction with, and integration into, 'the great national community' brought with it only benefits; and the idea that extending the socioeconomic ties of rural people (most especially those of Indian communities) ever further from the local level might entail greater, rather than lesser, risk was never entertained.

Why were Aguirre and other members of the postwar indigenista school unable to deal with the possibility that structural impediments to rural development might be as intractable within the context of a modernizing capitalist socioeconomic system, born of a nationalist

Indigenismo and functionalism, 1950-70   53

revolution, as within that of peripheral (merchant capitalist) remnants of colonialism? Several answers suggest themselves. The first has to do with indigenista ideology, and with the historical identification of indigenismo with Mexican nationalism. It has been illustrated at numerous points in the preceding pages that indigenismo grew out of continuous efforts to consolidate the Mexican revolution both politically (by winning the loyalty of groups at the most remote extremes of the national territory, and thereby presenting a united front to antirevolutionary forces, whether internal or external) and socioeconomically (through extending the social welfare benefits promised by the revolution to marginal and dominated elements of the national population). The construction of a new national society was a revolutionary, almost a utopian, task; and to criticize it constituted disloyalty.

The second reason why a more critical attention to the structural implications of integration beyond the regional level is not to be found in Aguirre Beltrán's work, or in that of his colleagues, would seem to be related to the influence of a rather fatalistic evolutionary perspective, attributable equally to Marxist and functionalist components of indigenista thought. For Aguirre Beltrán, urbanization and industrialization were inevitable,[23] as was the consolidation of the particular pattern of culture which accompanied those processes. The fact that the work of indigenistas, involved in breaking structural and cultural barriers between backward regions and the national society, implied integrating members of Indian communities more closely into an expanding capitalist socioeconomic system therefore did not give rise to any concern about possible damage to levels of living. Over the long run, no permanent improvement in the situation of dominated rural populations within refuge regions could be envisioned without breaking the bounds of caste relations and introducing members of Indian communities into a system of class conflict associated with the extension of capitalist relations of production to the limits of the national territory.

Finally, one can speculate, on the basis of scattered comments to be found throughout the work of Aguirre Beltrán,[24] that limiting the theoretical boundaries for an examination of the mechanisms of domination at work in the Mexican countryside strictly to the regional level, and eschewing rigorous structural analysis beyond that point, might have been a necessary tactical measure for indigenistas constrained to working within official institutions during a period characterized by extreme political conservatism. If any programs were to be carried out at all in Indian areas, reprisals against the budgets of indigenista agencies had to be avoided; and therefore it was not politically expedient to trace the threads of unequal exchange upward any further than the limits of remote, and politically peripheral, refuge regions. Isolation, it would seem, served as protection, both for indigenistas and for the national elites who distrusted them.

The action program of Regional Coordinating Centers: tying satellite communities more closely to the mestizo world

Basing its action program upon the vision of reality in 'intercultural regions' sustained by Aguirre Beltrán, the National Indian Institute proceded to delineate a number of those regions during the 1950s and 1960s, and to establish in each a Regional Coordinating Center headed by a professional anthropologist and staffed by middle-level technicians in medicine, veterinary sciences, education, agriculture, and semi-industrial trades. The primary purpose of each Center was to promote 'regional integration and development,' through working with both mestizos and Indians in an effort to provide new economic opportunities which would obviate the need of inhabitants of 'seniorial cities' to exploit ethnic minorities as castes in order to survive. 'The modernization or westernization of the mestizo city' was to be a key element in the strategy.[25] And the strengthening of economic links between the Indian hinterland and that city, so that members of rural communities could participate in the projected process of economic growth in each regional metropolis, was to be another. Both of these efforts, in turn, were to be supported by basic programs of 'induced culture change' designed to erase ethnic stereotypes and to encourage the formation of a single mestizo regional culture.

Such an approach rested upon what, in hindsight, must be described as a totally unrealistic evaluation of the political and economic strength of indigenista institutions. The kind of financial resources required to set in motion the industrialization of regional metropoli were never at the disposition of the National Indian Institute; they were managed by other federal agencies with only a modest interest in listening to the advice of anthropologists. And those agencies acted, as often as not, through the medium of existing regional elites. Modernization was therefore at least as likely to strengthen the structure of domination decried by indigenistas in 'refuge regions' as to weaken it. The hypothesized antagonism of interests between parasitic regional elites and national elites proved a poor basis for policy.[26]

Because that was the case, the second element in the program of Regional Coordinating Centers, 'tying satellite communities more closely to the mestizo nucleus' through building roads and teaching Spanish (once literacy had been achieved in native languages), tended to have contradictory implications for the welfare of rural people. Some members of newly opened communities were able to take advantage of 'modern' opportunities in regional centres; but, when 'open,' those communities also served as more accessible sources for accumulation of wealth by urban mestizos. Rural roads ran in two directions, and the greater experience and economic power of many inhabitants of the urban terminal gave the latter a definite advantage over the peasantry in putting new means of communication to profitable use.

At the local level, the program of Regional Coordinating Centers continued, in the tradition of incorporationist indigenismo, to center around community development work and the encouragement of 'acculturation,' understood (in general agreement with the definition worked out by applied functionalist anthropologists) to mean 'introducing the basic elements of industrial culture' while 'conserving those aspects of Indian culture which [gave] to regional integration its distinctive characteristics, its ethos.'[27] Aguirre Beltrán, and others of the postwar indigenista school, always insisted that this process was to produce a synthesis of non-Indian and Indian cultures — a national culture made up of both, rather than the simple imposition of the former over the latter. Yet in practice, Regional Coordinating Centers mounted a reinforced attack on the principal structural supports of Indian communities which, when successful, left little for indigenous peoples to contribute to a national culture except memories of the past.

The center of ethnic identity in all indigenous groups of Mexico, whatever the cultural differences distinguishing them, was the institution known as the civil-religious hierarchy, which functionalist anthropologists credited with requiring a special kind of local social organization fundamentally associated with maintaining the boundaries of rural communities in the face of fluctuating outside pressure toward incorporation. The civil-religious hierarchy was the repository of local political power, the mechanism through which status was defined within the community, and at the same time acted as an important channel for the redistribution of wealth through community service, rather than its accumulation for private gain. These characteristics, which anti-incorporationist indigenistas found of positive value in promoting rural development, were considered negative by those concerned with immediate national integration – including Aguirre Beltrán. By the time he had completed his stay in San Cristobal, Aguirre had concluded that the principal thrust of indigenista policy at the local level would have to be the replacement of the civil-religious hierarchy with modern political and economic institutions which would effectively break down local isolation and ensure the success of other 'acculturative' programs.[28]

To accomplish this end, Aguirre Beltrán proposed enlisting the assistance of the marginal, or 'acculturated' members of Indian and mestizo society, who had long fulfilled the necessary role of 'intermediaries between cultures in conflict.' Indian intermediaries, hired by Regional Coordinating Centers as 'cultural promoters,' were to advocate new practices and customs – including the institution of a modern structure of municipal authorities reporting upward toward state and national levels, as well as payment for services in money and the utility of accumulating resources for use in economic development projects or private investment – in their communities of origin. Mestizo intermediaries were to carry out simple technical assistance projects as teachers, carpenters, nurses or social workers. Together, they would set in motion a 'chain reaction' which would set Indian communities on 'that upward path which [was] the process of acculturation.'[29]

In the final analysis, then, the principal structural conclusion of the indigenista paradigm – that Indians were exploited as ethnic groups in a caste-like relation to backward urban mestizos – prompted those associated with the National Indian Institute not only to attempt to attenuate mestizo domination (a task at which they had relatively little success, in part because of the very nature of the links between regional and national elites which the indigenista paradigm could not consider), but at the same time to challenge the legitimacy of local ethnic identity. The latter policy was justified as necessary in order to provide Indian groups with the 'national culture' which was understood to be an indispensable weapon in the hands of those who would pass from an excluded caste to an integrated class within the larger social system. The policy was further imposed by the real conviction of postwar indigenistas that 'secularization, individualization, modernization, and integral development [were] successive moments in a permanent search for the liberty, wellbeing, and justice of all.'[30] Such a point of view was to be challenged with increasing insistence during the 1960s by those within both functionalist and Marxist schools who saw great

Indigenismo and functionalism, 1950-70

value in maintaining the ethnic identity of rural peoples, and who were not as sanguine as Aguirre Beltrán concerning the liberating influence of modern urban culture.[31] But postwar indigenismo nevertheless remained faithful to its incorporationalist calling, and followed the path first laid out by Gamio.

Collaboration between indigenistas and functionalists: the Harvard Chiapas Project

Aside from early work done by indigenista investigators on historical and contemporary elements conforming systems of regional domination (most particularly within the framework of interethnic and market relations, discussed above), the concerns of postwar indigenismo were congruent with two other general areas of research, which by the mid-1950s had largely overshadowed the former in importance. These were the study of elements of community development, or 'directed sociocultural change' in rural areas, on the one hand, and a more general interest in the dynamics of sociocultural change within Indian communities exposed to increasing contact with national society and culture, on the other. In contrast to the question of domination, which had required an understanding of situations of 'unbalanced reciprocity,' maintained by force, the latter two areas of investigation were traditionally fields of concern of structural-functionalists, whether applied or nonapplied. They were the topics around which collaboration between indigenistas and functionalist anthropologists had occurred from the 1930s onward; and as it became clear that, despite the new theoretical interest of postwar indigenistas in mechanisms of domination, the program of the National Indian Institute would be shaped by the same 'culturalist' emphasis as the program of the earlier Bureau of Indian Affairs, that collaboration was markedly strengthened.

The first area in which the National Indian Institute hoped to initiate long-term anthropological research on community development and cultural change was the Chiapas highlands, where the impact of the Institute's action program was to be evaluated not only in practical, but also in scientific terms. Therefore Alfonso Caso and Aguirre Beltrán got in touch with Evon Vogt, a graduate of the University of Chicago then on the faculty of Harvard. In the summer of 1955, Vogt went to Chiapas to investigate the possibility of setting up a joint Harvard-INI project there; and by 1957, he had obtained sufficient funding from the National Institute of Mental Health of the

United States to begin preliminary field work with the assistance of a single graduate student. During the coming years, additional grants from the Carnegie Corporation and the National Science Foundation permitted Vogt to expand the project until it included an interuniversity program of training for undergraduate students in anthropology (the Harvard-Columbia-Cornell-Illinois consortium) which brought up to fifteen of the latter to Chiapas each summer, as well as a smaller program for settling doctoral candidates from Harvard in the region during relatively long periods of dissertation research.[32]

The early goal of the project was ambitious, both in terms of the subject matter and the geographical area to be covered. It was, in the course of five years, to 'describe the changes that were occurring in the culture of the Tzotzil and Tzeltal as a result of the action-program of INI and to utilize these data for an analysis of the determinants and processes of cultural change.'[33] To study change in the entire Tzotzil-Tzeltal region, however, soon proved an impossible task. The area contained 200,000 people speaking dialects of Maya which varied markedly from each of thirty-seven indigenous communities to the next; and in addition, despite the fact that, in Vogt's opinion, the establishment of the Coordinating Center of the INI might have been 'the most important event to affect Indian cultures since the Conquest,'[34] the accumulated impact of the government program in most parts of the region remained limited. Therefore by 1959 Vogt abandoned any attempt to evaluate the work of the Center *in toto*, or to compare its impact in different indigenous communities throughout the region, and restricted the attention of the Harvard Chiapas Project to obtaining 'basic linguistic and ethnographic' material on one Tzotzil municipio, Zinacantan. Five years later, a second municipio, Chamula, was added to the universe of the study; but any principle of regional analysis (with the exception of attention to interethnic relations, to be discussed below) had been definitively discarded.

During the roughly twenty years covered by the Harvard Chiapas Project Bibliography, published by the Peabody Museum in 1978, students and senior researchers associated with the effort produced 27 monographs, 100 articles, and 21 dissertations, the great majority of which dealt with aspects of life in Zinacantan or Chamula. Clearly, the community as object of anthropological interest had experienced a renaissance within an influential sector of American structural-functionalism, precisely at the time when a number of anthropologists within the functionalist — as well as the cultural ecologist, Marxist,

Indigenismo and functionalism, 1950-70

and indigenista – paradigm were seriously questioning the utility of a community-study approach.[35] The way in which members of the Harvard Chiapas Project utilized the sociocultural material contained within the universe of two communities was, however, considerably different from that associated with earlier functionalist efforts. While Chicago-trained anthropologists like Tax and Pozas dedicated their time in Zinacantan and Chamula during the 1940s to producing monographs which attempted to take into account all the principal elements of community life, and to relate them as a meaningful whole,[36] members of the Harvard project chose particular problems of academic or practical interest and examined them in great detail within the setting of one community. Thus they participated in, and contributed to, a trend toward taking from the experience of a single community certain elements useful for the discussion of a broadly defined problem area, but not particularly for an understanding of the complex integration of the community itself. The negative effects of this fragmentation (from a functionalist point of view) were minimized in the specific case of the Harvard project by the fact that a comprehensive file containing the field notes of all participants was kept at the university, so that the cumulative result of partial efforts was the gradual formation of the basis for a single large community study, of the traditional kind, published by Vogt in 1969.[37]

Given the original concern on the part of both the INI and Harvard with the importance of studying change in the Chiapas highlands, what is striking about most of the academic output of the Harvard Chiapas Project is its relatively static nature. It is, as Vogt himself put it in his evaluation of the literature, generally 'descriptive ethnography,'[38] centered around the 'networks of beliefs, symbols, structural forms, and behavioral sequences that taken together form a consistent way of life' in Zinacantan and Chamula. This was a classic functionalist conception of culture, the 'decoding' of which would allow the ethnographer to 'behave properly in the myriad of settings and contexts he confront[ed] in Zinacanteco [or Chamula] society.'[39] Whether it could also effectively serve the practical interests of development workers associated with the National Indian Institute was a subject of debate among indigenistas.[40]

In order, then, to reach the deepest levels of understanding of culture in one Tzotzil community – in an effort which might be rather unkindly characterized, paraphrasing Clifford Geertz, as anthropological involution – members of the Harvard Chiapas Project collectively invested great amounts of time, over many years, examining cultural phenomena in the present tense. Although particular parts of a total discussion might have been worked out by a number of people on a number of different occasions, the result was presented as an integrated commentary on 'Zinacanteco culture' as such. When history was brought into the discussion, it tended to be pre-Conquest and colonial history, consulted in order to establish continuities and discontinuities in the cultural repertoire of Zinacantan or Chamula. Nineteenth- and twentieth-century social and economic history was very scantily covered, and its lessons very seldom incorporated into the literature of the project.

Frank Cancian and the impact of modernization upon the civil-religious hierarchy

One might, in consequence, be entirely justified in concluding that the Harvard Chiapas Project constituted the best and most consistently supported example of normal-science puzzle solving within the functionalist paradigm in the history of Mexican anthropology. Nevertheless, within the generally ahistorical and nonmaterialistic tradition of the endeavor, several of the products of the Harvard Chiapas Project made important practical contributions to an understanding of the process of rapid socioeconomic change which was indeed taking place in highland communities during the postwar period. This was true not necessarily because they provided an entirely convincing interpretation of the meaning of new patterns of relationships defining access to livelihood resources, but because the extremely conscientious field work on which they were based produced detailed information which could be utilized by readers of varying theoretical persuasions to obtain a picture of trends of change and to ask their own questions of the data. The work of Frank Cancian is a case in point.

Cancian was fundamentally concerned with a process which had been under way in Zinacantan since the 1920s: the seasonal migration of heads of families from their highland homes to the coastal lowlands of Chiapas, where pasture lands in the hands of private cattlemen could be rented and cleared for corn farming, thus supplementing the generally meager production of Zinacanteco plots. Before World War II, this endeavor had been carried out by the men of Zinacantan in a way congruent with the 'diffuse and particularistic economic and social roles that ... characterized the traditional Zinacanteco peasants.'[41]

Indigenismo and functionalism, 1950-70

Each peasant renter organized his own group of associates (often chosen with reference to kinship bonds), worked lowland fields with traditional techniques, and brought his own grain home on pack mules, where it was stored in his family compound for home consumption or eventually delivered to a small group of Zinacanteco middlemen for sale in the San Cristobal market. Transport difficulties, both for men and for grain, limited the distance from the highlands which could economically be travelled in search of acceptable land to rent.

This situation changed drastically during the 1950s, when the construction of a network of paved roads in the region made it possible for Zinacantecos to travel much further from their homes and therefore to rent virgin lands promising higher yields, despite increased transport costs. Some men began to expand their operations, taking on hired laborers from Chamula and utilizing buses and trucks to transport larger quantities of grain. Such an option was made particularly viable by the establishment, during the mid-1960s, of government receiving centers for grain in the lowlands, which offered a guaranteed price for corn and obviated the need to carry it up to the highlands after harvest. The net effect of these 'exogenous changes' on Zinacanteco economic life was to open up new lands for cultivation at a speed which more than kept pace with a high rate of population growth in the community, and to provide higher incomes from farming through raising and stabilizing corn prices. The effect on social organization was to undermine parts of the subsistence organization of families with a corn income from the lowlands and to hasten the transition from peasantry to small-farming entrepreneurs.

Cancian utilized this information specifically to explore a problem within the sociological tradition of 'diffusion of innovation' research, to wit, factors determining differential response to new opportunities under conditions of uncertainty. He did not look into the implications of such a remarkable change on the livelihood of different sectors within the population of Zinacantan, beyond saying that his information supported the hypothesis that 'some people are better off, but not that people on the whole are better off.'[42] He did not place the phenomenon of lowland renting within a regional context by asking what part Zinacanteco corn farmers played in maintaining the viability of extensive landholdings on which they gained permission to clear and cultivate a plot. (In fact, he noted that he had 'no data on the size of different [lowland mestizo] ranches,' but that the question was not important because 'from the [Zinacanteco] farmer's point of view . . . , almost any ranch is big enough and any landowner who is not malicious is good enough.'[43] He gave no indication that any element of exploitation, or unequal exchange, might be involved in a process through which land-hungry peasants cleared and capitalized badly overgrown lands on private holdings, often larger than the legal limit and therefore technically vulnerable to expropriation, paid 20 to 25 per cent of their harvests in rent to the landowner, and were required every few years to move on to new and uncleared areas. He did not discuss the long history of symbiosis between highland minifundia and lowland latifundia within which periods of 'opportunity' for Zinacantecos were inserted.

Nevertheless, Cancian had turned his attention, in an earlier book, to a question of fundamental importance for the future of Zinacantan as a community: the impact of growing economic surpluses on the cargo system through which rank was determined in the civil-religious hierarchy. Challenging the view that the cargo system functioned as a 'levelling mechanism' in Indian communities, preventing potentially conflict-generating socioeconomic differentiation among families by requiring the richest to spend the most on public ceremony,[44] Cancian showed (on the basis of very detailed analysis of personal cargo histories) that not only had there long been considerable differences of wealth and standing among Zinacantan families, but that these differences were to some extent passed on from generation to generation through the cargo system. Therefore the critical importance of the system lay less in the field of maintaining homogeneity than in that of 'requiring that wealth be used in an Indian way.'[45] And as lowland renting permitted growing numbers of Zinacantecos to aspire to cargos, the ability of the system to provide an Indian route to purchasing prestige grew relatively less adequate to the task at hand. Long waiting lists for cargos attested to the congestion of the system and seemed to herald its eventual breakdown. Then prestige commensurate with the increasing economic strength of a part of the community would have to be obtained through non-Indian means, implying the appearance of new mechanisms of village integration, or disintegration.[46]

Although Cancian did not say so, his information on socioeconomic change in Zinacantan supported to a certain extent the indigenista belief that bettering economic opportunities outside Indian communities, or connecting those communities by road with mestizo areas where new opportunities could be sought, was the key not only to raising levels of living but also to breaking down the cultural barriers which separated Indians from the national society. Cancian was not particularly sanguine

Indigenismo and functionalism, 1950-70 63

about long-term effects of the erosion of Indian identity upon the quality of life in indigenous communities; and an outside observer with a certain skepticism concerning the permanence of benefits from association by Indians with mestizo cattlemen might extend his concern from the cultural to the material areas of Zinacanteco life. (What would happen at the moment trends in national meat consumption made cattle grazing more profitable than renting out small plots of land to Indians? How would Zinacantecos survive if the possibility of farming lowland plots were suddenly cut off? Would the principal result of the experience be shown simply in the degree to which Zinacantan had become a highly stratified rural society in the process of cultural dissolution?) For indigenistas like Aguirre Beltrán, these were moot points. Zinacantan would anyway have progressed, even if only toward integration into a national lower class.

Functionalism and interethnic relations: evolution of the meaning of 'pluralism'

Despite the fact that Cancian's interest in the farming activities of Zinacantecos encouraged him to look beyond the boundaries of the community itself, and to study the effects of lowland renting on the central boundary-maintaining institution of Zinacantan, he was – like the great majority of the members of the Harvard Chiapas Project – fundamentally involved in understanding elements of Zinacanteco life which could be analysed without reference to the way members of the community were inserted in a wider system of interethnic relations of the kind emphasized by the indigenista paradigm. Nevertheless, the question of why there was so remarkable a degree of cultural diversity in the Chiapas highlands, and how interaction among ethnic groups was patterned, could not be ignored in any of the projects carried out by American or European functionalists in the region during the 1950s and 1960s. Not only was the topic of vital concern to the National Indian Institute, which provided official sanction for foreign projects, but it was also increasingly a central issue within a functionalist paradigm subjected to strenuous criticism and revision by its own proponents. Therefore the area around San Cristóbal de las Casas became, in the late 1950s and the 1960s, a laboratory for the study of interethnic relations by functionalist anthropologists, much as it had been in the 1940s and early 1950s for indigenistas.

Until the turn of the 1960s, the functionalist explanation for persisting cultural differences among rural people in predominantly 'Indian' regions like highland Chiapas was almost entirely based on two arguments: first, that ecological differences among local groups forced differential adaptation to varying habitats; and second, that the difficulty of communication among villages reinforced idiosyncrasy. Neighboring communities interacted only to the extent that products or services associated with one of them were not available in another; and in the course of time, a stable pattern of periodic regional exchange based on limited economic specialization (and thus ultimately on the characteristics of specific ecological niches) developed to reinforce localized ethnic differences. It was this view of cultural differentiation which first encouraged Evon Vogt to think in terms of orienting the Harvard Chiapas Project toward a broad-ranging comparison of cultural differences among Tzotzil and Tzeltal communities throughout the highlands (a course later abandoned, as noted above), and which had in fact moved the Department of Anthropology of the University of Chicago to set up a five-year project in 1957, dedicated to understanding cultural differences across the various ecological zones of Chiapas.[47]

Once the existence of distinguishable local cultures had been dealt with, functionalists went on to place these 'plural cultures' within a national setting (extending the boundaries of discussion from what might be called intra-Indian relations to Indian-mestizo relations) by utilizing the concept of a 'multiple society.' First proposed by Sol Tax in 1942, and apparently inspired by contact with the contemporary work of J.S. Furnivall, an Englishman concerned to describe the situation of national minorities forming relatively independent enclaves within colonial Burma,[48] the concept grouped all Indian communities, whatever their differences, into a single 'non-national segment,' members of which were concerned only with local affairs, relatively unfamiliar with national history and society, and uninvolved in the formulation of national policy. That segment was then contrasted with a 'national segment' of the Mexican population, containing people throughout the national territory who, in the words of Tax's student and colleague at the University of Chicago, Manning Nash, 'participated significantly in the national social and cultural life or [had] control over resources and communications of nationwide scope or impact.' It was in the latter group that 'political control [was] vested and ... political control contested'; and by virtue of its unique ability to determine national policy, it maintained a 'superordinate [position] over the smaller-scale societies within the political network.'[49]

Aside from ties of political control inherent in living within a single national territory, what held the two parts of these 'multiple' or 'dual' societies together was the participation of both national and nonnational segments in a single economic system. Functionalists like Tax and Nash placed great emphasis on the unity of that system, in explicit negation of theories of dual economies or capitalist and precapitalist modes of production, which contemporaries within both cultural ecology and indigenismo were employing to explain unequal exchange between Indian and mestizo groups. Within the multiple society, members of both national and nonnational segments were equally motivated by the principles of 'Western capitalism' and participated with 'differences of degree but not of kind' in the national – and even the international – economic arena.[50] That Indians were likely to enjoy less material prosperity than non-Indians had fundamentally to do with the fact that the former lacked prolonged contact with, and control over, the technological improvements 'which . . . in the end led to abundance' for those integrated into modern industrial society.[51] This was a problem stemming from isolation, and from the inherent inability of very small-scale productive units (peasant households) to invest on a scale sufficient to make productive use of industrial technology. It could be overcome only through extending investment and technical assistance activities of the national segment into areas where nonnational cultures were still predominant.

There was, then, nothing in this view of interethnic relations which implied that Indians were exploited through ethnic stereotypes, or that Indian cultures as such would have to be entirely integrated into a national culture before economic development could occur. Functionalists of the Tax-Nash group never accepted the validity of the indigenista concept of caste, whether in its implication of ethnically based domination or its emphasis on the rigidity of separation between Indian and mestizo groups. Rather, many held out for the study, long undertaken by applied functionalist anthropologists, of the relationship between 'economic development and cultural change' in specific cases, and for the recognition of positive elements inherent in cultural pluralism. In the tradition of applied functionalism from the 1940s onward, they heartily championed 'modernization,' understood to be the promotion of 'conditions under which different societies and cultures either discover, invent, or accept the essentials of the technological and economic revolution ushered in around 1750' in Europe.[52] But they assumed, as Tax put it, that 'people [made] adjustments necessary for industrialization while maintaining very different cultures, and therefore that the new economy [would] take different forms according to the soil onto which it [was] transplanted.'[53] Within such a framework, it was essential that 'the government avoid trying to impose specific directions for development..., but rather attempt to offer [viable] alternatives among which Indians [themselves] could choose freely.'[54]

The functionalist approach to interethnic relations was therefore considerably more voluntaristic than that contained in the indigenista paradigm. And it generally rejected any consideration of exploitation, whether by national or regional elites. Put quite simply, members of the Tax-Nash school supposed that Indians and non-Indians interacted principally because each needed the other and received a necessary service during exchange.[55]

By the late 1950s, this relatively conflict-free vision of 'plural cultures in a multiple society' began to come under attack, not only by indigenistas who affirmed that ethnic differentiation in areas like Chiapas had sprung from the historical experience of colonial domination, and that it was maintained in modern times through the continued exercise of a despotic power by mestizo elites, but also by functionalists convinced that the role of conflict in social interaction must be more adequately treated within the paradigm then orienting their work. In sociology, this conviction was embodied in the theoretical revisions of functionalism proposed by Robert Merton. In anthropology, it was particularly visible in the work of the new generation of English scholars grouped around Edmund Leach (at the London School of Economics and Cambridge) and Max Gluckman (at Manchester). The latter, in particular, applied their concern with conflict to the specific question of intertribal, or interethnic, relations; and in the course of the 1950s their approach was increasingly studied by Americans. The fact that both men tended to emphasize the constructive, or functional, ends served by conflict, much in the tradition of Simmel or Coser, made their ideas acceptable even at Chicago and Harvard, where ties with British structural functionalists continued, in the 1950s, as in preceding decades, to be strong.[56]

The young generation of functionalist anthropologists who worked on interethnic relations in Chiapas from the late 1950s onward, and whose finished studies formed part of the literature of the 1960s, therefore had a considerably wider explanatory repertoire from which to draw than had their earlier counterparts. They used new theoretical

Indigenismo and functionalism, 1950-70 67

openings toward the consideration of conflict in a number of ways. Some, like George Collier of the Harvard Chiapas Project, rather completely adopted the 'refuge region' explanation for the persistence of ethnic differentiation in southern Mexico. In the process of a long (and one might add, very interesting) study of changing patterns of land use in Zinacantan, Collier definitively discarded the premise that the distinctive characteristics of Zinacanteco culture had much to do, either historically or in modern times, with effective isolation from the mainstream of regional mestizo society. On the contrary, his study of archives showed continuous interaction, as well as continuous reaffirmation of Zinacanteco separateness, in a process of 'dynamic, active, and adaptive response to peripheral placement in a larger system.'[57] By 'peripheral placement,' Collier meant 'exploitation by peripheral elites'; and in the tradition of indigenismo, he predicted that 'only in so far as the hinterland and its control city [became] articulated with the national economy [would] ethnic patterns erode.'[58]

Others, notably Benjamin Colby and Pierre van den Berghe, integrated insights obtained from de la Fuente and Aguirre Beltrán into a far broader treatment of interethnic relations owing much to Max Gluckman. Van den Berghe had in fact worked with English functionalists of the conflict school in South Africa, during a period of time between his first experience in the Chiapas highlands and his later return to the Maya Ixil region of northern Guatamala;[59] and he was therefore particularly instrumental in transferring to Mesoamerican anthropology the new ideas on 'pluralism' concurrently being elaborated by Manchester Africanists.

Ixil Country, published in 1969, constituted a specific attempt by Colby and van den Berghe to 'bring together within a single analytical framework the "functionalist" and the "conflict" streams of sociological thinking' through reference to the question of ethnicity.[60] The concept of 'plural cultures in a multiple society' was taken over integrally from Nash; but to the latter's general presupposition of harmonious relations was added the firm possibility of domination. Thus Colby and van den Berghe noted that the bases of social integration uniting very different societies, sustained by very different cultures, into a single national system need not necessarily be related to common values or consensus. Integration could be promoted through a wide variety of political arrangements, from parliamentary democracy to colonial imposition. And similarly, patterns of economic interaction among ethnic groups could be shaped not only by a common interest in 'the values of Western capitalism,' as Tax and Nash had held, but also by a historical process through which the political control exercised by colonial powers had been turned to the task of reducing conquered peoples to a permanent state of economic dependence. In such cases, interaction often involved contact between different kinds of economic systems, based upon differing rationales, and could very well be founded upon the kind of 'interdependence' created by differential relations to the means of production.

What was most important in the opinion of Colby and van den Berghe, echoing Gluckman, was the need to take into account the total context of a plural society, within which no group could be understood without reference to the nature of its relationship with others. 'A plural society,' they stressed, 'was not a set of groups or "cultures" living side by side and "borrowing" traits from each other; it was rather a set of interacting groups which remained distinct by virtue of not sharing all their institutions, and which constituted a single society by virtue of sharing some crucial ones.' 'The area of institutional overlap ... determined both the form and content of ethnic relations' and 'constituted the very core of the plural society.'[61]

That such a formulation sounded very much like parts of Fredrik Barth's well-known discussion of *Ethnic Groups and Boundaries*, published in English one year after Colby and van den Berghe's book, was not fortuitous.[62] Barth was also associated with English 'conflict' functionalism; and in addition, one of Barth's colleagues from the University of Bergen, Henning Siverts, was at work in the Chiapas highlands around the time Colby and van den Berghe were there. Siverts utilized his stay in the Tzeltal community of Oxchuc to study the political and economic elements of relationships between Indians and mestizos which seemed to reinforce the ethnic identity of the former and concluded that, given the virtually complete control which mestizos exercised over all productive resources in the region except the communal lands of Indian villages, young men born into those villages were forced to adhere to the cultural standards of their communities in order to exert their rights to the only available means of support for themselves and their families.[63] Such a conclusion fit well into the growing consensus that ethnic differentiation was less a matter of cultural content than of structural placement — an affirmation which Barth carried to its logical consequence by noting that ethnic boundaries could in fact be maintained even though the culture of the group involved changed drastically.[64]

A final contribution by a functionalist anthropologist with experience in the Chiapas highlands to the reformulation of the way interethnic relations were considered by members of his school was made by Julian Pitt-Rivers, who progressed in the course of the 1960s from simple description of patterns of behavior exhibited by San Cristobal mestizos, when required to interact with members of Indian communities, to an historical analysis of the colonial roots of ethnic discrimination in Latin America.[65] Like Siverts, Barth, Colby and van den Berghe, Pitt-Rivers found those roots in the structural requirements of colonial society, and turned definitively against the 'culturalist' position of earlier structural-functionalists — including those at the University of Chicago who had first sent him to Chiapas.

One might therefore say in summary that the way interethnic relations were treated within a distintegrating functionalist paradigm by the end of the 1960s brought many members of that school very much closer to an historical structuralist interpretation than they could possibly have been a decade before. A considerable part of the postwar indigenista explanation of historical elements in the consolidation of interethnic differences had been accepted by the younger generation of functionalists, and early reliance on static analysis had begun to be significantly supplemented by recourse to study of the past. At the same time, the structural unity of Indian-mestizo interaction, stressed both by English conflict functionalists and by indigenistas like de la Fuente and Aguirre Beltrán, had also been incorporated into the work of anthropologists originally trained within the rather traditional functionalist atmosphere epitomized by Harvard and Chicago. 'Pluralism' was no longer simply a synonym for cultural difference, and the 'multiple' or 'dual' society not necessarily free of conflict.

3 Cultural ecology, Marxism and the development of a theory of the peasantry, 1950-70

The partial historical structuralist challenge to functionalism crafted by Mexican indigenistas in the early postwar period, and consequently reflected in the changing world view of foreign-trained functionalists conducting research in indigenista 'refuge regions,' developed at the same time that a second challenge to functionalism, also of a historical-structuralist nature, was being elaborated in the United States within the emerging paradigm of cultural ecology. While the indigenista revision of functionalist tenets revolved around the relatively narrow issue of ethnicity, that of cultural ecologists was of a much broader nature: the problem for cultural ecologists was not simply how to account for defensive cultural difference in predominantly Indian regions, but how to place all inhabitants of the countryside (Indian or not) in an historically informed, structural relation to the broader socioeconomic and political system of which they necessarily formed part. Therefore while indigenistas drew the outer boundaries of their theoretical interest at the borders of well-defined regions, and were paradigmatically unable to look critically at relationships linking local people to others outside those areas, the system envisioned by cultural ecologists extended upward from the rural community to national and international levels. And while indigenistas ultimately explained the exploitative phenomena with which they were concerned in terms of culture, thus giving primacy to mental over material elements of livelihood, colleagues engaged in the elaboration of the paradigm of cultural ecology accorded first priority to socioeconomic relations based on material considerations. The result was the construction of a theory of rural-urban interaction containing a number of concepts congruent with contemporary insights of indigenistas, yet arranged in a broader causal scheme which was as profoundly at odds with indigenismo as it was with functionalism. Let us look first at how the new paradigm began, in dialogue with functionalism, before discussing at much greater length the way in which it was utilized by

The development of a theory of the peasantry, 1950-70   71

Eric Wolf as a starting point for elaboration of a comprehensive theory of the peasantry, which definitively incorporated the insights of the European Marxist tradition into the prevailing anthropological understanding of the Mexican countryside.

Julian Steward's 'levels of sociocultural integration' and the paradigm of cultural ecology

Early critical attention to some of the least useful suppositions of functionalism, including its geographical localism and relative inattention to possible sources of socioeconomic and political conflict in the countryside, began to appear within the camp of American culturalist anthropology in the 1940s not only in the work of Oscar Lewis, already analysed, but also in that of Julian Steward, who argued from the vantage point of metropolitan American society for recognition of a tendency toward increasing interdependence between rural and urban people in most of the major areas of the world. Steward was a professor at Columbia University, and during World War II had served as director of the Institute of Social Anthropology of the Smithsonian Institution at a time when technical assistance funds were channelled toward support of some very localized, functionalist studies. Yet he had never been particularly convinced of the utility of studying rural communities in isolation, and had as early as 1943 suggested that priority be given instead to research on the historical development of regions.[1] Those regions, in turn, could not be fully understood without placing them within the context of the nation, as Steward himself did in his pioneering study of Puerto Rico, undertaken during the latter 1940s.

Expanding the boundaries of anthropological concern as far as the national level was an exercise which required not only a novel organization of field work, but also a fundamental reorganization of categories of observation, and a concomitant fashioning of new analytical tools: the traditional categories of anthropological functionalism, predicated upon the study of a single, integrated local culture (with widely shared norms and patterns of behavior), could not easily be adapted to the study of all the varied groups and relations contained within a nation state. Steward therefore concluded that 'the greatest need of contemporary social anthropologists [was for] an adequate conceptualization of the phenomena of sociocultural systems above the tribal level,' and to meet that need he offered, in 1951, the concept of 'levels of sociocultural integration.'[2]

As a research strategy, reference to 'levels of sociocultural integration' implied dividing 'total national culture' into the 'suprapersonal ... and often formally institutionalized' elements (such as government and banking, the legal and educational systems, military organizations and others) which could only be understood 'apart from the behavior of the individuals connected with them,' and were therefore supposedly not amenable to ethnographic methods; and sociocultural segments of the population (communities, ethnic groups, classes, occupational groups, and so on)[3] which could profitably be studied by 'methods of direct observation.'[4] This exercise allowed anthropologists to retain their commitment to the study of culture — through dealing with separate *subcultures* — in the face of increasing pressure to abandon their own special field of competence to the more generalizing disciplines of sociology, economics or political science.

'Sociocultural integration' was, however, more than a research approach, which allowed the separation of national society into subcultures and institutions at differing levels of complexity. It was also a way of looking at the process through which modification occurred in any element of a subculture, or in the relationship of all elements, as 'simpler forms' gradually became ... specialized, dependent parts of new kinds of total configurations.'[5] This was, to some extent, an elaboration on Redfield's 'disorganization and reorganization of culture'; but it differed in allowing for a significantly greater degree of complexity in the analysis of rural cultural change. 'Sociocultural integration' was entirely separate from the movement from rural to urban ways of life consequent upon increasing contact with the city; it could occur during contact between different subcultures in rural areas or in urban ones. And in addition, it was not posited that secularization or individualization would be necessary outcomes of contact between simpler and more dominant subcultures.

'Sociocultural integration' was also used by Steward to describe the static state of any subculture at any moment in time, as it had been shaped both by interaction with its physical environment and with the wider world. One might say, for example, that the kind of 'sociocultural integration' of the Tarascans was different from that of the Lacandones, because the first group lived in temperate cornfields and had sustained long contact with Spanish and Mexican culture, while the latter lived virtually isolated in the jungle.[6] The differing combination of elements which came to be characteristic of each culture (or within the national context, subculture) suggested that they could be classified as different 'cultural types.'

At this point, Steward made another important break with prevailing anthropological practice, for his cultural types were not based primarily upon analysis of the mental organization of reality within any given human society, but rather upon close attention to the kind of adaptation imposed by the material conditions of environment. While serving as editor of the *Handbook of South American Indians* during the 1940s, Steward came to the conclusion that it was misleading to classify the indigenous population of the content, according to traditional criteria, in 'culture areas.' Such a classification implied a degree of sociocultural homogeneity within given geographical regions which was often not true to reality: all members of a certain language group might exhibit certain similarities of culture, but the particular requirements of local environment, and local history, very often contributed to substantial differences among them. And in fact, those elements of culture which remained most common to the wider group were likely to be precisely the ones which were least fundamentally related to the basic problems of livelihood. Therefore classification should be based upon comparison of the material arrangements central to livelihood in an attempt to reach an understanding of common features which might conceivably be dispersed among culture areas as well as within them. Such a classificatory scheme rested upon hypotheses sufficiently incompatible with those of functionalism or particularism to warrant Steward's coining a new name for his approach of 'cultural ecology,' and specifically counterposing it to what he himself came to call the predominant form of anthropological 'culturalism.'

Fusing cultural ecology and Marxism: the 'closed corporate community' of Eric Wolf

Steward was clearly not a Marxist; and in fact, his 'cultural' definition of classes was anti-Marxist.[7] Yet his insistence upon giving priority, within the framework of 'cultural ecology,' to the interrelationship of the environment, productive technology, and associated social organization was very close to the central theoretical interest of Marxist thought. As in the case of the substantial overlapping of interests of Lewis Henry Morgan and Karl Marx, in the preceding century, it would seem that non-Marxist anthropology concerned with clarifying the material bases of different cultural types in the 1950s served as a useful starting point for a subsequent elaboration of Marxist theory —

in the latter instance, fundamentally concerned with explaining the historical development of the Mexican countryside. This gradual fusion of cultural ecology and Marxism is especially well illustrated in the work of Eric Wolf, a student of Steward whose familiarity with the European Marxist tradition permitted him to elaborate new analytical tools of lasting importance to the growth of anthropological theory.

Significantly Wolf's first approach to Mexican rural reality in the 1950s was made not through the medium of a prolonged stay in a single community, but through an extremely detailed review of existing archaeological, ethnological, historical and sociological material which allowed him to trace changing forms of sociocultural integration within the geographical boundaries of Mesoamerica from pre-Conquest times to the present.[8] He concluded as a result of this review that a most influential element in structuring the kind of social interaction which prevailed outside the urban areas of Mesoamerica throughout most of the post-Conquest period was the economic depression of the seventeenth century — a crisis which put an end to the 'cumulative development' of the sixteenth century and initiated a process of ruralization and retrenchment at simpler levels of integration in order to ensure subsistence to the population under difficult conditions. Two predominant patterns of organization emerged in the countryside at this time: the hacienda, which served to provide for the security of the Spaniards, and the Indian community, which accomplished a similar end for the conquered. Both erected barriers between the local group and the outside world in an effort to 'stem the tide of disorder';[9] both became largely self-contained political and economic units, stressing self-sufficiency in foodstuffs, limited involvement in a wider market, and local self-government. But while the hacienda could have ultimate recourse to the colonial 'apparatus of power,' in its efforts to extend control over land and labor, the indigenous community had no such option. The Conquest had destroyed the Indian political elite, leaving the mass of rural people in Mesoamerica subject to the authority of a state which was both socioeconomically and culturally foreign.

The roots of the social and cultural organization of Indian communities in Mesoamerica were thus not to be found in a timeless harmony of interests among members of isolated rural settlements, as functionalism tended to imply, but rather in the historical necessity imposed by conquest and depression to reconstruct a 'shattered countryside,'[10] and to defend a conquered people from extinction. It was not organic, but mechanical solidarity which motivated cooperation within indigenous communities, as they confronted the permanent challenge of defending their exiguous right to subsistence within a hostile environment. In order to maintain control over village land, upon which physical survival depended, Indian communities became endogamous and developed an extremely strong sense of territoriality, reinforced by religious belief, which precluded the alienation of communal property to outsiders. In order to deal with the constant threat of economic differentiation within the community, and the eventual identification of the wealthiest with non-Indian interests, the distribution of prestige within the community was tied not to ostentatious individual display but to an ostentatious donation of available surpluses to the community at large, through ceremonial expenditure. And to curb any tendency toward the concentration of power, political office was associated with religious participation, and therefore more with proven dedication to community service than with individual attempts to manipulate political loyalties. The 'levelling' tendencies inherent in the functioning of the political and religious systems served in the end to spread the risks of everyday living, to subject the formation of social classes to the requirements of village autonomy, and to promote a 'democracy of the poor.'[11]

This characterization of the post-Conquest Indian community, taken by Wolf as the basis for an ideal type which he called the 'closed corporate community,'[12] was, in its treatment of the formal internal organization of life in Indian villages, not very different from that pieced together during the 1940s by Redfield and his associates (most particularly Tax, Villa Rojas, Pozas and Cámara) in their studies of highland communities of Guatemala and Chiapas; in fact, Wolf's bibliography shows that he drew heavily upon the work of that group in constructing his typology. But until Wolf put the Indian community within the context of post-Conquest historical development, the interrelationship between 'Indian' institutions and the surrounding Spanish or mestizo economy and society – the dialectical or 'symbiotic' nature of the formation of both Indian community and hacienda – had not been brought out by an American anthropologist. With Wolf in the United States, as simultaneously with Aguirre Beltrán in Mexico, the Indian community became a creation of the wider society, not a subtraction from it.

Such an image implied a relation of reciprocal dependence between Indian and mestizo worlds which was only beginning to be visible to American anthropologists as they extended their framework for analysis outward from the community in the 1950s (although, it might be added, such dependence had long been visible to historians).[13] If both the Indian community and the mestizo hacienda formed part of an integrated answer to the livelihood dilemma of the colonial countryside, then neither could survive without the other: the very limited amount of land generally controlled by Indian villages made it imperative that part of the population work seasonally on hacienda lands in order to supplement the meager economic resources of their communities; and at the same time, the haciendas depended upon an occasional availability of Indian labor to complement the efforts of a permanent labor force during certain parts of the agricultural cycle. Over a decade before French Marxist anthropologists like Terray and Meillasoux were to take up and make popular the question of the symbiotic nature of the articulation of capitalist and precapitalist modes of production, Wolf had already clearly stated their case.

> Assured of seasonal laborers who would do its bidding at the critical periods in the process of production, the haciendas welcomed the presence of Indian communities on their fringes. For such a community constituted a convenient reservoir of laborers where men maintained their labor power until needed, at no additional cost to the entrepreneur. Suddenly we find, therefore, that the institution of the conquerors and the institution of the conquered were linked phenomena. Each was a self-limiting system, powered by antagonism to the other; and yet their coexistence produced a perpetual if hostile symbiosis, in which one was wedded to the other in a series of interlocking functions.[14]

Even the 'closed corporate' community, then, had periodic relations with a wider socioeconomic system, whether in the form of providing labor to the hacienda, tithes to the colonial church, or taxes to the state. And as the political and economic ties associated with the building of a Mexican nation were extended inexorably throughout the countryside during the nineteenth century, it became increasingly difficult for the 'closed corporate' community to maintain its boundaries. Only the most remote and least well-endowed villages could remain effectively at the margin of this modernizing drive — those whose reorganization by the national system would have required an 'amount of energy' which at the moment 'outweigh[ed] the capacity of the larger society.'[15] Among the rest, a considerable number entirely lost control over their own livelihood from the 1850s onward, as the agrarian laws promulgated by liberal supporters of small private property and the subsequent colonization laws passed by Porfirista proponents of large capitalist enterprise wrenched large tracts of land from communal jurisdiction and forced Indian cultivators into an extreme dependence upon haciendas. At this explosive juncture, it was the task of the Mexican Revolution to 'disestablish the twin foundations of the old social order, represented by Indian community and hacienda, and to bring in a new order unhampered by the narrow social boundaries and unbreachable cultural barriers of the past' — to insert the countryside within the new economic and political parameters of a modern state.[16] Such a process, made partially possible by the demise of the traditional hacienda and the community development efforts of the indigenistas, became characterized over the years by an increasing incorporation of rural inhabitants into wider market systems, the growth of extracommunal ties of kinship and friendship, the decline of the civil-religious hierarchy, and the translation of local competition for power into a question to be handled through national political channels.[17] 'Closed corporate' communities gradually evolved toward a second ideal type, the 'open' peasant community, in which land ownership was individual and private, levelling mechanisms gave way to a conspicuous display of personal wealth, and nonpeasants entered the community to engage in activities not before included within the limited division of labor of a near-subsistence economy.[18]

It is important to note that for all the immediate similarities between this 'closed-open' progression of Wolf, on the one hand, and Redfield's 'folk-urban' continuum on the other,[19] there were far more fundamental differences, implying entirely unlike results of the incorporative process. Wolf's 'open' peasant community was not necessarily on the way to being absorbed on equal terms into a modern urban culture, or a modern national economy, as Redfield's linear model suggested. It was not necessarily being 'depeasantized,' and might in fact oscillate in cyclical fashion between predominantly subsistence- and market-oriented production according to the conditions of the wider economy. In addition, it continued to be a dependent community, made up of families who still farmed marginal lands and utilized primitive technology, much like their more isolated Indian counterparts, and who found themselves often manipulated by outside intermediaries who reaped an advantage from maintaining a traditional peasant productive process rather than modernizing it.[20] The 'open' peasant community was thus a permanent part of the Mexican countryside, integrated into the wider economic and political system in a subordinate position and not likely to disappear in the near future.

Wolf briefly sketched several other possible types of peasantry in his early work on the subject. One was made up of families under permanent contract to deliver their produce to a financier (most particularly those associated with a plantation complex); another was the *ranchero*, or small-farming mestizo; a third was foreign colonists; a fourth shifting cultivators.[21] Each was characterized by a different relation to the market, as well as a different history of contact with the wider socioeconomic system. The legacy of Steward's 'cultural types' was clear, as was an eclectic application of Marxist theory, only recently taken up again by those concerned with the long coexistence of unlike modes of production in rural Mexico.

The 'folk' becomes the 'peasantry': roots of an academic debate concerning the nature of interaction between the peasantry and the wider society

The concern of both Steward and Wolf with changing forms of sociocultural integration, characteristic of particular types of insertion into the wider system, must be considered part of a more general trend among American anthropologists during the 1950s toward analysing the social mechanisms which increasingly seemed to link the inhabitants of rural communities with individuals and groups outside the confines of the village. Redfield, for example, found it necessary to ask himself (in a series of lectures delivered at Swarthmore College in 1955) what 'kinds of social relations . . . one comes to describe if one begins with some local . . . community and tries to do justice to the fact that many of its relations are with outsiders.'[22] A peasant community was, after all, not only a part-culture, but also a part-society (as Alfred Kroeber had put it in his classic definition of 1948); and in fact it might prove to be 'so incomplete a system that it [could] not well be described as a [self-contained] social structure,' any more than it could be pictured as a self-contained cultural system.[23]

This shift in emphasis from the rural community as a part-culture (the social structure of which was presumed to be largely independent of the wider world) to a part-society, the members of which were intimately related to the outside world, required a change in terminology, for the prevailing usage of 'folk' implied a virtually exclusive cultural dependence. Therefore in the course of the 1950s the 'folk' became the 'peasantry,' and the earlier term fell quickly into disuse. Not surprisingly, it was Steward who presaged the need for change by noting, in 1951, that Redfield's 'folk' really described a kind of integration rather than a particular culture content.[24] Foster followed with a similar comment in 1953.[25] And Wolf took the final step of insisting upon utilizing the 'term "peasant" [to indicate] a structural relationship, not a particular culture content,' in his analysis of types of Latin American peasantries of 1955.[26] His suggestion was taken up by Redfield during the same year and made applicable to all those small cultivators, throughout history, who farmed for subsistence, not for profit, and who 'look[ed] to or [were] influenced by gentry or townspeople,' constituting (as Foster had also noted) 'the rural dimension of old [urban] civilizations,' in constant interaction with the latter.[27]

The unanimous agreement among structural functionalists, cultural ecologists, and Marxists that 'peasant' be substituted for 'folk' did not mean, however, that all understood the nature of interaction between rural villagers and the wider society in the same terms. Redfield and Foster were quick to admit that the peasantry must, by definition, be politically and culturally dependent upon the larger sociocultural system;[28] and they recognized a reciprocal dependence of urban society upon the agricultural goods provided to noncultivators by the peasantry. Nevertheless, on balance, they consistently assumed the peasantry to be the more dependent of the 'two halves of the social system,' and therefore rejected any suggestion that a peasantry was likely over the long run to provide more to the larger system than it received in return.

Wolf, on the other hand, insisted that the peasantry was not so much dependent as exploited: it produced a volume of agricultural goods appropriated through the exercise of power by groups with superior claims over the means of production, or over the use of force. In return, it was true, the peasantry might receive protection or services of other kinds; but Wolf clearly did not consider these services a sufficient repayment for the value of goods delivered. The local village unit was in fact an inherently superior kind of survival system: its peasant households could survive through self-provisioning if ties with the wider socioeconomic system were broken, while the same could not be said of urban inhabitants or gentry. Therefore the latter were in the last analysis most dependent upon the former, and illustrated their dependence in the process of exploitation.[29]

At the heart of this difference between Redfield and Foster, on the one hand, and Wolf on the other, lay basically incompatible suppositions of the structural-functionalist and Marxist paradigms. As Alvin Gouldner has pointed out in his lucid essay on 'Reciprocity and autonomy in functional theory,' functionalism was – and is – premised upon the 'operation of a "principle of functional reciprocity,"' through which all interaction among groups and individuals within a given system was assumed to involve the exchange of equally valued goods or services. The very persistence of the system was taken as proof of the operation of a basically 'balanced' reciprocity, and exploitation was therefore definitionally impossible. Marxism, in contrast, supposed that an extremely 'unbalanced' reciprocity could be upheld over long periods of time through utilization of the compensatory mechanism of force.[30]

The element which seemed most clearly to serve as a 'balancing' mechanism within the structural-functionalist evaluation of the relationship between peasantry and nonpeasantry was the value placed upon the cultural contribution made by urban elites to the quality of rural life. Redfield said in 1955,

> It will not do to describe these relations only as relations of ruler and ruled or of exploiter and exploited, although these elements are likely to be present... The cultural relations between the two halves are to be emphasized. Sjoberg puts it well: '... the elite exhibits to the peasant the highly valued achievements... and provides the peasant's social system with a sophisticated justification for its existence and survival.'[31]

Thus in return for peasant's goods, the elite provided cultural standards, and in the process cancelled out the debt.[32]

The city was always the repository of the 'great tradition,' and therefore an adequate social framework for the elite within the structural-functionalist paradigm. The peasantry existed in relation to the city, as the entire folk-urban continuum made patent. But if one looked at the question from the point of view of Marxism, the key element in maintaining the relationship between peasants and nonpeasants of higher status was power, and power was exercised not by a city, but by a state. It is not surprising, therefore, that Wolf insisted upon defining the peasantry primarily as subjects of the state: '... it is only when a cultivator is integrated into a society with a state – that is, when the cultivator becomes subject to the demands and sanctions of powerholders outside his social stratum – that we can appropriately speak of peasantry.'[33]

The development of a theory of the peasantry, 1950-70

Investigating mechanisms of domination: the concepts of surplus and domain in Wolf

This definition, which Wolf presented in a book-length discussion of *Peasants*,[34] published in 1966, grew out of involvement in a wide-ranging effort, made by a number of members of Steward's school, to understand the dynamics of relations between countryside and city in historical and sociological perspective, from the earliest periods of urban development to the present time. Drawing on the contemporary work of Gordon Childe, in England, and Steward and Leslie White in the United States, Wolf and others of his generation at Columbia accepted the thesis that civilization, based upon a complex specialization of labor in urban centers, had only been made possible when sedentary agricultural populations began to produce a surplus of goods, above their own immediate physical needs, which could be channelled by persuasion or by force, as Childe put it,[35] toward the sustenance of nonproducing urban groups. The city thus first appeared 'as a center of power, not as a center of productive economic activities,' and maintained itself 'only by utilizing that power, whether religious, administrative, military, or mercantile.'[36] In that case, it became important, within the framework of 'multilineal evolution' proposed by Steward and accepted by his students at Columbia, to investigate a number of different ways in which an agricultural surplus might be extracted, and the concomitant forms of domination and control which might appear.

These were questions worthy of nineteenth-century historical sociology, to which Wolf and his colleagues immediately turned. They were aided in their study by the reappearance, during the 1950s, of a long-lost manuscript by Marx (the *Grundrisse*, or preliminary notes for *Capital* and the *Critique of Political Economy*, in which Marx specifically took into account the possible relations between different kinds of peasantry and nonpeasant elites), as well as by the circulation in the United States of the revisionist Marxist historical work of Karl Wittfogel, also in residence for a time at Columbia. With the analysis of the exercise of power in agrarian societies provided by Max Weber, these sources formed a considerable part of the sociological basis for Wolf's fully developed theory of the peasantry – supplemented by the testimony of modern ethnographers and the particular insights attributable to the discipline of cultural ecology.

In brief, Wolf held that

the distinction between primitives and peasants... does not lie in the greater or lesser outside involvement of one or the other, but in the character of that involvement... [I]n primitive society, surpluses are exchanged directly among groups or members of groups; peasants, however, are rural cultivators whose surpluses are transferred to a dominant group of rulers that uses the surpluses both to underwrite its own standard of living and to distribute the remainder to groups in society that do not farm but must be fed for their specific goods and services in turn.[37]

As a cultural ecologist, Wolf thought these surpluses could be analysed in objective terms; they were the amount of produce or of labor time which remained once three requirements of a peasant family had been met: (1) minimum caloric rations; (2) produce sufficient to replace basis production equipment (seed, feed, implements and tools) and to provide for the culturally defined physical subsistence of the family (housing, clothing); and (3) produce which could be destined to the maintenance of needed social relations through ceremonial expenditure. All production above such a level constituted a potential 'fund of rent,' which might be appropriated by nonpeasant groups through the exercise of power.

The question of whether it was indeed possible to speak in terms of an objectively perceivable surplus was, of course, immediately raised.[38] Were not the possible uses to which production could be put in different cultures too varied to allow for the definition of a surplus? In some societies, people might prefer to eat badly than to slight an apparently inessential ceremonial obligation; in others, enormous quantities of food might be required for bacchanalia which eliminated all possibilities of a surplus. To these objections, colleagues of Wolf, and most particularly Marvin Harris, responded that while any group could find ways to utilize all of its production, if the latter were not subject to liens by outsiders, such an alternative was not usually open to the peasantry. Goods and labor which might ideally be turned to the task of cultural elaboration had to be delivered instead to nonpeasant elites. The 'surplus' therefore had to be envisioned not as entirely unneeded by those who produced it, but as expendable under duress. The maximum limits of the surplus corresponded to the minimum limits of biological and cultural sustenance, beyond which no family could go without jeopardizing its present and future existence. This minimum limit was similar to Marx's lower margin for reproduction of the labor force: beyond a certain point, no elite would choose to extract an amount which threatened to destroy its source of income.[39]

The 'fund of rent,' which in practice was the equivalent of an 'extractable surplus' in Wolf's theory, constituted, then, an amount to be transferred from peasants to nonpeasants without adequate payment to the former. The ways in which this transfer might be realized, however, were extremely varied. In his monograph on *Peasants*, Wolf utilized Weber's insights into historical mechanisms of domination and control to sketch a number of forms of 'domain,' or institutionalized rights to extract tribute, which might come into play. The first of these was patrimonial (or feudal), in which 'control of occupants of land was placed in the hands of lords who inherited the right to domain as members of kinship groups or lineages.' Such rights formed a pyramid of obligations to higher lords, ending with a sovereign. A second was prebendal domain, from which officials drew tribute from the peasantry 'in their capacity as servants of the state.' In this case, grants of income were not inheritable. A third form of domain, sheared of the ceremonial aspects which characterized relations between lord and peasant in the previous forms, was mercantile: land became private property, 'an entity to be bought and sold and used to obtain profit for its owner.' And a fourth was administrative, involving the direct organization of production by a state bureaucracy. Wolf stressed that none of these types of social relations was mutually exclusive of the others; a single lord might maintain feudal obligations toward the peasantry while running his estate as a capitalist enterprise. Similarly, none was historically obsolete. In modern form, patrimonial, prebendal, mercantile and administrative domain stood behind the continuing phenomena of hacienda and plantation, sharecropping and renting, and various kinds of state-administered farming.[40]

Wolf, Palerm, and the 'asiatic mode of production'

As the preceding concepts began to emerge from the work of Steward's students at Columbia, and to integrate a distinctive position toward rural life within the newly proposed paradigm of cultural ecology, they were taken up with alacrity by a small group of Mexican anthropologists whose intellectual heritage was similar to that of the Columbia circle. The best known of the Mexicans was Angel Palerm, who collaborated with Steward and Wolf during the 1950s and early 1960s from his position first as editor of the *Revista Interamericana de Ciencias*

Sociales and then as director of the Office of Social Studies of the Panamerican Union in Washington.[41] Like Wolf, Palerm was an émigré from European fascism: forced to flee Spain during the Civil War, he settled in Mexico, just as Wolf, upon leaving Austria, travelled first to England and then to the United States. The familiarity of both with European social thought, and most particularly with Marxism, gave them a common ground not shared by many of their more insular American and Mexican colleagues; and it was therefore not surprising that they should engage in joint research concerning a topic of very great possible relevance to the prehispanic agrarian structure of Mexico: the 'asiatic mode of production.'

First discussed by Marx in the 1850s and subsequently taken up by Weber, the 'asiatic mode' implied a form of domination of small peasant producers by a bureaucratic elite which made no pretense of directly owning the peasants' land, but only of controlling the provision of goods and services essential to agricultural productivity. The elite worked at the service of a strong, centralized state in which ultimate title to all land was vested; and the pressing need of the peasantry for services monopolized by the state kept the former permanently subject to the latter. Such a model differed from administrative domain only in the fact that the asiatic mode of production permitted the continued existence of peasant communities, nominally in control of their own land.[42]

The asiatic mode entered the thought of Wolf and Palerm through the medium of Karl Wittfogel's work on 'oriental despotism.' Wittfogel's interest lay particularly in the study of how an ecological given, the need for large-scale irrigation works in order to maintain sedentary agriculture in certain regions, seemed historically to have encouraged the appearance of an asiatic mode of production, in which the dependence of otherwise self-sustaining peasant villages upon the technical and organizational expertise of a state bureaucracy, in control of an irrigation system, seemed to ensure the maintenance in power of a despotic elite. Such an idea sufficiently intrigued ecologists like Steward, Palerm, and Wolf to warrant their taking it as an object of empirical investigation in the early 1950s, not only in 'Asian' or 'oriental' settings, but on a more general level throughout world history. At Columbia, a seminar was held on irrigation civilizations in the old and new worlds; and in Mexico, Palerm and Wolf carried out a joint investigation of pre-Hispanic states which had depended to some extent upon the maintenance of irrigation works.

The development of a theory of the peasantry, 1950-70

Through this effort, Palerm and Wolf made a well-known contribution to the study of the urban revolution in Mesoamerica; the examination of hitherto unutilized written records (both Indian and Spanish) refuted previously held beliefs that prehispanic agriculture in Mexico had been extremely primitive, and sustained instead the view that there had been an efficient and productive Indian agriculture capable of producing substantial surpluses and therefore of sustaining a complex urban civilization. The precise interrelation of small cultivators, administrators, and the state within these hydraulic systems remained, however, unclear. The question of whether the concept of an asiatic mode of production is applicable to pre-Conquest Mexico remains open for investigation.[43]

New approaches to studying the economic behavior of the peasant household: cultural ecology and the domestic mode of production

At the base of any system of surplus extraction involving the peasantry, cultural ecologists like Wolf and Palerm saw a type of domestic economy characteristic of peasant households everywhere. Peasant families assured their own livelihood, and produced the surplus required of them by outsiders, through a particular kind of economic organization, in which the household provided both the management capabilities and labor force required to produce the overwhelming share of goods needed by the family itself, and at the same time constituted the framework for allocating and consuming most goods so produced.

Such a statement might have remained little more than a reaffirmation of the ethnological truism that peasant families engage in subsistence production. But in fact it constituted the point of departure for replacing long-accepted and fundamentally uncritical ethnographic description of peasant economic activity with analysis of the deeper rationale underlying the economic behavior of the peasantry. Such analysis was based upon both Marxist and non-Marxist investigation of the inner logic of what came to be called the 'domestic mode of production' — a concept which gained adherents in the course of the 1950s, as the subdiscipline of economic anthropology was strengthened by debate between those who felt that the terminology of classical economics could be applied to primitive and peasant settings, and those who felt that it could not.

The characteristics of subsistence agriculture, as traditionally conceived by anthropologists of both the particularist and functionalist schools, were amenable in large part to treatment within the confines of the prevailing vocabulary of freemarket economics. 'Subsistence farming' was simply very small-scale family farming, in which the paucity of local resources required their utilization in ways no longer necessary in more technologically advanced societies. Thus George Foster had written a doctoral dissertation, in 1942, which attempted among other things to calculate the monetary cost of cooperative traditions among the Popoluca of Veracruz — and which, incidentally, concluded that those traditions were economically unsound.[44] And Sol Tax had argued at length, in his *Penny Capitalism* of 1953, for the proposition that differences in economic activity between the peasants of Panajachel, Guatemala, and those of any family in Western society were basically only of degree, not of kind.[45]

Anthropologists who, in the 1950s, began to adopt the concept of a domestic mode of production were, on the other hand, quite convinced that economic activity in peasant society could not be treated as a simple small-scale extension of capitalist rationality, nor could that activity *per se* be neatly sorted out from the whole fabric of social relations and subject to formal scrutiny in the absence of a much more integrated understanding of peasant existence. They rejected, in other words, not only what they considered to be the ethnocentric bias of scientists brought up within a capitalist socioeconomic system, but also the formalistic bias of traditional structural-functionalism. And they argued instead for recognition of a specific precapitalist (primitive or peasant) mode of production, governed by its own peculiar laws, among the most fundamental of which were the inseparability of production and consumption units, and of economic and social units, as well as the predominance of motives of production for use over production for profit.

Marshall Sahlins, who like Wolf was associated with Columbia during the 1950s and engaged in an exploration of the theoretical possibilities of the domestic mode of production, has noted that fundamental inspiration for the concept came from ethnographies of primitive peoples, including efforts made by colonial administrators to understand the peculiar behavior of rural cultivators under their charge;[46] from the work of A.V. Chayanov, whose *Theory of Peasant Economy* was rediscovered by American sociologists in the 1950s, some forty years after it had been written; and from Marx. All agreed that a large part of the agricultural output of the world, in both contemporary and historical terms, had been produced by rural families

The development of a theory of the peasantry, 1950-70

fundamentally concerned with self-provisioning rather than production for profit. The kind of cost accounting applicable to capitalist agriculture was therefore simply not relevant to their endeavor; and the types of stimuli employed to raise productivity among farmers motivated by hopes of gain were woefully unlikely to elicit a similar response from a peasantry.[47]

Chayanov, in particular, was able to show (through analysis of a wealth of statistical data gathered among the Russian peasantry in the immediate prerevolutionary period) that the domestic mode of production was an intrinsically 'anti-surplus system.'[48] Peasant families invested sufficient effort in agricultural or handicraft production to satisfy what they considered to be their livelihood requirements. There was little incentive for the family to work past that point, for its members also valued their own leisure time; and there was no real use (in the absence of an interest in accumulation) to which excess production could be put, once socially necessary expenditures on ceremony and mutual assistance within the community had been made.

Such was the case, however, only in an optimum or at least a satisfactory situation, when both the physical and social resources at the disposition of the family were sufficient to permit weighing the benefits of work and leisure within a framework of culturally prescribed livelihood. If the demographic composition of the family were unfavorable (with many young or very old dependents in relation to able-bodied members), land insufficient, or outside liens particularly onerous, the very nature of the domestic mode of production required the intensification of labor effort to a point which would be considered irrational, or exploitative, by the standards of capitalist economics. In order to provide at least an absolute minimum of foodstuffs and necessary subsistence goods to all family members, peasants often invested inordinate amounts of labor to increase productivity by a margin which remunerated their efforts (in terms of cost accounting) at a sharply decreasing rate. They therefore won their right to subsistence through working extraordinarily hard for a meager, but vital, return. And when it was possible for them to rent, buy, or otherwise gain access to additional land on which to farm, the same principle entered into play: the necessity to meet an irreducible minimum quota of production impelled them to pay any price they could (even though higher than the normal market price) for usufruct of the land.

This tendency toward 'self-exploitation' within peasant households not in control of resources adequate to meet their own needs and those of superordinate claimants was noted by Wolf in *Peasants*,[49] as was the fact that the juxtaposition of domestic and capitalist modes of production might reinforce self-exploitation to the benefit of the capitalist system. Goods produced for use value within noncapitalist modes were likely, through exchange, to be drawn into the hands of capitalists who would turn their use to profit.[50] And since the rationale of a capitalist buyer was to keep the purchase price low, while the urgent need of the peasant seller was to meet minimum subsistence requirements not amenable to postponement during a long process of bargaining, the amount paid the latter was often not a true reflection of the value of his work in a wider market. Wolf stressed the likelihood of such unequal exchange in his analysis of peasant involvement in national market systems. Nevertheless, it was left to colleagues like Clifford Geertz to show how peasant households compensated for inadequate access to livelihood resources through carrying self-exploitation to a degree which Geertz termed 'involution'; and to Angel Palerm (among cultural ecologists) to dwell upon the implications of peasant self-exploitation for the maintenance of capitalist accumulation in the specific case of Mexico.[51]

Differing views of the social organization of the peasantry: Wolf's coalitions and Foster's dyadic contract

Once he had sketched the broad outline of relationships which seemed historically to have conditioned behavior in the countryside, as well as toward the countryside, Wolf went on to examine concrete ways in which individuals or groups might carry on their daily lives within the social parameters provided by their environment. He was, in other words, not content merely to analyse the basic structural constraints providing outer limits to social intercourse: the need to extract a surplus, the existence of various forms of domain, the inner logic of the domestic mode of production. Even given such constraints, there remained a wide area of discretion, within which peasant families and members of families, as well as nonpeasant elites, must find themselves daily forced to make decisions concerning the most efficacious way to further their interests.[52] It was important for anthropologists to understand this kind of behavior, which occurred from day to day within small groups, as well as large, and which could at times have the cumulative effect of changing structural boundaries themselves.

In British social anthropology, such a field of concern had come

The development of a theory of the peasantry, 1950-70

by the 1950s to be known as 'social organization' — a term proposed by Raymond Firth for dealing with 'the effects of choice and decision-making by individuals in the context of social relationships,' or the way choices were made in terms of available alternatives established by the social structure.[53] It was a particularly useful concept for those, like Steward and Wolf, who had turned to the study of national societies in all their complexity, and who therefore were confronted with the question of how to analyse both temporary and permanent ties forged among individuals not necessarily characterized by similar group interests. These 'interstitial, supplementary, and parallel structures,' including friendship, ritual coparenthood, and patron-client relations, might span wide geographical distances and bridge considerable gaps in socioeconomic status.[54] They formed what another British anthropologist, J.A. Barnes, called personalized 'networks,' growing out from single individuals acting on their own behalf, within the limits of the possible.[55]

Wolf dealt with the question of social organization within peasant society by asking, quite simply, how a peasant household might arrange social resources in order best to withstand the constant pressures engendered by a basically exploitative structural setting. His answer was framed in terms of 'defensive strategies' involving a number of different kinds of temporary alliances or 'coalitions.' The latter might unite two persons (in which case the coalition was called dyadic) or more than two (polyadic); it might involve partners of equal (horizontal) or unequal (vertical) status; and it might be designed to cover a single interest (singlestranded) or many interests (manystranded). Some coalitions were far more enduring than others — an extreme example of the most enduring being the closed corporate community, in which peasant households formed a corporation in defense of a common territory.[56]

The concept of coalition provided Wolf with a counterweight both to the formalism inherent in prevailing structural-functionalist paradigms and to an overly rigid application of Marxism. It allowed him to link local actors with others at any level of society and to look at processes which might have economic or political implications without being contained within formally economic or political structures. At the same time, it was possible to consider questions of conflict and adaptation outside the boundaries of a strictly defined class system. While seeing the peasantry as a class-in-itself, determined by a structural relationship of subordination to nonpeasant elites, Wolf could look at heterogeneity within the peasantry and at forms of cooperation between peasants and nonpeasants for specific purposes.

Such an approach, for example, led Wolf and his colleagues toward a systematic analysis of patron-client relations, often manifested in ritual coparenthood, or *compadrazgo*. In certain social situations, ties of this kind, involving a 'lopsided friendship'[57] with outsiders of higher status, offered individual members of peasant communities what seemed to them their best opportunity to maximize access to needed physical and social resources. When the nature of opportunities within and without the community underwent qualitative change, however, the weaving of ties of coparenthood might better be accomplished within the peasantry itself, as an expression of 'horizontal' solidarity rather than 'vertical' dependence. The nature of personalized networks of mutual assistance was flexible and depended fundamentally upon the 'amount [and kind] of sociocultural and economic mobility, real and apparent, available to an individual in a given social situation.'[58]

When groups or individuals at both local and national levels urgently needed to communicate with each other but institutionalized channels for doing so tended to be very limited, Wolf observed the appearance of networks constructed around the figure of the 'broker,' who stood 'guard over the crucial junctures or synapses of relationships which connect[ed] the local system to the larger whole.' The 'basic function' of this broker was 'to relate community-oriented individuals who want[ed] to stabilize or improve their life chances, but who lack[ed] economic security and political connections, with nation-oriented individuals who operate[d] primarily in terms of the complex cultural forms standardized as national institutions, but whose success in these operations depend[ed] upon the size and strength of their personal following.'[59] If the broker utilized his virtual monopoly over communication to ensure his own political and economic hegemony within the community or communities involved, he was likely to become a *cacique*. In any event, his position ultimately depended upon maintaining tensions, not resolving them; he was required to 'serve some of the interests of groups operating on both the community and the national level' and to 'cope with the conflicts raised by the collision of these interests,' but not to eliminate the conflict altogether, for that 'would abolish his usefulness to others.'[60]

Wolf's interest in various kinds of social networks cutting across class lines has been taken by some sociologists as reason to classify him as a 'methodological individualist,' fastening upon 'specific types of social relationships subjected to analysis *per se*, independently of the totality of social relationships to which they relate.'[61] This, in the light of Wolf's constant concern with structural constraints upon peasant action, is indeed a superficial reading of his approach. There was, however, a very clear element of methodological individualism in the work of George Foster during the late 1950s, and it is instructive to compare his analysis of personal networks in peasant society with that of Wolf in order to understand the very different implications which apparently similar concerns could have.

During the course of his field work in Tzintzuntzan, Foster found that all social relations there (and by extension, in any peasant setting) were based upon a 'dyadic contract,' binding pairs of contractants, never groups. 'Each person [was] the center of his private and unique network of [dyadic] contractual ties, a network whose overlap with other networks [had] little or no functional significance.' In that case, community-wide cooperation, and even the cooperation of small groups, was impossible. There were 'no vigorous voluntary associations or institutions in which an individual recogniz[ed] identical or comparable obligations to two or more people.'[62] The only defensive strategies open to members of peasant families therefore involved kinship (defined in dyads), friendship (between two people), and patron-client relationships. Network analysis under such conditions seemed firmly to support Marx's often-quoted comparison of the peasantry with a sack of potatoes.

Wolf, on the contrary, gave increasing attention to the 'polyadic' element of social organization among the peasantry — to the kinds of defensive strategies, required in concrete social situations, which implied a coalition of many members of the peasantry in confrontation with nonpeasant elites, as well as alliances between groups of peasants and nonpeasant supporters.[63] Kinship and friendship could become key elements in fomenting wider solidarity, just as patron-client relations could be turned to the cause of a political movement. And in the last analysis, it was through personal contact between peasants and nonpeasants that class conflict took form within rural society. Therefore network analysis could serve as a tool for understanding class conflict, rather than for negating it.

Cultural ecology, Marxism, and limits on research during the 1950s and 1960s

Perhaps it would be wise, before leaving this discussion of cultural ecology, to summarize briefly the implications of the paradigm for research of the period. Cultural ecology, as understood and developed by Wolf and Palerm in work often related to an examination of Mexican materials, was fundamentally concerned with understanding the processes through which rural cultivators assured their own livelihood within a framework of broader socioeconomic systems the very existence of which was predicated upon the success with which nonfood producers could obtain agricultural goods from food producers. The geographical boundaries of enquiry therefore extended as far as one could trace existing relations of socioeconomic and political interdependence — almost certainly beyond the community (except in the extreme case of an entirely closed community), and with modernization, often beyond the region toward national and international systems. Privileged relations for investigation, which seemed to be of strategic explanatory power, were those concerned with the exploitation of physical resources through technological and social means, involving a process of allocating labor to certain ends and then of allocating the product of labor among certain groups. This implied constant attention to questions of power, not only as they might be approached through an orthodox examination of class relations, but also as the accumulation of control over the allocation of resources in the hands of individuals or groups might be related to the position of the latter in personal networks based upon kinship, friendship or patron-client relations.

In the terminology of Marxism, Wolf and Palerm examined the specific characteristics of capitalist and noncapitalist modes of production; and through their association with Steward's concept of 'levels of sociocultural integration' as well as their familiarity with modern Marxist thought, they came to deal in great detail with what must now be referred to as the articulation of differing modes of production in specific social formations. Yet perhaps in part because of the militant anti-Marxism characteristic of the official political and intellectual climate of the period, neither Palerm nor Wolf utilized the terminology of the Marxist paradigm in major publications of the 1950s and 1960s.[64] They were wary of the distortions which ideological debate could introduce, and of the damage which a very rigid adherence to all elements of Marxist doctrine could cause to the ongoing process of anthropological investigation. Palerm, in particular, began a long-standing dialogue with proponents of doctrinaire Marxism in Mexican anthropological circles, in which he stressed the need to place Marx's contributions to the social sciences within the historical context of the nineteenth century, to take from Marx what was applicable to contemporary conditions and to discard what was not. In disagreement with both the traditional Boasian particularists and structural functionalists, on the one hand, and the most uncompromising Marxist students, on the other, Palerm abandoned the National School of Anthropology in 1968, three years after his return to Mexico from Washington, and moved to the Department of Anthropology of the Iberoamerican University, where he could shape the program of studies in conformity with the specific requirements of cultural ecology.[65]

What fundamentally separated the Wolf-Palerm school of cultural ecology from that of orthodox Marxists in Mexican anthropology was the concern of the former with culture, not as a necessarily simple reflection of production, but as an adaptive system developed by particular groups of people confronting particular ecological and historical situations.[66] Within such a framework, capitalism − to take an example of greatest relevance − was more than a mode of production; it was a culture. Thus Wolf spoke in his conclusion to *Peasant Wars of the Twentieth Century* of a 'great overriding cultural phenomenon, the world-wide spread and diffusion of a particular cultural system, that of North Atlantic capitalism.' The hallmark of the system, he continued, has been 'its possession of a social organization in which labor is sold, land is rented, capital is freely invested,' through the functioning of the market. As a result of its incidence upon peasant culture and society (most particularly during the nineteenth and twentieth centuries), 'where previously market behavior had been subsidiary to the existential problems of subsistence, now existence and its problems became subsidiary to marketing behavior.'[67]

Like Karl Polanyi, from whom cultural ecologists took partial inspiration for their discussion of the impact on livelihood of the development of the capitalist market system, Wolf and Palerm saw the outcome of a confrontation between capitalist and peasant sociocultural systems in pessimistic − one might even say tragic − terms. This was the case not only because absorption into the market system could imply increased exploitation of small producers, but more importantly because it tended to cut away the personal relationships which had provided a measure of security and identity to peasants long exploited under less individualistic forms of domination.[68]

Capitalism 'liberated' man as an economic agent, but the concrete process of liberation entailed the accumulation of human suffering against which anti-capitalist critics, conservatives and radicals alike, would direct their social and moral criticism. This liberation from accustomed social ties and the separation which it entailed constituted the historical experience which Karl Marx would describe in terms of 'alienation.' The alienation of men from the process of production which had previously guaranteed their existence; their alienation from the product of their work which disappeared into the market only to return to them in the form of money; their alienation from themselves to the extent to which they now had to look upon their own capabilities as marketable commodities; their alienation from their fellow men who had become actual or potential competitors in the market: these are not only philosophical concepts; they depict real tendencies in the growth and spread of capitalism.[69]

Thus while many Marxists of the 1950s and 1960s might have argued in terms of the dialectic, that the destruction of peasant society was a necessary prelude to the introduction of industrial socialism, into which rural people would be integrated on equal terms with all other citizens, and structural functionalists engaged in programs of applied anthropology tended to suppose that modernization and urbanization would proceed through an inevitable reorganization of rural culture, making it more congruent with predominant patterns and therefore viable in livelihood terms, cultural ecologists like Wolf saw members of peasant communities travelling a long road toward insecurity, as the 'accustomed institutional context to reduce ... risks' was undermined and 'alternative institutions [were] either too chaotic or too restrictive to guarantee a viable commitment to new ways.'[70] Such insecurity, when carried to its logical (or physical) extreme, would produce a livelihood crisis of such proportions that peasants might become involved in rebellion and revolution. The new configuration emerging from armed struggle would nevertheless not necessarily be favorable to the peasantry.[71]

Wolf's particular interpretation of the impact of incorporation upon the livelihood of the peasantry in general, his insistence upon studying questions of security, risk, and adaptive or survival strategies, his attention to possible cycles of participation in and withdrawal from various kinds of wider social networks, have shaped the thought of a generation of later students of peasant life.[72] Yet until the 1970s, few of those students were Mexicans or worked systematically in Mexico. It is ironic that a paradigm so indebted to scrutiny of the

Mexican experience was employed by only a small minority of the anthropological profession in that country throughout the 1960s, and that among the latter, most were dedicated to an examination of the pre-Conquest, rather than the modern, period.

Palerm has explained the lack of greater opportunities for Mexicans to work outside structural functionalism, particularism and indigenismo during the 1950s and 1960s as a consequence of the prevailing climate of conservatism within such official institutions as the National Institute of Anthropology and History, and its related School, which had virtually complete control over national financial resources for teaching and research.

> The policy of economic developmentalism, combined with... strong political and intellectual repression..., was applied at the level of anthropology with the same efficacy as at the level of the nation as a whole. [This] left the field open for foreign social research. National research did not interest the administrators of the INAH, unless it fit within the limits of archaeological antiquarianism or Boasian ethnography.[73]

Such a policy was to fall to pieces in the period of confrontation and renovation following upon political crisis in 1968. But in the meantime, many students and investigators particularly concerned with the structural determinants of livelihood, including Marxists and cultural ecologists, could do little more than leave the country for study or work abroad, find foreign financing, or concentrate their attention upon topics the temporal boundaries of which precluded incursions into contemporary questions of rural livelihood.[74]

At the same time, there was no place for anthropologists of the cultural ecology school within official programs of an applied nature, both because government institutions working in the Mexican countryside were not interested in asking questions which might touch the sensitive nerves of a highly complex and uncertain political system, and because cultural ecologists themselves found prevailing community development efforts to be based upon 'notoriously inefficacious manipulatory techniques.'[75] 'Community development,' Palerm noted, 'frequently [tried] to substitute, or even to eliminate, any consciousness of the need for structural change' and thereby 'reached the point of tacitly attributing to [rural people] the responsibility for their own [unsatisfactory] situation.'[76] Like other cultural ecologists, he rejected the idea of a need for separating 'applied' work from the whole body of the anthropological endeavor, which in his view must inevitably be concerned with understanding basic problems of livelihood and therefore with providing new intellectual and practical tools for improving the quality of life.

4 Anthropology and the dependency paradigm in Mexico, 1960-75

During the same years when anthropologists from Wolf to Aguirre Beltrán to Pitt-Rivers – working within the paradigms of cultural ecology, indigenismo and functionalism – were all turning to an analysis of the specific historical experience of colonialism in an effort to understand the nature of certain central institutions in the Mexican countryside, the groundwork was being laid throughout the social sciences for a significant expansion of the explanatory utility of colonialism as a generic concept, applicable in modified form not only to historical situations of direct colonial domination but to the contemporary structure of socioeconomic relations between and within nominally independent nation states as well. Much that had been puzzling to anthropologists, confronted with patterns of social interaction for which traditional functionalist theory could not account, was also puzzling to economists and sociologists attempting to analyse the complex phenomenon of underdevelopment with the theoretical tools of the liberal heritage. If economic 'backwardness' and social 'traditionalism' were really nothing more than the result of isolation from the mainstream of technological and socioeconomic change associated with modernization in early industrial centers, as liberalism or structural functionalism held, there was no way to explain why the process of urbanization and industrialization moving with varying degrees of speed across the underdeveloped world from the 1940s onward was apparently not producing prosperous and relatively egalitarian industrial democracies, in which everyone received some relative material benefit from modernization, but rather increasingly polarized societies composed of an opulent 'modern' and an impoverished and excluded 'traditional' sector. Why was modernization increasing the 'dualistic' propensities of 'backward' societies, when all the predictive force of the prevailing paradigm would have indicated an opposite trend?

The answer might, of course, be sought by simply turning to the traditional Marxist conclusion that the advance of capitalism within any society implied polarization and inevitable misery. But it could also be sought by carrying out a more specific examination of the place of underdeveloped nations or territories within the world capitalist system, and therefore of the peculiarities of the socioeconomic, political, and cultural environment within which modernization occurred outside the original geographical core of the industrial revolution. Such an examination, begun shortly following World War II, seemed to suggest that the historical experience of subordination to the requirements of empire had so deformed the economy and society of underdeveloped regions that existing socioeconomic structures in the latter were incapable of autonomously directed development. Mechanisms of political domination, cultural manipulation and unequal market exchange, responsible in the first instance for the phenomenon of underdevelopment within an earlier context of colonialism, continued, even after formal independence, to condition the process of modernization in the Third World and to channel its benefits toward a dependent domestic elite and its foreign sponsors.

This conclusion came, by the 1960s, to constitute the core of a distinctive school within historical structuralism, centered around the concept of 'dependence,' which was fundamentally to influence the nature of social science research in Latin America. It was a multidisciplinary approach, to which economists, sociologists, anthropologists and psychologists contributed; and its use therefore encouraged expanding the boundaries of concern of each discipline into realms previously reserved for all others, at the same time that the geographical limits of the system under study were moved from the national to the international level. In the specific case of the study of rural livelihood, the problems of the peasantry could then be understood only if they were analysed in relation to the broad trends of development in a world capitalist system. Before discussing the way in which Mexican anthropologists made use of, and contributed to, dependency theory from the 1960s onward, let us turn for a moment to a more detailed discussion of its early intellectual formation.

The emergence of a concept of dependence within the Economic Commission for Latin America (ECLA)

To a considerable degree, the study of dependence has been the study of imperialism, and much inspiration has undoubtedly been drawn from early twentieth-century Marxist thought on that subject. Lenin, in fact, observed the existence of 'two main groups of countries' outside the industrial centers of capitalism: colonies and 'diverse forms of dependent countries which, politically, are formally independent, but in fact, are enmeshed in the net of financial and diplomatic dependency.'[1] The continued subjection of both kinds of countries constituted, as Rosa Luxemburg was the first to suggest, an indispensable condition of capitalist expansion if one followed Marx's reasoning to its logical conclusion.

Nevertheless, it would be mistaken indeed to suppose that the growth of dependency theory has simply reflected the transposition of Marxist thought on imperialism into the realm of contemporary Latin American sociology. Such an uncritical transfer would have represented acceptance of the very kind of 'intellectual colonialism' against which dependency theorists stood, for European Marxists could not help but see the modalities of imperialism from the standpoint of their own continent. The dependency paradigm, on the contrary, was constructed by those who looked at imperialism from the perspective of the periphery and attempted to utilize 'categories specific to underdeveloped countries.'[2] Interestingly enough, the earliest of these contributors in Latin America were not Marxists at all, but economists trained within the liberal tradition — just as, at the turn of the twentieth century, the first contributor to the study of imperialism had been an English liberal, John Hobson.[3]

The occasion for initial consideration of unequal commercial exchange, which would become a central element in the dependency paradigm, arose in the aftermath of World War II, when the United Nations Economic Commission for Latin America (ECLA), under Raul Prebisch, began to work with the hypothesis that the economic growth of the region was fundamentally constrained by consistently unfavorable terms of trade between manufactured products exported by the most modern industrial nations and primary products exported by Latin American countries. In part, this imbalance was associated with a relatively smaller elasticity of demand for primary products, which limited the bargaining strength of nonindustrial exporters. And in part, it was attributed to the fact that gains in productivity within primary sectors tended to be reflected in lower unit prices, while similar gains within manufacturing often did not. The conclusion drawn by ECLA economists from this analysis was that Latin American countries could best encourage economic growth through a program of import-substitution industrialization.[4]

In fact, however, the course of postwar industrialization in Latin America did not produce a particularly noteworthy shift in the bargaining power of 'peripheral' industrial economies. A late industrializing firm clearly confronted structural problems not countenanced a century before: it could dispose in an independent manner of neither the capital nor the technology at the command of competitors in advanced capitalist economies and generally remained associated in a subordinate position to decisionmaking centers in the latter. Observers of the process soon qualified it as 'dependent,' in the sense that the course of Latin American development continued to be subjected to the requirements of growth within foreign nations controlling vitally needed resources, including markets.

The dependent aspects of late industrialization in Latin America were related in part to insertion in an international economy increasingly characterized by the monopolistic or oligopolistic practices of firms and nations. Latin American economists therefore began to turn with interest to studies of monopoly capitalism, among which those by Baran and Sweezy were especially influential.[5] The insistence of the latter on the need for investigating the 'political economy of growth' — for examining the contributions made by some groups and nations to the development of others — proved an inspiration to any number of economists (and sociologists) soon to question the liberal conception of development.[6] The best-known of these was undoubtedly Celso Furtado, whose series of books on historical and contemporary aspects of Latin American economies made a forceful case for the contention that underdevelopment was the result of a consistent contribution to the development of Europe and the United States, rather than of isolation from the mainstream of capitalist modernization.[7]

By the 1960s, then, two lines of thought were converging toward the study of dependence by economists: one particularly concerned with quantifying and explaining postwar terms of trade unfavorable to late-industrializing countries (or to primary products), not necessarily requiring the use of a Marxist vocabulary; and another attempting to place the phenomenon of unequal exchange within a broader analysis of the political economy of growth, associated with twentieth-century revisionist Marxism. These two approaches were supplemented during the decade by contact with a third way of focusing on dependence, offered by sociologists. The tendency of economists to stress the external causes of underdevelopment was tempered by the insistence of Fernando Henrique Cardoso, Aníbal Quijano, Theotonio dos Santos,

Anthropology and the dependency paradigm in Mexico, 1960-75 101

and others, that although 'dependent development' was indeed the product of an historical experience with colonial domination, extended past formal independence through mechanisms of neocolonial economic and political manipulation, and although its study certainly required understanding 'how underdeveloped [or dependent] economies [had been] historically linked to the world economy,' it was equally important to examine 'the way in which *internal social groups* were constituted which managed to define the kind of outward-oriented relations which underdevelopment presuppose[d].'[8] Dependence involved, at bottom, the existence of a decisionmaking process *within* nominally independent countries which produced an outcome molded to fit the interests of developed countries. And in the series of interdisciplinary discussions taking place at the United Nations-sponsored Latin American Institute for Socioeconomic Planning (ILPES) in Santiago de Chile during the 1960s, sociologists insisted that the concept not be considered 'an external point of reference but rather a fundamental element in the interpretation of . . . [national] history.'[9]

A sociological contribution to the dependency paradigm: the concept of the 'colonial situation'

There was, in fact, a separate and very well-elaborated tradition of work on dependence by European social scientists, on which Latin American sociologists and anthropologists could draw as they fused their insights with those of economists to form the dependency paradigm. That tradition — already noted briefly in Chapter 2 with reference to Max Gluckman and the Manchester School — grew out of the systematic study of colonialism (and later of neocolonialism) from the late 1940s onward within a framework which rejected any partial analysis of isolated elements of the experience and attempted instead to come to grips with what Georges Balandier called 'the concept of the colonial situation.'[10] To do so required 'passing from classic ethnology to total sociology,' multidisciplinary in nature and multicultural in focus, incorporating the insights of the colonized as well as the colonizers and making an effort to explain the social and psychological organization of both in terms of each other.[11] The process began with an exhaustive review of the existing literature on imperialism and colonialism, continued through perusal of ethnographic materials, and gave sustained attention to the testimony of the intelligentsia of colonized territories, often involved in national liberation movements. It shared important areas of concern with contemporary work by C. Wright Mills and Gunnar Myrdal, whose application of a critical sociology to problems of social inequality and racial discrimination were also carefully studied by Latin American social scientists of the embryonic dependency school.

Colonialism, it was generally agreed by all, rested in the economic and political sphere upon the exercise of monopoly control over economic exchange and information by a dominant group of foreigners, who interposed themselves by force and administrative fiat as the single intermediaries between a dominated group and all others, and thereby eliminated the element of competition which would otherwise have provided a certain bargaining power to the colonized. In the psychological and cultural sphere, colonialism implied as well the manipulation of racial or ethnic stereotypes which justified the existence of domination to the colonizers and which were absorbed into the mentality of the colonized in a way which frustrated their own awareness of injustice. It was particular interest in this latter aspect of colonialism which encouraged Balandier to equate a colonized state with 'dependence' — a term first in vogue among psychologists, but utilized by Balandier by the turn of the 1950s as a virtual synonym for the effects of all forms of colonial domination.

The implications of the 'colonial situation' for patterns of social interaction within both the colonial center and the colonized periphery were extraordinarily complex, for systems of stratification in each case were determined in part by the quality of interaction with the other. There was no self-contained frame of reference within which to work out the comparative position of various groups in a single region, but rather a shifting field of relative privilege or privation based upon the interaction of class, race, ethnicity and territorially based domination within a worldwide system. Furthermore, the position of each group or stratum grew out of historical experience and changed in relation to concrete opportunities presented or foregone. Therefore a classical Marxist analysis of stratification, which took neither ethnicity nor geographically based exploitation (colonialism) into account, and which assumed that class relations in non-European settings would ultimately be the same as those taking form in the industrial powers of the nineteenth century, was not — in the opinion of postwar students of the sociology of colonialism — adequate to the task at hand.

To do justice to the complexity of social relations within a 'colonial situation,' European social scientists concerned with the topic — and most particularly the group of sociologists and anthropologists associated with Balandier in Paris — adopted a position somewhat similar to that of Claude Levi-Strauss in its concentration upon interrelations among levels of social reality.[12] One could not look at 'traditional' social organization within a colonial territory, for example, without asking how it had been, and was being, modified by interaction with 'modern' forms emanating from the colonial metropolis, how the latter had been affected by the existence of the former, and how both interacted in a constant process of redefining the bases for assigning social status, whether through recourse to economic, racial, cultural or political (territorial) distinctions. There was, as Balandier put it in a telling paraphrase of the Marxist vocabulary, a 'coexistence of heterogeneous modes of social stratification,' among which those based upon modes of production were only one.[13]

Latin Americans studying in Paris, including the majority of the sociologists making outstanding contributions to the paradigm of dependency during the 1960s, absorbed this way of envisioning social interaction in a colonial (or neocolonial) situation and concluded that just as it was unlikely that the development of capitalism in underdeveloped countries would follow exactly the same course as that in developed ones, so it was essential to 'discard the idea that class action ... [would] be of the same kind in dependent countries in the original phase of their development.'[14] The existence of territorially based political and economic domination meant that all groups within a dominant region or nation could benefit to some extent from the transfer of resources from all groups within a dominated or dependent region or nation, irrespective of unequal distribution of gain or loss among classes on each side of the transaction; and such an eventuality implied the need to develop new approaches to the study of Latin American (and indeed, European or American) society.

Concretely, the bourgeoisie of colonial or neocolonial centers, for example, could exploit the working class within its own national boundaries less than might otherwise be expected through passing a part of the burden supposedly borne by the latter on to the working class of peripheral nations. In that case, bourgeoisie and workers at the center became to some extent allies. And within dependent countries, the relation of the bourgeoisie to the national working class was influenced not only by the need of the former to extract a surplus for its own use, but for the use of neocolonial groups as well. This led in practice to rapid technification despite the abundance of the labor force and to a consequent limitation on the size of the industrial working class, which became a privileged group relatively uninterested in political struggle.[15]

In such a scheme, the behavior of the political and economic elite of dependent nations or regions was obviously of strategic importance. To the extent that the elite attempted to maintain a margin of national or regional autonomy and to deal with certain issues of economic organization in ways responding to the needs of a national majority, some form of development, within dependency, might in fact be possible. But if it simply served as a conduit for orders emanating from the industrialized center, then a dynamic process of underdevelopment would continue to beset dependent regions. Members of the dependency school were divided among themselves, it might be added, on which of these courses was the more likely in present-day Latin America. Some, like Gunder Frank, held that the consistent worsening of the livelihood conditions of the majority was inevitable within a capitalist framework and that only a socialist revolution could reverse the trend. Others, of whom Cardoso is perhaps the best-known representative, felt that the 'ambiguous' position of national elites in dependent countries allowed for the definite possibility of 'dependent development.' Peripheral elites were, after all, not only allies of elites within industrial centers, owing a part of their continued hegemony over their own peripheral society to ties with the latter, but also to some degree competitors. Exactions were made from the elites of dependent countries, as they were from the masses; and such a situation created friction between the bourgeoisie of peripheral and central economies which could imply some kind of nationalistic alliance among classes within a peripheral society.[16]

González Casanova, Gunder Frank and the analysis of exploitative mechanisms in a chain of metropolis-satellite relations

As Latin American sociologists utilized the concept of colonial exploitation to look deeper into their own societies toward the end of the 1950s, the consensus began to emerge that the same patterns of power visible at an international level were also distinguishable on intra- and inter-regional levels within the boundaries of a single nation state. To the extent that groups within certain metropolitan areas or regions of any given Latin American country had been historically successful in establishing themselves in a position of monopoly control over goods and services needed or wanted by groups within other geographical areas of the same country — or that the former had simply come to control the political and military instruments of domination — and to the extent that some of the benefits of that position of dominance were likely to accrue to all classes within a hegemonic city or region, it was possible to speak of 'internal colonialism.' Furthermore, the simile could be drawn down through progressive geographical levels, in which a chain of exploitation linked 'capitalist world and national metropoli to regional centers, . . . and these to local centers, and so on to large landowners or merchants who expropriate[d] a surplus from small peasants or tenants, and sometimes even from these latter to landless laborers exploited by them in turn.[17] Latin American society was therefore divisible into a hierarchy of sociogeographical divisions, each containing exploiters and exploited, and each serving at the same time as satellite of a more powerful entity and as metropolis of a less powerful one.

The research possibilities opened up by such a concept, and the difficulties inherent in it, can be illustrated by turning to the work of Pablo González Casanova, who was one of the first and most influential proponents of its use.[18] González Casanova, by the end of the 1950s director of the School (later to become the Faculty) of Political and Social Sciences of the National University of Mexico, was integrated into the group of Latin American sociologists concerned with dependency both through his training in Paris (where he had been a student of Georges Gurvitch) and through his participation in the Latin American Faculty of Social Sciences (FLACSO), founded by UNESCO in 1957 to encourage the systematic interchange of ideas among academic institutions throughout the hemisphere. His early efforts to come to grips with the fundamental nature of underdevelopment reflected the ambiguities of Latin American social science during the period when it turned from a past dominated by functionalism toward a future more closely aligned with Marxism. The literature in which he first presented his views on the nature of socioeconomic inequality within and among nations was therefore characterized by a tendency to stress the differences between developed and underdeveloped regions in a way somewhat similar to functionalism: colonialism encouraged the formation of 'dual' societies, made up of modern and traditional sectors, the interrelation between which was not particularly well specified.[19] This utilization of the vocabulary of dualism won him the criticism of André Gunder Frank.[20] Yet of all the members of the dependency school, González Casanova (in his later writings) was probably closest to Frank, both in his conceptualization of a chain of metropolis-satellite relations and in his contention that the functioning of the chain, as it drew resources up from the most remote rural hinterland toward the industrial center, constituted a vital element in the continued development of European and American capitalism.

A central problem of both González Casanova and Frank was how to coordinate a simultaneous analysis of geographical and class-based exploitation. Frank addressed the question by defining exploitation very broadly, as 'the expropriation of economic surplus from the many and its appropriation by the few.'[21] That process could occur by virtue of exercise of control over the means of production by nonworkers (which involved class, but not exploitation of one region by another); and it could come about through commercial confrontation, in which more powerful capitalists in one region extracted a surplus from less powerful ones in another.[22] Thus regional elites which might have accumulated a surplus from workers or peasants (or a local middle class) within the sphere of their own control would be forced to pass a part of that amount on to elites at a higher level when subjected to the monopoly control of the latter over needed inputs, outputs, credit, and/or merchandise. Through the transaction, possibilities for autonomous development of the satellite would be reduced while augmenting the freedom of maneuver of more powerful elites in their relations with subordinate groups in their own region.

Frank buttressed his concept of a chain of exploitation with evidence drawn primarily from a detailed study of the economic history of Argentina, Chile and Brazil, in which concern with unequal commercial exchange almost entirely overshadowed consideration of class relations. He also began a study of mechanisms of colonial domination in Mexico, during a year's stay at the National University in 1965, in which he hoped to correct what he considered to be serious deficiencies in the existing historiography of the nation; but the project was discontinued when Frank discovered that a new group of Marxist historians was producing works which made his own effort largely unnecessary.[23]

González Casanova was much more explicit than Frank in his recognition of the theoretical difficulties of sustaining, within the broad outline of Marxist analysis, the simultaneous existence of geographical and class-based exploitation. To deal with the question, González Casanova turned not to history, as Frank had done, but to mathematics; and in *La Sociología de la Explotación*, published in 1969, he carried out an extended analysis of the mathematical possibilities inherent in adapting Marx's definition of exploitation occurring during *production* (surplus value divided by socially necessary labor time) to a situation of neocolonial *commercial* interaction. The result was a series of equations which represented hypothetical ways in which 'transfer [of value] might benefit or affect different classes operating in different [geographical or productive] units.'[24] In some of the hypothesized situations, the fruits of exploiting a working class within a given region might indeed be passed on indirectly to the working class of a superior link in the chain of domination; in others, they might not. But in all cases, the existence of geographical (or sectorial) transfers increased the mathematically expressed 'degree of freedom' of elites to dispose of the economic surplus at their command in ways which might enhance their own power.

González Casanova and the quantification of rural marginality

To be operationally valuable for most sociologists, González Casanova's later mathematical efforts, presented in *Sociología de la Explotación*, required a more qualitative application to concrete cases, historical or contemporary, which was not immediately forthcoming. In the meantime, however, that part of his theoretical concern most readily taken up by anthropologists and sociologists interested in rural livelihood was not his attempted contribution to understanding the mechanisms of domination in a chain of geographically or sectorially based exploitation, but his interest in illustrating the effects of capitalist development in Mexico upon a countryside integrated into that process in a permanently subordinate position.

For this purpose, González Casanova turned during the early 1960s to the quantification of what was, at that time, coming to be called 'marginality,' and was generally taken as a synonym for lack of participation in the material and sociopolitical benefits of economic growth. The phenomenon was first observed in the burgeoning peripheral shantytowns and 'lost cities' of Latin American metropolitan areas, swollen by rural immigrants in search of opportunity. The chronic lack of access to adequate housing, urban services, education, and remunerative employment which plagued such populations, combined with their political disorganization or manipulation, suggested that large segments of Latin American society, far from enjoying the fruits of modernization, were being uprooted from traditional settings without being integrated on favorable terms into the growing urban industrial (and presumably democratic-participatory) sector. They were suspended, in a sense, between two worlds and seemed to have the worst of both of them.

González Casanova extended this perception of urban marginality to rural areas, sustaining the thesis that most of the marginal population of Mexico was to be found in the countryside, where neither revolution nor economic modernization had succeeded in breaking the mechanisms of political control which kept much of the peasantry in a state of economic deprivation and political impotence little different from prerevolutionary times. The principal cause of such continuing rural marginality was, González Casanova thought, subsumed within the historical development of the Mexican state, which in the postrevolutionary period had been forced to subdue or integrate rebellious factions at the local, regional and state levels and thus to form a common front with which to face a constant threat of external domination and control. The very forms of cooptation, combined with threats of possible repression, which held the political system together also tended to concentrate the benefits of economic development in the hands of a minority, and to encourage individuals seeking socioeconomic mobility to ally themselves with the more powerful above them rather than to promote the solidary organization of compatriots fighting for a common cause. This chain of individual loyalties left most of the rural population without the political means necessary for insisting upon a more equitable distribution of the benefits of growth.[25]

In order to quantify the phenomenon of rural marginality, González Casanova turned to the only statistics widely available — those of the national census and national election returns. Taking as indicators of marginality such census entries as percentage of the urban and rural population eating wheat bread or tortillas, wearing sandals or shoes, consuming certain sources of animal protein at given intervals, as well as rates of monolinguism and illiteracy, and from election returns summary information on abstentionism in elections, he put together a statistical picture with which to sustain the thesis that despite advances in the relative strength of the 'participatory sector' as a result of political restructuration and socioeconomic modernization in twentieth-century Mexico, the absolute number of Mexicans receiving no benefits from modernization continued to grow inexorably — and the greatest number of them were in the countryside.[26]

Such an attempt to quantify the extent of disadvantage or marginality within the Mexican population, and to suggest its geographical location, was not entirely new. It had been essayed by Nathan Whetten in his classic study of *Rural Mexico*, published in 1948.[27] And it had formed a part of the indigenista strategy for dramatizing the situation of Indian groups, as well as for justifying expenditures. During the 1960s, however, González Casanova's work presaged the formation of a growing school of development sociology particularly concerned with the analysis and mapping of census data, usually divided into urban and rural categories. Not surprisingly, as planning began to assume greater importance within private and governmental circles, this school gained concomitantly in numbers.

Efforts like those of González Casanova served the useful purpose of reminding academics, policy makers, and the general public alike of the very real possibility that economic growth would not automatically 'trickle down' to the population at large, and that development at one level of society might imply underdevelopment at another. Nevertheless the methodology underlying the use of existing census statistics by González Casanova, and others who followed his example, was problematic to an extreme. Not only was the information-gathering process upon which the national census rested notoriously untrustworthy, but it depended in the last analysis upon a series of questions which could be considered real indicators of deprivation or exclusion only through the most strenuous recourse to mental gymnastics. The conclusion, for example, that the rural population of Mexico was made up of 'an immense number of [people] who have nothing at all,'[28] because the latter ate less wheat bread and more tortillas, were more likely to wear sandals than shoes, were more likely to be illiterate or monolingual, and did not consume certain relatively expensive sources of animal protein popular among urban dwellers, was highly debatable. Yet if one felt compelled to utilize statistics to confirm a general (and indeed well-founded) suspicion of low levels of living in the postwar Mexican countryside, the range of possible indicators of consumption or wellbeing provided by the national census left few alternatives.

Theoretical debate on the meaning of marginality

The methodological problems of quantifying marginality during the 1960s were compounded by a thick layer of confusion surrounding the meaning of the concept itself. González Casanova, for example, obviously understood marginality to mean exclusion from participation in the benefits of development, but not exclusion from participation in the productive process as a whole. To be marginal was to be poor, politically impotent, and exploited, but in no sense to be superfluous to the functioning of the capitalist system. On the contrary, the entire argument of dependency theorists like González Casanova and Gunder Frank was based upon the working of a chain of exploitation which placed the 'final burden [of capitalist development] in the rural periphery of the Third World.'[29] The 'marginal' were therefore 'central' to the continued existence of modern industrial society.

A second current within dependency theory, however, did reach the conclusion, after investigating the nature of urban industrial growth in Latin America in the postwar period, that the particular requirements of international monopoly capitalism (including the use of advanced technology and the maintenance of a restricted internal market oriented toward the production of luxury items for the Latin American middle and upper classes) were in fact encouraging the formation of an increasingly large group of people who were marginal not only to the benefits of development but to the functioning of the economic system as a whole. Torn free of traditional economic activities in the countryside by the advance of capitalism in agriculture (or simply born into a situation of overpopulation and restricted economic opportunity), many Latin Americans were coming to form part of a 'marginal mass' for which no productive employment was possible. Some might represent an alternative to employed workers, if capitalists should decide to threaten the latter with dismissal; and in that case, they fulfilled the function of the 'industrial reserve army,' conceived by Marx as serving to maintain the salaries of the employed at a constantly low level. But most were so badly prepared for the relatively specialized tasks required by modern industry and commerce that they were unemployable on a permanent basis. Their only means of survival was therefore to engage in a precarious provision of minor services, with which Latin American cities were increasingly saturated, or to beg.[30]

If one adopted this approach, it was no longer possible to quantify marginality by searching for statistics which simply illustrated poverty and political exclusion, whether urban or rural. One had, in addition, to look at figures which gave an idea of economic activity, for among a group of people badly fed and badly educated, some might contribute to the functioning of the national (and international) economy while others might not. But here again, the categories within which census and other national statistics were presented often concealed as much, or more, than they revealed. Marginality could most often be measured only in terms of an extremely low income or a state of unemployment, not in any sense an adequate reflection of the phenomenon at hand. It should be noted that in addition to the two approaches to marginality just presented, both of which fell broadly within the paradigm of dependency, there was a third, and very interesting, interpretation of marginality which shared some common elements of the first two, but which was far more concerned with subjective elements of social change. It was contained in the work of Gino Germani, a functionalist whose seminal treatment of the process of modernization during the 1950s and 1960s included a reformulation of the Redfieldian question of disorganization and reorganization in terms which included the possibility of fundamental imbalance, or asymmetry, in the process of socioeconomic and psychocultural change characteristic of the transition from 'traditional' to 'modern' society. Germani's view of asymmetry was in many respects like Ogburn's vision of 'lag': it implied differing rates and forms of change at differing levels and dimensions of the social system, and therefore the likelihood of stress, whether psychological, cultural, or socioeconomic, within social units undergoing modernization. One correlate of such stress was the creation of marginal men, and marginal masses or groups, mobilized but not yet entirely integrated (for lack of adequate patterns of behavior or material or social resources) into modern national society.

Marginality, in Germani's scheme, was thus equated with less than full participation in 'spheres which, according to [culturally] determined criteria, one should participate.'[31] On an individual level, the concept had a very strong normative element, for it counterposed expectations of adequate fulfillment of roles against existing socioeconomic, political and psychological impediments to reaching that goal. If there were no 'consciousness of marginality' there could be no marginality as such. At an aggregate level, however, it could be utilized simply to designate any 'social category [or] geographical area ... to be found in a situation of backwardness, exclusion, or increasing deterioration [relative to others] whether as a direct result, as a cause, or even as an indirect consequence of the development of other areas.'[32] This was very much the meaning given marginality by González Casanova.

Indigenismo and dependency theory: similarities and differences of 'refuge regions' and 'internal colonies'

If it was Latin American sociology which most thoroughly explored the theoretical implications of superimposing geographical or sectorial forms of domination upon class relations, as the concepts of colonialism, neocolonialism and dependence implied, it was anthropology which provided much-needed perspective on the third dimension of the generically colonial situation: ethnic discrimination. A significant part of the population of the continent might be exploited not only as citizens of a neocolonial country, members of a dependent (underdeveloped) region, and a class, but also as members of an ethnic minority. And Mexican anthropology, with its strong component of indigenismo, was well accustomed to deal with the peculiarities of that status. In doing so, however, Mexican anthropologists associated with the dependency school brought into question a number of the fundamental precepts of indigenismo and, in fact, set the stage by the end of the 1960s for a thorough revision of the paradigm upon which official treatment of indigenous groups had long been based.

As it was pointed out in chapter 2, the indigenista theory developed during the 1950s shared significant common elements with the consideration of the 'colonial situation' by European anthropologists which contributed to the formation of the dependency paradigm. The similarity was perhaps most clearly reflected in the frequency with which the dependentista term 'internal colony' came to be used interchangeably in Mexican social sciences with the indigenista term 'refuge region.' In fact, the two concepts existed within total theoretical frameworks containing very different views of the nature of insertion of indigenous regions within the national (or international) context. But they could be made virtually synonymous by ignoring the wider context and looking only at interethnic relations within any single region in isolation.

Indigenistas like de la Fuente and Aguirre Beltrán had, when elaborating their interpretation of the social relations characteristic of refuge regions, stressed both the need of populations within 'seniorial cities' to exploit a surrounding rural hinterland by exercising a monopoly control over the disposition of its surplus, and the existence of an ideological justification for that domination, expressed in racial and ethnic terms. At the same time, through categorizing interethnic relations as caste-like, they made it clear that all socioeconomic strata within mestizo society benefited from the subjection of all socioeconomic strata within Indian society.

González Casanova, Gunder Frank, and others associated with the dependency paradigm therefore utilized indigenista literature prolifically in illustrating their theories of geographically based or colonial exploitation; and González Casanova in fact incorporated the theoretical construct of the refuge region virtually without change into his earliest discussions of internal colonialism.[33] An internal colony was not simply any given regional link in the chain of exploitation which extended from the colonial metropolis to the countryside; it was in addition the product of the specific historical experience of conquest of one 'civilization' by another and therefore rested in the last analysis upon racial and ethnic discrimination. Many members of the Latin American dependency school did not find such a qualification of ethnic difference necessary to their definition of internal colonialism; but the legacy of indigenismo required it in a Mexican context, and it has remained a central element of the concept as it is generally understood by dependency theorists in that country up to the present time.[34]

While a refuge region was by definition, however, isolated from the mainstream of national development, an internal colony was an integral part of the national and international capitalist system. The exploitation of its Indian population served not only to maintain a parasitic regional elite, but to provide a surplus skimmed from the hands of the latter by more powerful elites at higher levels. Therefore dependency theorists could not accept the indigenista belief in a benevolent national society, nor in the benefits which would necesarily accrue to Indian communities linked more directly to it. Neither could they support the indigenista attempt to reduce or eliminate ethnic differences as a precondition to more egalitarian participation in national life. One might say that indigenismo pioneered in the study of mechanisms of regional domination, but subsumed its findings in an ever-increasing concentration on promoting cultural change. Dependentistas, on the other hand, remained concerned with the early preoccupations of radical indigenistas and extended the scope of their investigation in an effort to understand the broader context of structural disadvantage, of which culturally defined defensiveness was more a symptom than a cause.

Bases for a dependentista challenge of indigenismo: Stavenhagen on class and caste in interethnic relations

The way in which dependency theory was integrated into Mexican anthropology during the 1960s can be particularly well illustrated by looking at the work of Rodolfo Stavenhagen, who played a central role in transposing the theoretical conclusions of the new Latin American sociology into the realm of anthropological concern. Stavenhagen was both an anthropologist (trained by indigenistas and functionalists at the National School of Anthropology and the University of Chicago) and a sociologist (studying for his doctorate under Georges Balandier at the University of Paris). In addition, he was, like González Casanova, active in establishing the Latin American Faculty of Social Sciences at the turn of the 1960s, and occupied the post of secretary general of the Faculty's Center for Research in the Social Sciences, in Rio de Janeiro, at the time when the dependency paradigm was in the process of formation. He was therefore particularly well prepared to bring together the threads of Mexican, French, American and Latin American thought on the 'colonial situation' and to contribute in that way to the formation of a new approach to indigenismo.

Stavenhagen's criticism of the indigenista paradigm — and one of his contributions to the understanding of ethnicity in Mexico — grew out of an attempt to deal in a new way with the long-debated question of the relative importance of caste and class in interethnic situations. Indigenismo, it will be remembered, had presupposed a dichotomy between caste (or ethnically justified domination) and class: one or the other predominated and, in practice, it was caste which shaped the process of social differentiation in the refuge regions with which indigenistas were fundamentally concerned. Therefore it was necessary to do away with ethnic identity (as the cultural basis of caste) before Indian minorities could be inserted into a national class system which would allow them the possibility of fighting for their own liberation.

For anyone aware of the complex forms of domination being considered within the paradigm of dependency, this seemed an unnecessarily rigid conception of the issue. Caste, class, and many other forms of stratification could conceivably exist simultaneously and interact upon one another, just as geographical forms of exploitation were superimposed upon relations to means of production. The problem was to understand the nature of the interrelation among systems of differentiation, not to construct a continuum in which one form excluded another.

In the specific case of the Chiapas highlands, which Stavenhagen took as his point of reference, it seemed that the mass of Indians, who had been exploited as a class of peasant tributaries before the Conquest, and as an ethnic group during the colonial period, were transformed following independence from Spain into a 'subjugated class of poor peasants' by the expansion of capitalism throughout the countryside and the gradual elimination of communal barriers to outside penetration.³⁵ The class nature of their subjection was nevertheless closely linked to their ethnic identity, which reinforced and sanctioned, in the eyes of mestizos, the extraction of a surplus from Indian communities. Class and caste coexisted, in Stavenhagen's view, and had done so for more than a hundred years. To say, as indigenistas were doing at the time, that the substitution of class for ethnic relations would represent an historical advance toward national integration could therefore not be a valid prescription for policy. The nation had been integrated along class lines since the nineteenth century, and inclusion within the broader capitalist system had done nothing to improve the position of the Indians.

On the contrary, it was precisely the progressive penetration of Indian communities by the market, their increasing involvement in commercial agriculture, their recourse to wage labor and to the sale of land as private property, which had served over the preceding century to transform them from traditional societies into underdeveloped ones.³⁶ Indians as a whole were less and less able to satisfy the minimum requirements of livelihood; and to strip them of their ethnic identity could only eliminate one more element of protection between them and an exploitative capitalist environment.

Stavenhagen was particularly concerned, in his review of the effects of the indigenista attack on ethnicity, with the probable stimulus given to the growth of a marginal population by the breakdown of Indian identity. While indigenistas generally assumed that individual 'passage' from the status of Indian to that of mestizo, and group-wide acculturation toward a mestizo pattern, were signs of upward mobility, Stavenhagen pointed out that they were more often concomitants of proletarization or marginality. And the economic elements of dispossession were compounded by an accompanying syndrome of anomie: 'The problem [arose] when . . . "national incorporation" of the Indians at a structural level of marginality [was] accompanied by an accelerated process of deculturation without any accompanying process of cultural integration.' The resulting psychological and cultural malaise was roughly equivalent to that of the culture of poverty, encountered by Oscar Lewis.³⁷

The similarity of this view to the picture of capitalist penetration in the Mexican countryside drawn by Eric Wolf (the formation of classes in the nineteenth century, the often negative effects of the process on livelihood, the danger of alienation) was striking. The difference lay, however, in the emphasis which Stavenhagen, and others within the dependency school of Mexican anthropology, placed upon

116 *Anthropology and the dependency paradigm in Mexico, 1960-75*

the importance of ethnicity, largely left aside in Wolf's treatment. Such concern put them in a better position to challenge the prevailing wisdom of indigenismo, and ultimately to change it.

Dependentista support of cultural diversity: Bonfil and the decolonization of ethnic relations

Despite his defense of Indian identity, it would be wrong to suppose that Stavenhagen or any of the other young anthropologists beginning to apply the concept of the colonial situation to an analysis of the indigenista paradigm in the 1960s was unaware of the negative elements contained within the cultures of indigenous groups. They were not. In fact, the new school, working within the broad framework of dependency theory, was only too clearly prepared by its contact with anti-colonial writers like Fanon to understand the distortions which could be introduced into the way of life of dominated peoples by the necessity to adapt to long subjection. Therefore just as Moisés Sáenz had found some of the groups with which he came in touch to be 'miserable people, terrorized and exploited,' and Ricardo Pozas described the population of Chamula as 'afraid of life,'[38] dependentista theorists often characterized Indian cultures as 'inauthentic' and 'oppressed.'

The very fact that such inauthenticity grew out of deformations worked by external domination nevertheless offered hope of cultural renaissance for some groups, if not for all. A concerted effort to eliminate the objective elements of exploitation by non-Indians might permit the least decimated of the nation's indigenous peoples to salvage from their own traditions those aspects of behavior of greatest value outside the parameters of discrimination. And in the process, the 'national culture' itself would be changed, for it existed in a dialectical relation of 'master' and 'slave' which was as detrimental to the former as it was to the latter.

The most articulate spokesman for this position, which implied reorienting indigenismo toward a frontal attack on exploitative non-Indians rather than on ethnic identity, was Guillermo Bonfil, a contemporary of Stavenhagen equally influenced by radical indigenismo and dependency theory. Bonfil took up the threads of analysis of interethnic relations left by de la Fuente and Aguirre Beltrán, and agreed with them that 'the category of Indian denoted a colonized position and [made] necessary reference to a colonial relationship.' It implied an historical experience in which local cultures had been 'compulsively altered, mutilated, stripped of all [capacity] for autonomous development...' But 'Indianness' could be separated from ethnic identity, which referred not to a process of subjection but to a concrete local tradition. Therefore

> the liberation of the colonized − the disappearance of the colonial order − [might] signify the disappearance of the Indian; but the disappearance of the Indian [would] not imply the suppression of ethnic entities. On the contrary, it [would] open the possibility that the latter [could] once again take control over their own history and shape their own destiny.[39]

The evident conclusion toward which such reasoning led was the value of maintaining a pluricultural nation and of rejecting the prevailing indigenista inference that cultural homogeneity was a necessary precondition for national unity.[40] This was in essence a return to the anti-incorporationist stance of Sáenz and Lombardo Toledano; and like the position of the latter, it required not only permitting but encouraging the political organization of indigenous groups. The hallmark of a unified and democratic nation state was the active participation of all citizens in the political process, whether through the medium of organizations representing economic interests, parties, occupational blocks or ethnic groups. There was no reason why ethnicity should not serve the positive function of uniting disadvantaged rural people and providing them with a means for expressing their demands within a system which had for too long relegated them to silence on the supposition that they were culturally unfit to speak.

This point of view, consistently pressed by Stavenhagen, Bonfil and others within the broad confines of the new anthropology during the second half of the 1960s,[41] found an echo during the presidential period of Luis Echeverría, from 1970 to 1976, when the rapid deterioration of levels of living in the Mexican countryside, combined with a growing crisis of agricultural production and of political accommodation, strained the bases of popular support for the postrevolutionary Mexican state to an extent not equalled since the early 1930s. Echeverría, like Cárdenas, responded to the crisis by reorienting federal policy toward meeting the demands of least advantaged groups; and to carry out that policy, he required the visible political support of the masses. The founding of representative councils for each Indian group, and their integration into an Indian Coalition within the National Peasant Confederation, became one important element in the Echeverría strategy, as it had been in the earlier Cardenista example.

The degree of Indian mobilization obtained during the 1970s was, however, far more significant than that of the 1930s, because the network of communications tying Indian groups to the broader society was of a qualitatively, as well as quantitatively, different order. That the Mazahuas, Tarascans or Nahuas of the 1970s were no longer as parochial as they had been forty years before could not have been more clearly illustrated than in the form of their participation in the new councils, compared to the old. With the assistance of a large group of bilingual promoters, formed during decades of incorporationist indigenista effort in the countryside, members of the Indian Councils of the 1970s spoke out strongly for an end to discriminatory practices of all kinds, which transferred the fruits of their own labor to mestizo intermediaries and urban dwellers. They demanded equality within a legal system long vitiated by discrimination; access to services long concentrated in urban areas; the right to form productive and commercial organizations free of mestizo domination; and the right to preserve their own customs. These were, by all accounts, not demands placed in their mouths by outsiders; they were a locally generated commentary on the vicissitudes of dependence and marginality, and they far surpassed the expectations of those who had hoped to organize support for the state without paying a significant price for it.[42]

Mexican anthropologists of the dependency school responded to this surge of political organization among Indian groups – which, it must be noted, eventually resulted in active collaboration among different ethnic councils in the name of a national Indian movement – by interpreting and defending it within national news media and within the National Indian Institute,[43] as well as by initiating programs to defend elements of ethnic tradition from extinction. The Viceministry of Indian Education, within the Ministry of Education, previously in the hands of incorporationist indigenistas, was reoriented through the founding by Rodolfo Stavenhagen of a Department of Popular Culture in the latter 1970s, and a program intended to provide support to beleaguered Indian languages (through the formation of Indian linguists) inaugurated by Guillermo Bonfil. This was not simply the functional equivalent of traditional anthropological efforts to preserve novel or beautiful elements of the human heritage for posterity; it was in addition an expression of the conviction that a situation of colonial domination could only be broken through utilizing cultural reaffirmation as a weapon in the struggle to achieve integration on equal terms within a pluricultural state.⁴⁴

Anthropology and the redistribution of knowledge

In the 1960s and 1970s, then, the nature of the socioeconomic and political balance within Mexican society itself, and the changing position of rural and Indian people in particular, brought sharply to the attention of many anthropologists the fact that they were approaching an end of the time when it could be thought that levels of living in the countryside could be raised through the intervention of conscientious outsiders, manipulating the local culture in ways designed to produce positive adaptation to the requirements of modernity. Whether anthropologists and community development workers were aware of the cultural idiosyncrasies of a particular group or settlement seemed suddenly far less important than whether local people possessed sufficient awareness of the working of regional or national society to permit them to make headway in defense of their own interests. The new task of anthropology, in that case, was not only to study the poor and powerless, but also the rich and powerful, and to make its findings available to the former in a process of 'redistribution of knowledge' among social groups consciously conceived as a parallel to the process of redistribution of wealth.⁴⁵

There was a strong precedent for this point of view within the structure of the dependency paradigm itself, for dependency or neocolonialism was defined in part as a state of exclusion from access to needed resources, including information, monopolized by powerful outsiders. If one applied this perspective to the anthropological endeavor, it could clearly lead to the conclusion that anthropologists had played a generally conservative role throughout the twentieth century, by making information on local people available to more powerful regional and national groups without concurrently providing peasants, Indians, or the working class with similar information on elites. The point might in fact have been moot at a time when none of the former seemed interested in having such information. But with the increasing incorporation of rural areas into national society, the growth of communication networks, and the spread of literacy, an effective demand for knowledge on the part of certain previously excluded sectors concerning the working of the wider socioeconomic system has clearly been created by the end of the 1960s; and anthropologists began slowly to respond to that demand.

As they did so, however, they began to move much closer to the realms of sociology and political economy. Interestingly enough, the kind of information which seemed to be required for understanding the principal mechanisms inserting rural people on an unequal basis within national and international systems did not often center around the question of the culture of elites, but rather around their control over resources. There was a certain baseline of knowledge concerning the ways in which material and political power could be, and were being, exercised which had to be covered before anthropologists could allow themselves the luxury of becoming immersed in the subtleties of culture which were their stock-in-trade; and Stavenhagen and others of the dependency school urged their colleagues to attend to those points on a priority basis, or run the risk of 'deifying culture' at the expense of social relevance.[46]

That this was not a negation of the importance of culture must surely be clear from the preceding discussion of the role of representatives of the new school of Mexican anthropology in defending cultural pluralism. It was a call for meeting the immediate requirements of disadvantaged groups through setting in motion a new kind of applied anthropology less concerned with changing values than with changing the structure of access to needed resources – an attack, in other words, upon the prevalent functionalist and indigenista premise that the most serious problems of the countryside could only be approached through inducing modification of attitudes and ideas.[47] Within the realm of longer-term anthropological research, however, anthropologists like Stavenhagen and Bonfil gave continuing support to the study of cultural change, among elites and the disadvantaged alike. Among the most interesting investigations of this kind associated with the dependency paradigm were Bonfil's own doctoral thesis on the revival of religious traditionalism within stagnating lower-income groups of the provincial mestizo town of Cholula, in which traditionalism was shown to be a response to a particularly stultifying form of dependent modernization,[48] and a series of studies on the American community in Mexico, as well as the impact of American cultural models on various sectors of Mexican society.

Abandonment and renewal of interest in agrarian reform among anthropologists and rural sociologists in Mexico

Perhaps the clearest example of the practical and theoretical pitfalls entailed by the tendency to 'deify culture' observed by the new school of Mexican anthropologists in earlier work on rural life was the paucity of attention paid before 1960 to non-Indian communities, and most particularly to the socioeconomic implications of agrarian reform. The preoccupation of functionalist and indigenista anthropologists with deciphering the peculiarities of Indian culture had not encouraged them to look at mestizo land reform communities with the care which both the numbers and the sociopolitical importance of the latter would have warranted, nor had anthropologists played any significant part in assessing the broader structural implications of agrarian reform for Mexican society as a whole. With very few exceptions,[49] agrarian reform had, until the 1960s, been the terrain of political sociologists, historians and economists.[50] Anthropologists might refrain from mentioning the subject even when villages under their scrutiny had passed through long years of struggle to obtain land, water, and/or credit.[51]

The relative lack of work on concrete local or regional experiences with agrarian reorganization, compared with the vast array of material produced by anthropologists on problems of community development and cultural change, was compounded by the long-standing weakness of rural sociology as an academic discipline in Mexico. Despite the fact that the Institute for Social Research of the National University had been directed from the late 1930s onward by a dedicated rural sociologist, Lucio Mendieta y Núñez,[52] and that Mendieta had for many years entertained the idea of carrying out a comparative study of land reform communities which would supplement the anthropological 'monographic method' with recourse to a regional framework, the project languished throughout the 1940s and early 1950s while the Institute's contribution to the understanding of rural Mexico continued to be made by ethnographers whose articles on elements of the culture of numerous Indian groups were indistinguishable from those of other particularists of the period.[53]

By the mid-1950s, however, currents of renovation and change began to appear within the field of rural sociology, as they were concurrently appearing in anthropology. Mendieta y Núñez's comparative study was set in motion, and produced by the end of the decade an invaluable commentary on the socioeconomic impact of agrarian reform in three communities judged representative of predominant tendencies in rural Mexico as a whole.[54] A National Sociological Congress (the sixth, held in 1955) was dedicated to rural questions for the first time; and although the tone of discussion was decidedly traditional, the effort marked a beginning for new projects, the fruits of which were clearly visible in the next national congress on a similar topic (agrarian reform) held nine years later.[55] Finally, Mendieta and a number of colleagues, who were in constant contact with the agrarian and agricultural problems of the Mexican countryside through their work as agronomists or agricultural economists within official agencies attending the ejido sector, succeeded in founding a Center for Agrarian Research (Centro de Investigaciones Agrarias), funded by the government, through which a start could be made toward addressing selected topics on a multidisciplinary basis.

The reasons for growing interest in the sociological study of rural problems during the latter 1950s, in Mexico as in many other countries, could not have been entirely academic. In fact, it was a time of increasing unrest in the countryside of a number of Third World nations, the population of which had begun to feel the impact of the modernizing drive upon traditional agrarian structures with particular force, whether as urban consumers discontent with the relative inefficiency of stagnating landed estates (haciendas) or as peasants driven to the limits of physical endurance by loss of land or employment to capitalist agricultural enterprises. The need for some form of agrarian reorganization, brought about under the aegis of Latin American governments, began to be discussed with frequency; and in Mexico, the problems of an agrarian reform already three decades old began to be reexamined in the light of lessons which might be learned, as well as new measures which might be taken to deal with the obviously serious livelihood situation of large numbers of rural people.[56]

Anthropologists who tended to collaborate in the renewal of interest in agrarian affairs during the latter 1950s in Mexico and, in the process, to provide an early stimulus for erasing any rigid disciplinary division between anthropology and rural sociology, were to be found within that small minority of students and teachers at the National School already encouraged by familiarity with the nascent paradigm of cultural ecology or by their association with Marxism to look at the structural problems of rural areas outside the parameters of ethnicity. Among teachers, Ricardo Pozas should particularly be mentioned; and among students, the majority of the group soon to contribute to the formation of the dependency paradigm.[57] By the mid-1960s, when those students were completing their graduate studies and had become associated with a way of approaching rural reality which made the integrated study of

Anthropology and the dependency paradigm in Mexico, 1960-75 123

all groups in the countryside — and indeed of the relation between countryside and city within a world capitalist system — a necessity, the stage was set for a definitive turn toward anthropological concern with the agrarian structure of Mexico.

The Center for Agrarian Research and the multidisciplinary study of agrarian and agricultural problems: designing a new research strategy

It was in keeping with the multidisciplinary nature of the dependency paradigm that the first large-scale study of the socioeconomic parameters of livelihood in the Mexican countryside as a whole, and of the particular place of agrarian reform in determining those parameters, should be carried out by a team of anthropologists, sociologists, economists and agronomists collaborating in an international program of hemispheric scope. The study, which began in Mexico in 1965, was one of seven in Latin America sponsored by the Inter-American Committee for Agricultural Development (ICAD) and financed jointly by the Organization of American States, the Economic Commission for Latin America, the United Nations Food and Agriculture Organization, and the Inter-American Development Bank. Its official purpose, as that of all ICAD studies, was to examine the causes of agricultural stagnation and agrarian unrest and to propose ways in which the agricultural sector, as an economic abstract, and the rural population, as a social one, could be integrated into a more satisfactory form of national development in the future.

Obviously, the ideological preferences of the various groups and agencies united behind the study at an international level varied markedly, from a patent interest in maintaining prevailing patterns of capitalist development within some quarters to a well-defined desire to alter them in others. The majority of the research staff was nevertheless influenced by new currents in Latin American social thought and skeptical of continuing to utilize the theoretical tools of liberalism or functionalism in attempting to come to grips with rural problems at hand. The overall analytical framework utilized in all studies was in fact elaborated by social scientists with strong ties to the ECLA-affiliated Latin American Institute for Socioeconomic Planning (ILPES) and the Latin American Faculty of Social Sciences in Santiago de Chile, both centers for discussion of dependency theory, and with a personal history of long dedication to the promotion of structural change in the Latin American countryside.[58]

In order to combine the traditional concern of participating governments for production and productivity, on the one hand, with a new insistence upon the need to elucidate the structural problems of rural livelihood on the other, all ICAD studies included macroeconomic analyses of agricultural census statistics, broken down into categories of producers designed to reflect more than simply the size of holdings or the kind of land tenure involved. These new categories, first suggested by Andrew Pearse, were based upon the capacity of agricultural production units to sustain a family at culturally acceptable levels, through providing both employment and income.[59] Their utilization made it possible to construct a sociological picture of the countryside out of statistics formerly used for rather traditional economic commentary, illustrating not only the extent to which rural families were impeded from making an adequate living from the land, but also the maldistribution of land and other inputs which contributed to that situation. Taken as a whole, the statistical mosaic emerging from each country study provided a basis for discussion of a distinctive 'agrarian structure,' within which various groups of producers, with differing access to resources and forms of social organization, were interrelated among themselves, and interacted with the wider nonagricultural society.[60]

The ICAD studies were, of course, not only statistical in nature. Qualitative research on different forms of agrarian systems, or agrarian institutions, in Latin America had in fact begun to enjoy a certain importance within the social sciences from the early 1950s onward, when cultural ecologists like Mintz, Palerm and Wolf had set in motion a series of investigations of haciendas, plantations and latifundia, the institutional center of which became the social research division of the Organization of American States. The ICAD effort inherited the fruits of that work, as well as those of a growing concern by historians with the socioeconomic characteristics of the Latin American countryside, evidenced particularly in the 1960s.[61] The social history of agrarian structure in each country covered by the project therefore was given considerable emphasis in most ICAD reports and was stressed in the field work carried out by multidisciplinary teams sent into selected regions to construct detailed pictures of specific local experiences.

These teams dealt not only with matters of history, but also engaged in direct investigation of contemporary problems of agricultural production and rural livelihood, at times utilizing questionnaires, at times interviewing key informants, and at times participating in an anthropological fashion in the daily round of activities associated with gaining

Anthropology and the dependency paradigm in Mexico, 1960-75 125

a living within various groups of agricultural producers. It is important for an understanding of the innovative nature of this research to stress that, in accordance with the comprehensive scope of the dependency paradigm, it involved studying elites as well as peasants — large landowners, businessmen and government officials, as well as smallholders, renters and landless laborers — and that it did not shy away from the detailed examination of politics. In fact, the study of peasant organization, counterposed against that of elite organization, constituted a significant part of the exercise.

Obviously, the possibilities of such a large-scale investigation of agrarian structure for contributing to the renovation of rural studies in any country — for broadening the horizons of anthropology in particular, and for giving marked impetus to any incipient process of fusion between the disciplines of social anthropology and rural sociology, were remarkable indeed. They were reinforced in the Mexican case by the fact that the ICAD study was carried out by Mendieta y Núñez's Center for Agrarian Research, at the time under the leadership of Sergio Reyes Osorio; and that Rodolfo Stavenhagen shared with Reyes Osorio the direction of the project. In the midst of an academic atmosphere still dominated by a marked preference for the study of Indian cultures, Stavenhagen put a number of students from the National School of Anthropology in mestizo peasant communities, or regional complexes, and directed their attention toward prerevolutionary agrarian history and the postrevolutionary transformation of agrarian institutions. Emphasis was placed upon understanding the internal functioning of land reform settlements, both as communities in the anthropological sense of the term and as ejidos, or institutional constructs of land reform legislation. And that task could not be completed without also studying the relations between ejidatarios and a network of economic and political institutions extending from the local to the national (or even international) level. Anthropologists, in the company of sociologists, therefore found themselves turning to subjects they might previously have ignored altogether, including the agricultural marketing and credit system, the intricacies of state and local politics, and the nature of the Mexican State.[62]

A macrosociological and macroeconomic view of the Mexican countryside in the postrevolutionary period: the ICAD report

The macroeconomic picture which emerged from the ICAD study in

Mexico was one of an agricultural sector which systematically provided more to the national economy as a whole than it received in return, and which thus supported industrial growth at the expense of the increasing decapitalization of agricultural activity. Through maintaining low food prices, providing cheap labor, producing large volumes of export crops and making a relatively small claim on credit supplies, agriculture subsidized postwar economic growth up to the early 1960s, when signs of stagnation in farm production began to suggest the declining capacity of the sector to continue along the path traced for it by the existing model of capitalist development.

There were, however, great differences in the structural position of the various groups of producers integrating the sector. Almost one-half of all holdings surveyed by the agricultural census were so small and badly endowed with productive resources that they provided full employment for less than one person and produced crops worth an average of only 750 (1960) pesos per year. These 'infra-subsistence' holdings belonged to families which obviously obtained more of their income outside agriculture than within it, who were only marginally engaged in farming, and who contributed less than 4 per cent of the entire agricultural product of the country in 1960. They were followed by another large category of 'subfamily' holdings which absorbed the labor of less than two men per year, and produced an average of 5,000 pesos worth of crops, most of which were consumed by the family itself and did not find an outlet in the market. These holdings constituted 34 per cent of the total in the nation and provided 17 per cent of the value of the agricultural product. In sum, then, 84 per cent of all the landholding families within the agricultural sector of Mexico, according to available statistics, formed an impoverished group of minifundistas who could not make an adequate living from the land. Family-sized holdings, fully occupying the labor force of a farming household and requiring the occasional use of hired hands (the statistical category foresaw the employment of two to five persons) constituted only 13 per cent of the national total and provided 25 per cent of the agricultural product. The greatest part of all the food and fiber supplied by the agricultural sector (54 per cent) came in consequence from only 3 per cent of all holdings, made up of 'medium'- and 'large'-scale multi-family farms, operating on extensive tracts of land and utilizing modern capital-intensive technologies. The latter category, in particular, contained postrevolutionary latifundios, generally exceeding the legal limits set by agrarian reform legislation and owned as private property by families equally likely to be influential in politics as in regional and national nonagricultural economic life.[63]

To explain the persistence of such an unequal distribution of productive resources among the agricultural population of Mexico, despite revolution and agrarian reform, the ICAD study turned to an analysis of the development strategy followed by postrevolutionary governments and to the sociopolitical foundations underlying that strategy. It became clear, in the course of the review, that government policy had systematically favored large private farming over peasant production, investing disproportionate sums in modernizing the physical and financial infrastructure of the former and subsidizing its expansion at the expense of smallholdings. Agrarian reform, in turn, had been utilized more as a tool of political control than as a vehicle for the economic development of the countryside: land reform beneficiaries had been integrated into a cumbersome hierarchy of bureaucratic institutions which ensured their economic and political dependence, but not the possibility of participating in accordance with their numerical strength in the formation of a modern Mexican nation.

The end result of this peculiarly distorted process of capitalist modernization in the countryside was the increasing underdevelopment of many agrarian communities, concurrently with a wasteful 'overdevelopment' of large private agriculture. The overwhelmingly superior political and economic position of large landowners permitted them ever greater control over the productive resources of the peasantry (including their labor at a low price), while many of the latter, unable to survive on their own plots, joined the ranks of wage laborers on a temporary or permanent basis. This was to some extent an example of the classical pattern of social differentiation in the countryside foreseen by Marx and Lenin, but it was tempered by the existence of a large reform sector whose land could not easily be alienated.

Although it did not go into great detail concerning the dependent position of Mexico within a world capitalist system, then, the ICAD study consistently dealt with questions of unequal exchange within the socioeconomic configuration of the agricultural sector, between that sector and others at the level of the national economy, and within the broader political structure of the nation. It was particularly concerned to show that the simple redistribution of land from latifundistas to the peasantry was not in itself sufficient to transform situations of domination into situations of equality. Peasants with nominal control over the means of production could still be exploited through any number of mechanisms, ranging from the working of the price system through the manipulation of credit to the collection of taxes and bribes by an oppressive bureaucratic superstructure. This was an example of a chain of transfers, one of the most important modern elements of which was what Stavenhagen called the 'rural bourgeoisie,' 'a new regional upper class whose pre-eminence [did] not come from property of land [although its members often did own private properties], but rather from the monopolistic control of commerce, the distribution of goods and services, and regional political power.'[64] In the last analysis, the rural bougeoisie, operating in the small and medium-sized towns which took the place of the hacienda as centers of power in the Mexican countryside following the revolution, were the central part of a machinery which continued to channel the surplus produced by the peasantry toward urban, and international, destinations, land reform notwithstanding.

The functioning of this exploitative machinery eventually rested upon the continued, indeed enforced, political impotence of the peasantry — upon the working of a political system which controlled from above rather than responding to demands formulated from below, and which systematically eliminated independent organization through cooptation of peasant leaders or, if made necessary by the failure of the former strategy, through repression. The presentation of the ICAD study, written by Reyes Osorio and Stavenhagen, in fact placed particular stress upon this element in the continuing agrarian crisis of the country by concluding with the statement that support for locally controlled and locally responsive peasant organization must necessarily be 'the fundamental task of the future' in Mexico.[65] It was a subject to which Stavenhagen, like González Casanova, had given considerable attention in the past, and on which he systematically encouraged others to work in coming years.[66] Political anthropology, under the impact of the dependency paradigm, became by the end of the 1960s a necessary element in the multidisciplinary study of the Mexican countryside.

Contradictory currents within the dependency paradigm

In the decade which followed the path-breaking work of the Center for Agrarian Studies, the network of relationships determining access to productive resources in rural areas, mestizo or Indian, was studied with ever-increasing frequency and depth; and the dependency paradigm continued to be very much associated with most treatments of the subject. Nevertheless, by the 1970s, it was clear that the ambiguities inherent in the paradigm since its first appearance in the 1950s were straining its coherence, and that dependency was being considered in contradictory ways leading to radically different policy conclusions. One group of dependentistas, leaning more toward association with a revisionist Marxist position on the inevitability of capitalist expansion from European and American centers of industrial capitalism to the most remote corners of the globe — and consequently the collapse of capitalism if that expansion were halted — assumed that increasing exploitation and declining levels of living in Third World satellites, and most particularly in the rural areas of those satellites, were inevitable and would be detained only through the revolutionary advent of socialism. Members of this group tended to study the international manifestations of dependency, with emphasis on the growing role of transnational corporations, banks and technological transfers in the agriculture of Third World countries.[67]

A second group of social scientists also concerned with dependency leaned toward a somewhat more probabilistic view of the future. In keeping with the nature of the original anthropological contribution to the dependency paradigm, made by Balandier and others concerned with the 'colonial situation,' they stressed the resiliency of local (dominated) groups of people, their capacity to adapt to the impositions of the metropolis without entirely surrendering. This resiliency was grounded in culture, and it could impel a subjected peasantry or ethnic group to respond to domination in a way with which even the modern machinery of capitalism could not adequately cope. It might therefore conceivably not be inevitable that liberation from exploitative ties would come only after the development of capitalism had run its entire destructive course. Some sort of earlier 'delinking' from the world capitalist system might obviate that necessity.

Probabilistic dependentistas were, in addition, not as sanguine as their more deterministic counterparts concerning the equation of liberation with state socialism. Dependency, it was true, had necessarily to be seen in the Third World as an historical concomitant of the expansion of capitalism from the sixteenth century onward. But the phenomenon of dependence was not simply a facet of capitalism. It existed as well in relations between socialist metropoli and their satellites, and in social relations among groups within any socialist country. It seemed particularly to be associated with extreme levels of urban industrialism. Given that fact, the prevalence of consistently unequal transfers from rural to urban areas, from one region to another, and from one class to another might best be attacked by attempting to create an entirely different kind of development — less centralized, less technologically predatory, and less dehumanizing than that of either industrial capitalism or industrial socialism. In such a new order, the rural community had a key role to play.[68]

Within this latter framework, the study of dependency was generally turned inward toward an examination of the incursions of capitalism in rural society, and toward the specific domination of the peasantry by representatives of the modern Mexican state, rather than toward a study of the peculiarly transnational elements of domination. The approach shared much with cultural ecology; and in fact, by the 1970s the work of probabilistic dependentistas and cultural ecologists — most especially when touching upon the relation between the peasantry and public or private expropriators of a surplus — was distinguishable only to the extent that cultural ecologists gave particular attention to the more technically 'ecological' aspects of their subject. Leading dependentistas, like Stavenhagen and Bonfil, shared with Palerm, Warman and others among cultural ecologists a program of action for anthropological research and teaching, as well as a belief in the need to influence national policy toward the pursuit of 'another development,' which they were soon to be given the chance to further. That, however, will be the subject of the following chapter.

5 Historical structuralism and the fate of the peasantry, 1970-80

During the 1970s, three currents within Mexican social anthropology, separated for decades by differences in research priorities as well as by a somewhat more fortuitous geographical dispersion of principal representatives of each group, converged around the need to understand the present and future of the peasantry. All three schools – cultural ecology, dependentismo, and orthodox Marxism – drew inspiration from Marxist theory. But the first two had been concerned, from the time of their formation, with adapting the Marxist tradition to the apparent peculiarities of socioeconomic organization within peripheral groups, regions or nations. They were, in other words, revisionist in that they challenged the universal applicability of concepts originally proposed by Marx to explain the dynamics of social relations in core areas of Western industrial capitalism, and that they suggested new approaches for elucidating mechanisms of dependence and exploitation in a world capitalist system. Orthodox Marxists, by definition, had not engaged in a similar endeavor.

The distance between orthodoxy and revisionism had been maintained for decades within historical structuralism in Mexico not only by differences in temperament and academic formation among members of various schools, but also by material differences in access to specific documents within the body of literature produced by Marx in his lifetime, and by the first generation of European Marxist scholars following his death. Cultural ecologists and dependentistas, generally trained outside Mexico in the 1950s and early 1960s, came into contact with a broader range of literature – whether in German originals or French or English translation – than orthodox Marxists restricted to analysis of the basic works available in Mexico at the same time. While the former, including Marx's own *Grundrisse*, the works of Chayanov, Luxemburg, Wittfogel, and Preobrazensky, opened new avenues of investigation and discussion concerning such issues as colonialism, socialist accumulation, and the nature of precapitalist socioeconomic formations, the latter focused almost exclusively upon an examination of 'pure' capitalism, as an ideal type.

The difference in emphasis between the kind of analysis contained in classical translated works of Marx, Engels and Lenin guiding orthodox Marxists in Mexico until the late 1960s, and that to be found in untranslated manuscripts and books within a flourishing European revival and re-evaluation of Marx, had far-reaching implications for the study of the peasantry. Confining the boundaries of enquiry rather strictly to the socioeconomic requirements of fully capitalist formations, as orthodox Marxists tended to do, in fact left little place for the peasantry, except as a residual historical category destined for prompt extinction. But if one expanded those boundaries through a consideration of coexisting capitalist and noncapitalist forms, it was possible to examine not only the elements permitting a long persistence of the peasantry, but also the role of the latter in the complex web of regional and class-based exploitation characteristic of internal and international colonialism.

The urgency of adopting the second approach was made clear in the late 1960s by several developments, both within the peasantry itself and within the groups which studied it. To begin, agricultural census figures for 1960, released toward mid-decade, pointed sharply to the fact that while most rural families could no longer maintain themselves (if indeed they ever had) through the kind of largely autonomous self-provisioning which had once provided the objective basis for functionalist anthropological theory, neither were they dissolving into a proletariat. On the contrary, despite the increasing necessity to supplement limited agricultural production with income earned as seasonal laborers on large capitalist farms or in the cities, a sizeable part of the total population of the nation survived through ultimate recourse to activities centering around peculiarly peasant-like forms of production and exchange.

The fact that the peasantry had not disappeared in the postwar period, but rather was increasing in absolute numbers (while declining in relative ones), constituted a challenge to orthodox Marxist theory almost as serious as that posed by the disproval of self-sufficiency to traditional functionalists. The extent of the challenge was reinforced by the political behavior of virtually landless and landless rural laborers, who continued with great insistence to petition for land, and thus to stress the peasant, rather than the proletarian, nature of their commitment. To attempt to classify the families of these men, or most other families in rural Mexico during the late 1960s, as either *petite bourgeoisie*

Historical structuralism and the fate of the peasantry, 1970–80   133

or proletariat, in deference to an orthodox interpretation of capitalist development, simply failed to provide a particularly productive research strategy. A new approach to the problem was obviously needed.

Roger Bartra and the study of precapitalist modes of production

In order to adapt the theoretical tools of orthodox Marxism to the stubborn persistence of the peasantry in Mexico, Marxist anthropologists began in the late 1960s to turn to an analysis of the possibilities inherent in Marx's own discussion of the coexistence of various forms of production within single socioeconomic units. This was a subject treated tangentially by Marx in *Capital* and other classical works long available to Marxist scholars in Mexico. But it was developed more fully in untranslated manuscripts the content of which was only brought to the attention of the latter shortly before the *Grundrisse* was published by the Fondo de Cultura Económica in 1965, and at a time when the early work of French structuralist Marxists like Althusser and Godelier began to be widely read in Mexico.

The role of introducing the theoretical possibilities of this new literature into the discourse of those working within the classical Marxist tradition in Mexico fell in large part to Roger Bartra, a young archeologist whose work at the National School of Anthropology had been oriented by a reading of Gordon Childe toward consideration of mechanisms through which an incipient Aztec state expropriated the surplus required for its formation from peasant tributaries within and without the Valley of Mexico. Not surprisingly, Bartra — like Wolf and Palerm a decade before — found Marx's concept of the asiatic mode of production, elaborated in the *Grundrisse*, of particular relevance to Aztec society; and in his first analysis of precapitalist modes of production he concentrated exclusively on an historical explanation of the transition from classless to class-based society in pre-Conquest rural Mexico.[1] This was in a certain sense a remarkable replication of the experience of cultural ecologists upon coming into contact with the same material at the turn of the 1950s, occurring independently within orthodox Marxism in the 1960s and carrying with it the possibility of a common — if not harmonious — discussion between members of two schools not in the past accustomed to communication.

In 1969, Bartra edited what was to become a seminal work on the asiatic mode of production, thus firmly establishing the latter as a subject of investigation within Marxist anthropology in Mexico.[2] At the same time, however, he turned increasingly away from archeology and history, toward the study of the role played by precapitalist forms of socioeconomic organization in determining the nature of contemporary Mexican society. Here he initiated a radical departure from existing orthodox Marxist scholarship. To talk of precapitalist modes of production in the past tense, and most particularly of asiatic forms applicable to the Aztec period, was not in fundamental disaccord with the mental framework of those who traced the development of human society from barbarism, or the natural economy, through classical antiquity and feudalism, to capitalism. New categories were simply added to an established evolutionary pattern. To argue that certain precapitalist modes of production continued to exist in articulation with modern capitalist modes, in mid-twentieth-century Mexico as well as much of the rest of the Third World, was, on the contrary, extremely debatable.

In making his case for the necessity to look at contemporary forms of precapitalist socioeconomic organization, it should be stressed, Bartra did not deny the evolutionary, historical elements of traditional Marxism. Despite a brief period of study during 1970 at the Sorbonne of Althusser, Balibar and Godelier, he did not accept the ahistorical structuralism of the French. While the latter argued that one could theoretically consider almost any combination of modes of production, each of which could be determined empirically at any given moment, Bartra considered relevant only those macrosociological categories specifically discussed by Marx in his lifetime, including 'the primitive community, the asiatic mode of production, the slave mode of production, the feudal mode of production, the simple mercantile economy, capitalism ... and socialism.'[3] And he tended to suppose that they followed an evolutionary order over the long run, although (as Marx had noted) earlier forms could continue to exist during long periods of time within more highly developed ones.

It was the dependent nature of Mexican development, from the time of the Conquest onward, which − for Bartra as for dependentistas and cultural ecologists − determined the incomplete realization of a capitalist transformation, and the continued existence within a dependent capitalist structure of important precapitalist elements. The country was in effect stalled at a transitional stage, in which indigenous capitalists were not capable of completing the destruction of earlier forms of socioeconomic organization in the countryside, and in which, furthermore, the destruction of the latter would be highly prejudicial to the interests of capital formation in a dependent setting. The influence of Rosa Luxemburg, as well as of dependency theory in general, was clear.

One precapitalist mode which could still be found in certain extremely remote areas of the Mexican countryside was the natural economy, or primitive community, in which daily life flowed on with virtually no need for exchange with the wider society. But the precapitalist form of socioeconomic organization obviously of most significance in rural Mexico, was that in which direct agricultural producers and artisans were continually drawn into a process of exchange from which they themselves expected only to assure necessary elements of their subsistence, but from which capitalist buyers of their goods extracted the raw materials with which to make an eventual profit. This was the situation which Marx described as a 'simple mercantile economy,' and which Bartra found best to categorize the position of the peasantry in contemporary Mexican society.

Whether such a relationship was of sufficient comprehensiveness to warrant considering it a mode of production, and in fact whether Marx himself had so considered it, was to become an issue of bitter debate in the coming years. But in the meantime, use of the concept permitted Bartra to bring the peasantry into Marxist discussion of the Mexican countryside as a separate social class, which was neither proletariat nor bourgeoisie, while avoiding any challenge to the orthodox understanding of class structure within capitalist society. The peasantry constituted a class only — or precisely — because it still survived *outside* capitalism, as part of an entirely different precapitalist mode of production.[4] And it interacted with capitalist classes from a position of secondary importance, of exclusion, which could only be remedied once its members had been absorbed into the predominant capitalist mode as workers or entrepreneurs. In the tradition of Lenin, Bartra thus predicted the eventual dissolution of the peasantry and the disappearance of the simple mercantile mode.

The peasantry, then, re-emerged through Bartra in Mexican Marxism as a substantial unliquidated remnant of precapitalist social organization, articulated with and dominated by a capitalist mode of production, but moved by a noncapitalist rationale. The person who had most carefully studied that rationale was Chayanov, to whom Bartra turned at the suggestion of Gutelman. In a widely read article of 1975, as well as an introduction to the first translation of Chayanov published in Mexico, Bartra in effect extended to 'all those dedicated to the study of agrarian problems' 'an invitation to read' the Russian economist's work in order to understand the 'laws which regulate[d] the internal structure of the peasant economy.'[5] Such a reading added yet another common element to the vocabulary of orthodox Marxists, cultural ecologists, and dependentistas, although not to the evaluation which each made of the future of the peasantry.

The articulation of capitalist and noncapitalist modes

In order to analyse the particular ways in which those included within a simple mercantile mode of production were indeed linked to — and subordinated by — the predominant capitalist mode in Mexican society, Bartra and others looked at a number of points of contact (or 'articulation') between the systemic requirements of the two kinds of socioeconomic organization in question. The principal point of contact was, of course, the market, in which peasants could exchange their own goods for others produced in the capitalist economy, and capitalists could obtain fruits of peasant labor to be utilized in generating a later profit. This was the intersection of the cycle 'commodities-money-commodities' and 'money-commodities-money' about which both cultural ecologists and dependentistas had commented from the 1950s or 1960s onward.

Marxists like Bartra were, however, wary of stressing mechanisms of circulation at the expense of a more detailed examination of mechanisms of articulation operating at the level of production. The peasantry not only engaged in a process of exchange premised on criteria different from those characteristic of capitalism, but it also organized production in a way which was consonant with satisfying needs for subsistence, rather than profit. As a result, peasant families did not accumulate a surplus which could be reinvested to raise the technological level of their farming activity; and this relative technological disadvantage of peasant holdings, when articulated through a common marketing structure with capitalist holdings, made the former increasingly inefficient, both as competitors in the capitalist-controlled market and as sources of sustenance for small cultivators. In Marxist terms, the peasantry was drawn by operation on the fringes of the capitalist market into the sphere of influence of the capitalist 'law of value,' and that law inevitably worked against the continued viability of semi-subsistence production units.

The way in which Bartra brought Marxist theory to bear on the question of articulation of capitalist and noncapitalist modes of *production*,

Historical structuralism and the fate of the peasantry, 1970-80 137

as distinguished from *exchange*, can perhaps best be illustrated by turning to his *Estructura agraria y clases sociales en México*, published in 1974.[6] Drawing upon insights gained during field work in the Mezquital Valley, the coast of Michoacán and Guerrero, and the Venezuelan Andes, Bartra presented a reinterpretation of, and commentary upon, the ICAD study, which (as noted in Chapter 4) was associated with the dependentista paradigm in Mexico. The ICAD report, it will be remembered, had quantified for the first time the extent to which livelihood in the Mexican countryside hovered dangerously around infrasubsistence and subfamily levels; and it had attributed such a situation clearly to both the political subjection and the economic exploitation of the peasantry. The desperate economic plight of most rural people was, however, analysed in general terms as stemming from the failure to provide adequate official support for peasant production as well as from mechanisms of unequal exchange which systematically transferred resources from the peasantry to the rural and urban bourgeoisie. The idea that the social organization of production within peasant units themselves was of a kind which destined them irrevocably to extinction was never entertained. On the contrary, smallholding family enterprises were shown to be by far the most efficient in their utilization of scarce resources; and it was a principal conclusion of the study that all official support be given to strengthening peasant agriculture in Mexico.

Bartra specifically set out first to adapt the ICAD study (and by association, the dependentista diagnosis of the dynamics of rural change) to the requirements of class analysis by rephrasing the ICAD stratification of agricultural producers in class terms. Thus, following the general scheme proposed by Lenin, the 'large multifamily' category became the 'landholding bourgeoisie'; the 'medium multifamily' category became 'rich peasants'; 'family' holdings, 'medium peasants'; and 'infrasubsistence' or 'subfamily' holdings, 'poor peasants.' The rural proletariat remained, of course, unchanged. One then confronted three distinct classes in the Mexican countryside — bourgeoisie, peasantry and proletariat — in proportions the arithmetical basis of which were drawn without modification from ICAD.

In itself, this was hardly a fundamental challenge to the intentions of dependentistas.[7] But the next stage of Bartra's discussion was indeed so. By reworking the calculations of ICAD economists concerning the input-output ratio of small (peasant), medium and large holdings, Bartra proceeded to shift large capitalist enterprises from the lowest level of efficiency, where they had been placed in the ICAD study, to the highest, and peasant productive units from the highest to the lowest. Thus the dependentista argument for the superior productivity of small family enterprises was made to seem untenable.

The theoretical debate which lay behind this reversal can only be understood by remembering that dependentistas working on the ICAD study had tried to evaluate peasant agriculture on its own terms. Since the peasantry itself did not value family labor in terms of a wage, and did not insist upon payment of a wage for the expenditure of labor, that element of production was not valued in the ICAD calculation of efficiency. Labor was treated, in other words, as an abundant and unremunerated factor. And once the cost of labor was excluded from input-output matrices, it could be shown that small family holdings utilized available physical resources far more efficiently than large capitalist ones.

Marxist analysis, on the other hand, was predicated fundamentally upon a labor theory of value. What invested any material good with value for society was precisely the amount of time and effort expended in producing it; and that effort had of necessity to be remunerated at the average rate established by the state of technological advance prevailing in the economic system at the moment. The fact that the peasantry might not think in terms of perceiving such remuneration did not alter the need for imputing a wage; it only pointed out one of the areas in which a subsistence rationale could permit capitalist society to take advantage of the peasantry.

As soon as peasant labor was assigned the value of the prevailing minimum wage in the countryside, however, the inefficiency of small family holdings in a capitalist system seemed patent. Furthermore, the competitive position of the peasantry would inevitably worsen, according to Marxist theorists, for it was constantly affected by the changing average productivity of labor within the wider society as a whole. As capitalist development proceeded, that part of the total social product attributable to human labor constantly declined, while that attributable to technological innovation constantly increased. Workers on capitalist farms could produce more and more with relatively less and less effort − a trend reflected in the price structure for agricultural commodities, which tended to increase only in proportion to the average amount of labor expended in production. But family labor on peasant holdings, deprived of any meaningful possibility of increasing output through technological innovation, could not produce more without expending more effort. Therefore the relatively low prices which peasant produce could fetch in regional or national markets would not adequately remunerate producers for their effort and would force them to work ever harder in order to satisfy the minimum needs of their families.

It was this kind of reasoning, then, which led Marxists of Bartra's school to conclude that the ultimate significance of the articulation of simple mercantile and capitalist modes of production through market mechanisms was not to be found in the sphere of circulation itself, but in that of production. Peasant participation in a capitalist market could only serve over the long run to force family productive units into an unequal competition with capitalist ones, thereby distorting the allocation of resources within the former and eventually ensuring its extinction.

Inefficiency and exploitation within the framework of articulated modes of production

While the kind of emphasis on articulation of peasant and capitalist forms of socioeconomic organization through the sphere of circulation stressed by dependentistas in the ICAD study suggested, therefore, that small family holdings might enjoy a secure future if guaranteed just terms of exchange, the classical Marxist-Leninist emphasis on articulation at the level of production, through the working of the law of value, negated such a claim. The peasantry was innately inefficient; and even when remunerated adequately for its products — at the average level determined by the socially necessary labor time within the wider society — it could not perform well enough ultimately to guarantee an adequate livelihood for its members.

The fact that Marxists like Bartra visualized peasant economic activity as occurring within the theoretical equivalent of inefficient capitalist enterprises was of considerable relevance to the way members of that school discussed the question of exploitation. If an extraordinary expenditure of labor were required to produce any given output within a capitalist enterprise, such a departure from the mean simply indicated uncompetitiveness. The possibility that surplus value would be produced over the cost of production was reduced or nullified; and exploitation (defined as the ratio of surplus value to the necessary consumption of workers) declined toward zero. As a number of Marxists summarized the situation, surplus value which was not created could not be transferred; and therefore the extremely labor-intensive methods of the peasantry (qua enterprise) implied no more than the donation to the wider society of an astonishing amount of human effort for which inadequate compensation was obtained – a development as deplorable as it was unjust, but which served no useful purpose for the process of capitalist accumulation as a whole.[8]

The peasantry was not, then, from this point of view, exploited in the process through which its component families invested inordinate amounts of labor to produce goods remunerated at an average level established to cover the much less labor-intensive requirements of efficient capitalist enterprises. It was, however, exploited as soon as peasant producers received less for their output than the average price in force for the sector as a whole. This latter development was a concomitant of unfair manipulation of the terms of trade by commercial intermediaries, and was generally linked to the practice of usury. Through controlling not only the scarce fund of capital required to meet the minimum requirements of peasant production, but also the knowledge of prevailing market conditions, transport and urban buyers necessary to put the goods of smallholders up for sale outside the community, locally or regionally based intermediaries could buy below value, thus depriving the peasant enterprise of a part of its legitimate remuneration. At an analytical level concerned only with the relationship between an enterprise and the wider system, such a process could best be characterized as unequal exchange, not necessarily affecting internal rates of exploitation; but given the undeniable fact that the peasant enterprise was nothing more than a concentration of family labor, any reduction in its socially necessary remuneration could as well be seen as a direct appropriation of a part of the labor time of its workers, and denominated exploitation.

The kind of accumulation associated with the activities of commercial intermediaries and moneylenders in rural areas was not necessarily functional for the capitalist system as a whole. The traditional intermediary harmed not only the smallholders whom he dominated but also the interests of industrial capitalists who depended upon obtaining raw materials and foodstuffs at low prices in order to produce efficiently and to maintain a workforce at an acceptable subsistence level without paying high wages. He was in effect a retrograde, and over the long run could only be pushed aside by the advancing tide of capitalism.

A second form of exploitation to which many members of the peasantry were subject – that inherent in the absorption of an increasing number of rural people into the labor force of capitalist enterprises on a

Historical structuralism and the fate of the peasantry, 1970-80   141

temporary or permanent basis — was, in contrast, of positive value for the progress of capitalism and thus, by extension within the logical framework of Marxism, for the progress of civilization. While the operations of commercial intermediaries were characterized by the parasitic expropriation of a part of the extremely limited product of rural family labor, the transfer of value which occurred through the direct exploitation of peasant workers by capitalist entrepreneurs grew in theory out of the production of goods in greater volume than the simple reproduction of the labor force required. The resulting surplus was in consequence ideally to be attributed to increased productivity, fostered by the technological superiority of capitalism, rather than to the forced reduction in already precarious levels of living from which the monopolistic intermediary drew his profits.

At the same time, the form of exploitation to which members of the peasantry were subject as they entered the wage labor force of the capitalist sector encouraged, by the very nature of the social relations of production involved, the growth of class consciousness, and therefore of a potential for political activity impossible in an unproletarianized rural setting. This was, without question, the heart of the argument for the progressive nature of the proletarianization of the peasantry, and underlay the convinced optimism with which Marxists like Bartra greeted the absorption of ever-increasing numbers of peasants and their families into the wage labor sector of rural and urban Mexico. To be exploited as a peasant offered no political future; to be exploited as a proletarian laid the groundwork for socialism.

Political subordination of the peasantry in a secondary mode of production

The low esteem in which many Marxists held the political acumen of the peasantry grew directly out of the conviction, often found in the classical writings of Marx and Lenin, that the dispersed settlements of rural people, their relative autonomy and limited knowledge of the wider society, did not permit the formation of class consciousness among them. The peasantry was a class-in-itself, when analysed by observers, but not a class-for-itself; and in practice, it was generally manipulated by the bourgeoisie for the benefit of the latter. As Bartra put it, quoting Marx:

> the peasantry [was] unable to assert class interests in its own name,

whether within a parliament or a convention. It [could] not represent itself, but [had] to be represented. And its representative [had] to appear at the same time as its lord, as a superior authority, an unlimited power protecting [the peasantry] from other classes and granting it from above the sun and the rain.

> Therefore it was 'condemned to disappear without engendering a class consciousness which might constitute itself in revolutionary alternatives.'

And until it disappeared, it served in fact to support the hegemony of the bourgeoisie, to the detriment of the proletarian cause.[9]

The utility of the peasantry to dominant groups within Mexican society was, for Marxists of Bartra's persuasion, a principal reason for its unusually prolonged survival. In the face of an inexorable advance of capitalism, implying ever greater conflict between workers and bourgeoisie, the continuous reconstitution and protection of a large but apathetic constituency of the state in the Mexican countryside was vital to the continuity of the postrevolutionary political system. Each presidential period was characterized by efforts to mold this rural mass 'in its own image'; and thus 'in different historical moments, the Mexican peasant acquired his present characteristics.'

> Obregón and Calles imagined him as a North American farmer; Cárdenas as a minifundista trapped in the capitalist market, with collectivist elements but fundamentally linked to the apparatus of the state; many years later, López Mateos ... generalized the image of a semiproletarian granted a small piece of arid, or mountainous, land ...

From this process of official manipulation, the peasantry emerged, 'a result of intrigues and alliances which at the time expressed the correlation of political forces, without the peasants ever having enjoyed any effective intervention' in the outcome.[10]

Such an extraordinarily passive picture of the peasantry in politics fit well into the general scheme of an articulation between two different modes of production, with qualitatively distinct forms of social relations in each. While maintaining the peasantry outside the mainstream of capitalist socioeconomic organization, one could also suppose it to be excluded from relevant political activity; and one could then hypothesize that political power, like economic advance, would only come once the process of absorption of noncapitalist modes had been completed.

Historical structuralism and the fate of the peasantry, 1970-80 143

Acceptance and rejection of the concept of articulated modes of production

The analytical framework just summarized, constructed by those closest to the classical Marxist-Leninist tradition at the turn of the 1970s around the concept of articulated modes of production, gained such acceptance within Mexican social sciences throughout the following years that certain terms associated with it came to form part of standard academic usage. Social relations of all kinds between rural and urban people began to be denoted with frequency, for example, as 'articulations'; and any number of different ways of earning a living from the soil were referred to as 'modes.' This popularization of the terminology of Marxist peasant studies, and most particularly of that utilized by Roger Bartra, was not welcomed either by Bartra or by Marxist colleagues engaged in an effort to debate the theoretical validity of his construct. The proliferation of an often misunderstood vocabulary transformed the literature on rural society into a battleground in which endless pages were devoted to clarifying the meaning of terms about which there was considerable uncertainty.

Leaving aside the superficial confusion which arose as a result of the popularization of only half-understood concepts, however, there was at the same time a deeper and much more fruitful discussion among Marxists concerning the applicability of the concept of articulated modes of production to the situation in the Mexican countryside. On the one hand, this debate was centered around the purely logical elements of the theory, and around the adequacy with which the spirit of Marx's work had been reflected in the construct presented by Bartra and his school. On the other, historical and contemporary sociological evidence was brought forward to challenge the empirical relevance of a model of articulated modes of production to twentieth-century rural Mexico.

The crux of Marxist criticism of the theory of articulated modes of production, on the level of internal consistency and compatibility with the established understanding of Marx's work, was quite simply that a 'mode of production,' as Marx seemed to define it, was a complex combination of physical and technological means of production, social organization, and political and ideological superstructure, which contained the means of its own reproduction. It also contained, with the exception of the primitive or communal mode, a particular pattern of conflict between those who labored and those who benefited from the receipt of unremunerated labor, or in other words, between classes; and it was dialectically impelled toward a particular kind of change by the inevitable strain between productive forces and social relations of production. A mode of production, as thus understood, was a macrosociological construct of far wider dimensions than the 'simple mercantile mode' within which Bartra had placed the peasantry. To gain a portion of one's livelihood by exchanging home-produced goods for needed but locally unavailable products, without any consideration of profit, represented a kind of survival strategy possible under many changing circumstances. It was more a characteristic of family units than of classes, and specified neither a single necessary kind of political superstructure nor a single predominant form of exploitation. To consider it a 'mode of production' was therefore logically indefensible.[11]

At the same time, a number of Marxists pointed out the incongruity of supposing that a socioeconomic system as comprehensive and internally coherent as a mode of production could, under any circumstances, logically be articulated with another. It could, over time, evolve into a different mode altogether; but that change emerged from the internal dialectic of the system, not from articulation with another. Furthermore, the proposition that one mode of production could be subordinated to another, as the peasantry were within the capitalist system, was an incomprehensible contradiction in terms. Socioeconomic and political domination occurred at the level of classes, not modes of production.

A corollary of this criticism grew out of questions concerning Bartra's own discussion of the subordination of the peasantry. If the proletarianization of the latter was indeed continually being effected by the working of the law of value — if, in other words, the productive structure of peasant units was being systematically undermined by competition on unequal terms with capitalist enterprises — the integration of the peasantry into the capitalist system was surely greater than that implied by placing it in a separate mode of production. The entire thrust of Bartra's work pointed toward the existence of an organic link between peasantry and capitalism which would have tended, in the absence of compensatory mechanisms employed by the state, to destroy the former. In such a situation, there could by definition be no separate peasant mode of production, but only a particular subordinate position within the overall capitalist conformation.

In addition, if the continued support of the peasantry was largely the work of the bourgeoisie, incarnate in the state, then obviously the political and ideological superstructure which corresponded to the hypothesized 'simple mercantile mode of production' was generated not by the peasantry itself, but by the capitalist system. Both capitalist and noncapitalist socioeconomic groupings shared the same political universe. To reply, as Bartra did in *El poder despótico burgués*, that 'the category "mode of production" refers fundamentally to the economic base of society' and not to political and ideological superstructures,[12] could hardly satisfy the majority of scholars formed in a broadly Marxist tradition.

At bottom, Bartra's own work seemed to show that the Mexican peasantry, although still organizing productive activities in the twentieth century in a predominantly precapitalist way, could not have survived (or in Marxist terms, reproduced itself) for long without continuous recourse to resources controlled by, and contained within, a capitalist mode of production. And Marxist historians were quick to point out that this was far from a recent phenomenon. Sergio de la Peña, for example, argued forcefully that capitalism had predominated throughout the Mexican countryside from the mid-nineteenth century onward, and that 'by the beginning [of this century] there were no conflicting modes of production, except in nuclei of lost tribes. By then the stage of violent primitive accumulation had ended and the law of value operated fully.'[13]

Perhaps the best-documented case made by a Marxist anthropologist, and historian, for the long insertion of even apparently isolated peasant communities in the overall socioeconomic system of capitalism was that presented by Robert Wasserstrom of the Harvard Chiapas Project. After a number of years' work in Highland Chiapas communities, as well as in ecclesiastical and secular archives, Wasserstrom presented evidence to refute both the ahistorically functionalist picture of peasant life to which members of the Harvard program had habitually ascribed and the idea of Bartra's school that the peasantry could be considered in a separate precapitalist mode of production. Both currents of thought, he noted, suffered equally from a dualistic bias which kept them from appreciating vital interaction between members of peasant communities and surrounding capitalists within the context of regional economies from the time of the Colony onward. In the specific historical experience of Chiapas, a significant part of the entire Indian population of the highlands had, since the first half of the nineteenth century, made a living as temporary wage laborers and sharecroppers on lowland capitalist farms. This was not a relation which could be categorized simply as an isolated moment of 'articulation,' but rather a form of interaction which had fundamentally modified the social structure of highland Indian villages and contributed to the appearance of classes within them. To characterize these communities as part of a 'secondary and classless' mode of production, in the tradition of Bartra's school, was as empirically indefensible as the functionalist tendency to treat them as a homogenous and isolated social universe.[14]

Defining the peasantry as a subordinate class within the capitalist mode of production: the circulationist argument

Toward the latter half of the 1970s, then, a consensus began to emerge within Mexican Marxism that while it was undoubtedly necessary to integrate the peasantry into an analysis of contemporary Mexican society, and while it was fruitful to do so by comparing the way in which noncapitalist and capitalist organizing principles interacted both to support and to destroy the peasantry, the original formulation of articulated modes of production was too rigid a theoretical instrument to be defended further. It required considering the peasantry within a socioeconomic system so separate from the rest of Mexican society, and so analytically cumbersome, that an adequate understanding of the real situation of rural people could not be gained. The study of the structural position of the peasantry by Marxist social scientists therefore evolved rather quickly toward consideration of a *single* socioeconomic formation, in which the capitalist mode of production predominated, and in which other productive forms were articulated.'[15] The peasantry was in this way liberated from the macrosociological category of a noncapitalist mode of production and placed firmly within the dominant capitalist system, in a subordinate category or 'form.'

Such an alteration in the conceptual boundaries surrounding the peasantry implied a necessary admission that — contrary to the widely accepted tenets of most Marxists in Mexico — advanced capitalist society might in fact contain classes which could not be analysed within the framework of a single antagonism between proletariat and bourgeoisie. The artifice of treating the peasantry as a separate mode of production, in order to discuss the relation of direct agricultural producers to capitalist society without placing them unequivocally within the class structure of the capitalist mode, had temporarily obviated this difficulty; but with its disappearance, fundamental reconsideration of the criteria of class could no longer be delayed.

If one chose as the central determinant of class the traditional criterion of nature of relation to the means of production, the peasantry was a *petite bourgeoisie* and could not be exploited. But there were parts of *Capital* and other works in which Marx put equal emphasis upon the importance of determining class by reference to the mode of labor-exaction, to the way in which surplus labor was appropriated by nonproducers from producers; and in this case, reference to ownership of the means of production was only one element (although obviously a vital one) in the overall discussion. The peasantry, for example, could be exploited in the sphere of circulation, rather than production, and could constitute a class at odds with the bourgeoisie despite continued formal ownership of land.

There were also, it seemed upon further review of the theoretical components of the concept of class, a number of supplementary criteria which could be utilized to judge the structural position of the peasantry within a capitalist formation. As Héctor Díaz Polanco pointed out in a round table discussion of social class in the Mexican countryside in 1977, Lenin had proposed a cluster of interrelated factors, including not only relation to the means of production, but also role played in the social organization of work, place occupied in the overall system of production, and form of receiving any given part of the overall social product.[16] Utilizing most particularly the latter variable, Díaz Polanco suggested that the peasantry as a class was distinguished by assigning itself a wage, while the bourgeoisie claimed a part of the social product in the form of profit, and the workers were allotted a wage by the bourgeoisie.

The redefinition of class which accompanied the abandonment of the concept of articulated modes of production and the final integration of the peasantry into a single capitalist formation was fundamentally encouraged at this point by the appearance in Spanish of works by Kostas Vergopoulos, Samir Amin, and Claude Meillassoux, all of whom held the conviction that, as Vergopoulos put it, 'social class is not determined as a function of a place in the productive process in a strict sense . . . , but rather as a function of the nature of social relations and above all those related to the process of circulation.'[17] The peasantry could thus constitute an authentic class within the capitalist system without ever being entirely proletarianized, or at an opposite extreme, converted into capitalist farmers. In fact, 'the development of capitalism [did] not imply the advance of a capitalist mode of production in agriculture' at all, but only the quickened ability of industrial capital to extract a surplus from various subordinate forms of production and to turn that surplus to its own use.

Such insistence upon examining the circulation of capital within single (heterogeneous) systems carried with it a corollary emphasis on the complementarity, rather than the incompatibility, of peasant agriculture and capitalist development, and therefore upon the likelihood that, at least over the 'short and medium term,' direct producers of agricultural goods would be supported by capitalist society.[18] The difference between this position and that of Roger Bartra's school should be clearly noted: for the latter, the constant 'refunctionalization' of the peasantry by postrevolutionary capitalist society, represented by the Mexican state, was an outgrowth of conditions of dependent development, and of the consequent inability of a stunted capitalist manufacturing sector to absorb the labor force which should be liberated by the total proletarianization of the peasantry. Refunctionalization was thus a stopgap measure, a necessary exercise in sociopolitical manipulation, geared to the maintenance of political peace in the countryside. But peasant production was never seen as fitting efficiently into the overall economic design of capitalism.

For circulationist Marxist students of the peasantry, on the contrary, the fact that the latter seemed to have been absorbed into the modern capitalist system on a worldwide scale was taken as an indication that direct producers indeed met a concrete economic need of advanced capitalism. And that need was as visible in the economies of the 'center' as of the 'periphery'; it did not depend upon the subordinate nature of Third World development. Amin and Vergopoulos in fact drew examples for their discussion of the way in which the capitalist economy integrated and controlled peasant families from a study of the position of smallholders in France; and their conclusions were then extended to the nature of peasant insertion within capitalism in the Third World as well.

This was an appeal to the lessons of concrete historical processes. It was equally possible, however, to make a case for the utility of — and indeed the necessity for — the integration of peasant agriculture into the broader circuit of capital by turning toward a strictly theoretical examination of the logic of capitalist development, as Marx had presented it. And it was at this level that the hardest battles among Marxist students of the peasantry in Mexico were fought. Since the central concept in the discussion was 'rent,' no presentation of the dominant theoretical tendencies of the late 1970s can fail to consider the way

Historical structuralism and the fate of the peasantry, 1970-80

this concept was presented, or the logical conclusions which were drawn from its use.

Differential rent and the utility of the peasantry within advanced capitalist systems

Marx conceived rent, like capital, to be a social relation between men, based upon an exaction made for the utilization of a scarce and irreplaceable resource — the land. Those who controlled land could exact a price from others for its usufruct; and when land was utilized in a capitalist manner, that price formed part of the cost of production. In the particular case of capitalist *agriculture*, however, rent assumed an importance for the entire functioning of the system which it did not have in the case of capitalist industry. The value of agricultural output depended fundamentally upon the quality of the land involved: good land (fertile, well-watered, level, near lucrative markets) could produce extraordinary profits; bad land produced poorly. This existence of natural limits within the productive process of agriculture, which could not be entirely overcome by any artifice of technology, introduced rigidities and promoted monopolies interfering with the free play of capitalist competition. Those controlling the best agricultural land could constantly produce above the average for the sector as a whole, and those with the worst land would constantly produce below the average. In the process, no maximally efficient mean could be reached, as it could, on the contrary, in industry. The entire capitalist system suffered the negative effects of such rigidity in agriculture, for the prices of farm products never fell to a level optimum for the purposes of capitalist accumulation.

The simple fact that a juridical monopoly over land could force the exaction of a payment for its productive use was, then, denoted by Marx an 'absolute rent.' And the additional importance of the varying quality of land in agricultural production gave substance to the concept of 'differential rent.' The opposing conceptions of the place of the peasantry in capitalist society developed among Mexican Marxists were in turn associated with whether the first of these concepts was emphasized, or the second.

Roger Bartra and others sharing a theoretical commitment to articulated modes of production had drawn from their study of the phenomenon of rent the conclusion that a fundamental element slowing the advance of capitalism in Mexican society was the continued application of an absolute rent by a traditional class of (semi-feudal) landlords, as well as by a large group of refunctionalized, noncapitalist peasants. Capitalist entrepreneurs, from this point of view, were penalized by failure to gain access to resources over which noncapitalists held a semi-monopoly, whatever the quality of the land; and capitalism could only be unfettered with the disappearance of precapitalist forms, after which modern farmers would exert control over this most basic of productive resources through recourse to a totally capitalist market.[19]

Those who subscribed to the existence of a single capitalist socio-economic formation, containing a subordinate peasant sector, on the other hand, pointed out (with Vergopoulos) that even the most fully capitalist system was beset by the problems inherent in the existence of a differential rent, based upon the varying quality of agricultural land. The rigidities of agriculture continued once all land was entirely within the domain of capitalism, as long as the price structure for farm products was based upon the undeniable need to remunerate less well-endowed capitalist holdings at a rate which would not force them out of business. In such a situation, entrepreneurs controlling exceptionally good land could continue indefinitely to reap exceptionally large profits, and that unnecessarily high charge against the entire social product constituted a permanent drain upon industrial development.

The simple abolition of absolute rent, through the removal of non-capitalist landholders (landlord or peasant), thus in no way dealt with the fundamental problem which the continued existence of differential rent posed to the capitalist system as a whole. And in fact, the only way in which the latter seemed able to offset the negative charge made by well-endowed agricultural holdings against the total fund of social production was precisely to recuperate value from least-endowed holdings by forcing remuneration for their products to sink below the minimum required to maintain a capitalist enterprise – to restrict, in other words, the operation of capitalist relations of production in a certain part of the agricultural sector by continually supporting the survival of the peasantry. It was the need for such a counterbalancing mechanism which made the coexistence of large private farmers, on good lands, with peasant cultivators, on bad lands, the virtual hallmark of the world capitalist system in the nineteenth and twentieth centuries.[20]

The problems created by the phenomenon of differential rent could, of course, be theoretically obviated if it were argued that production obtained from relatively good land were sufficient to satisfy the agricultual requirements of a capitalist system. Then cultivation of poor land could simply be abandoned, and with it the need to maintain noncapitalist forms of socioeconomic organization in the countryside. A supposition of this order seemed to lie unstated behind the concern of Roger Bartra and others with the overwhelming importance of eliminating enclaves of noncapitalist control over land (absolute rent). Circulationist Marxists nevertheless took the physical limitations of agricultural land seriously, and supposed that modern societies could never afford to do without the agricultural product of those who, under ideal conditions of capitalist accumulation (unfettered by an inferior quality of land) would be considered chronically inefficient. In that case, the peasantry, with its peculiar capacity to operate on the margin of capitalist rationality, must be a vital and continuing element in the productive process of capitalism.

Armando Bartra, Luisa Paré, and the 'exploitation of peasant labor by capital'

Furthermore, the form of socioeconomic organization characteristic of the peasantry — circulationist Marxists argued — made it the ideal vehicle through which capitalist investors could reap extraordinary profits from agriculture, and consequently through which a maximum amount of surplus value could be channelled out of the countryside and into industrial development. The basic attributes of a 'peasant economy,' already so extensively commented upon by other schools within historical structuralism, were precisely those which assured that direct agricultural producers could withstand exactions which for either small capitalist entrepreneurs or a landless proletariat would be intolerable. Since peasant families could always fall back upon some self-provisioning activities, they could survive with lower monetary incomes than members of the urban working class; and since they did not expect to make a profit, they did not express the demands of a bourgeoisie. In fact, their only really mobile resource was their labor, which unlike the capital of an entrepreneur could not be easily shifted from one endeavor to another, most especially given the insoluble tie between land and labor within the overall structure of family livelihood. Their bargaining position was thus so minimal that they were virtually forced to accept any remuneration for their effort, even if it did not cover the full value of labor expended.

The commercial sector of the capitalist system could take advantage of this situation in a number of ways. First, as all previous analyses had noted, it could 'buy cheap' – appropriating in its entirety the surplus value, or potential profit, embodied in peasant commodities. Second, it could extend the range of exploitation beyond the simple appropriation of surplus value, and fail to remunerate direct producers even with an amount which would cover the cost of reproducing their own labor force. At this stage, capitalists engaged in super-exploitation, which was only made possible because members of peasant families – including most especially women and children – engaged in subsistence activities which kept them all from starving. Third, capitalists could 'sell dear,' taking advantage of the fact that goods needed for survival by the peasantry would be bought on conditions not acceptable to capitalist enterprises. And finally, they could charge exorbitant interest rates, the acceptance of which rested in the last analysis upon the same requirements of small producers to obtain financing at any cost.

All of these mechanisms of unequal exchange, operating ostensibly within the sphere of circulation, constituted upon closer inspection direct charges against the product of peasant labor. They therefore served the same function as the appropriation by capitalists of the surplus value of the proletariat and justified fully the discussion of the insertion of a peasant economy within the broader capitalist context in terms of 'the exploitation of peasant labor by capital.'[21]

This phrase, utilized by Armando Bartra as the title of a book published in 1979, succinctly illustrated the distance which had grown up between modes-of-production and circulationist Marxists during the latter half of the 1970s in Mexico. What for the modes-of-production school was nothing more than a large group of inefficient producers being exploited by a retrograde faction of commercial capital was for circulationists a reservoir of cheap (in fact captive) family labor on which rested the profits, and therefore the growth, of a considerable part of the modern capitalist system.

The degree of integration of much of the peasantry into the very center of the process of capital accumulation was especially visible when one looked at credit arrangements, both traditional and modern, surrounding agricultural production on smallholdings. A significant proportion of all peasant families in the country could not begin cultivation each year without obtaining money from outsiders; and the latter, whether local moneylenders or transnational corporations, very often tied their loans to the use of particular products, obtained from particular merchants and utilized in particular ways. Peasant borrowers therefore often found themselves in a position structurally quite similar to that of cottage laborers: although maintaining a noncapitalist organization of work within the family, the flow of resources through each productive unit was determined by entrepreneurs situated outside it. The peasantry was in that case little more than a putting-out system for capitalism, providing agricultural commodities at a cost which, as in primitive industrial cottage industries, covered neither payment for the physical installation within which work went on (rent) nor full (average) remuneration of the work force.

Luisa Paré, an anthropologist and colleague of Roger Bartra at the Institute for Social Research of the National University, brought this point forcefully to the attention of students of the peasantry in a series of articles and books published during the 1970s.[22] Paré had been involved since the 1960s in field work oriented toward understanding what she originally envisioned as being the articulation between noncapitalist and capitalist modes of production. Her examination of the place of the peasantry in regional, national and international markets, and most especially the way in which credit facilitated the control of capitalists over the output of direct producers, soon convinced her, however, that nothing as autonomous as a precapitalist mode existed. Her material proved rather to be in accord with the kind of theoretical framework then being proposed by Vergopoulos and Meillassoux, and she oriented her discussion accordingly.

The regions in which Paré worked, including the coast of Michoacán, the Mezquital Valley, and the state of Puebla, all included areas in which eminently commercial crops were cultivated (copra, alfalfa, coffee, sugar). And the structural position of the peasant families who tended those crops was closely analogous to that of domestic laborers in cottage industries. The case of sugarcane growers was especially illustrative, because they were likely to be land-reform beneficiaries living in areas which had been designated by law as primary suppliers of cane to publicly or privately owned sugar mills, and they therefore depended heavily upon the provision of credit and inputs by the mills. Bureaucratic inefficiency and corruption assured that they received very limited profits from their cane, if indeed they received any profit at all — a situation which consequently reduced their remuneration from agricultural activities to monthly payments which might be considered little more than a wage.

Paré designated all peasants of this kind a semi-proletariat, and included them with the landless wage laborers of the Mexican countryside in a single broad category of all

> those producers (whether or not they own[ed] land...) whose output [was] financed and organized by a private or public enterprise and generate[d] a surplus appropriated by capital, and who [did] not obtain in recompense more than an amount which permitted them to reproduce their labor force.[23]

They were in effect salaried through credit; and therefore, as Paré's colleague Armando Bartra noted, programs set in motion by agents of capitalist enterprises, including the state, to increase productivity through fomenting greater investment and promoting technological change were not likely to transform this part of the peasantry into a *petite bourgeoisie*. Ostensible investment in peasant agriculture was simply a way in which capital increased the likelihood of appropriating surplus value through more progressive and effective forms of exploitation of its landed rural labor force, without granting the latter any further control over the productive process.[24]

Class action and the peasantry: the validity of the struggle for land

Removing most peasant families from the category of independent farming units, or enterprises, where they had been placed by members of the modes-of-production school, to that of a semi-proletariat, proposed by circulationist Marxists, allowed social scientists within the second group to see much larger contributions on the part of the peasantry to the overall fund of social production within the capitalist system than those envisioned by the first. As enterprises, peasant families might simply be judged inefficient when they devoted an excessive amount of labor to agricultural production. But as members of the working class, they expended energy all of which contributed to the formation of social value:

> what a worker in an enterprise [was] obliged to cede [was] the total of his surplus labor, embodied in surplus value; and that [was] entirely independent of whether the latter [should be] more or less than the profits realized by the enterprise which hire[d] him.[25]

The peasantry, in consequence, was not so much inefficient as exploited. And the extraordinary lucrativeness of obtaining control over the points of exchange between direct rural producers and capitalist society — the 'zones of exploitation,' as Armando Bartra called them —

combined with the equally unusual diffuseness of the physical and social boundaries of those zones, contributed to the frequent utilization of force by representatives of the capitalist system in a position to appropriate the surplus labor of the peasantry. The right to exploit labor was, in the industrial sector or on capitalist agricultural holdings, a concomitant of ownership of the means of production; it was an arrangement sanctioned by law and custom, and not likely to be challenged by force. The same could be said of arrangements, like production contracts, established through appeal to modern legal procedure. But the right to exploit the peasantry through the myriad complex forms of unequal exchange associated with usurious financing, 'buying cheap,' and 'selling dear,' was only gained through establishing a monopoly which excluded interaction between direct agricultural producers and any other possible intermediary. Therefore the history of rural areas in Mexico was one of constant violence, not only between *caciques* attempting to expand or defend their spheres of influence, but also between exploiters and exploited in a situation of institutionally unlimited rapacity.

Among circulationist Marxist students of the peasantry, it was Armando Bartra who assumed the lead in emphasizing the importance of class struggle in protecting direct producers from extinction. Although it was no doubt true, Bartra argued, that at a general level the continued survival of the peasantry was functional for the capitalist system, and that the state might play a significant role in protecting the overall interest of capital toward that end, it was equally true that individual capitalists often recognized no boundaries in their search for profit and might drive their workers (or tributaries) to the brink of disaster. There was 'no [purely] economic mechanism which guaranteed, by itself, the retention of the necessary value of labor by the small producer' in the capitalist system.[26] The guarantee of sufficient income to meet minimum needs came only through the political activity of the exploited. And the very logic of this fact, combined with the lessons of countless cases of peasant mobilization and protest, invalidated entirely the position of more orthodox Marxists who saw in direct rural producers little more than the passive clay from which political conformity was molded by factions of the bourgeoisie in power.[27]

Furthermore, given the nature of the insertion of a peasant semi-proletariat within the wider logic of capitalism, direct agricultural producers were forced to give primary attention to preserving or ensuring their access to land, just as industrial workers were forced to fight for the preservation of employment opportunities. Each constituted an irreducible condition for survival. And to the extent that the demand for land was placed within a context emphasizing control by the producers of wealth over the fruit of their labor, the challenge by the peasantry to capitalist domination could be as profound as that presented by the industrial proletariat. Together, the two groups were destined 'to dig the grave of the bourgeoisie.'[28]

Campesinistas and descampesinistas: a debate over the future of the peasantry

In contrast to those who organized their discussion of the relationship between the peasantry and surrounding capitalist society in terms of articulated modes of production, and who saw the eventual dissolution of the peasantry as the only future of rural people, a second important group of Mexican Marxists thus put forward an analytical framework, centred around the subordination of domestic forms of production within the capitalist system, which went so far as to predict a probable role for the peasantry, in league with the industrial proletariat, in the future construction of socialism. By the latter 1970s, these two theoretical positions had come to form part of a debate between 'campesinistas' and 'descampesinistas' — between those who stressed the resiliency and ability of direct agricultural producers to contribute to the future conformation of Mexican society, and those who stressed the anachronistic nature of their enterprise — which had immediate implications not only for public policy, but also for personal political activity.[29]

Within the descampesinista camp, there was general agreement that the devastating dispossession of the peasantry implicit in the course of capitalist development should be allowed to run its course without interference from more progressive forces, and in fact that any attempt to mitigate the inevitable destruction of the peasantry could only constitute a 'populist' plot to prolong the agony of a class in extinction. As Roger Bartra put it, populist reliance upon 'ideological propositions destined to "protect" the development of capitalism through the application of palliatives which slowed the decline of levels of living within the rural population' constituted 'flights of romanticism ... which in the end protected the exploiter more than the exploited.'[30] Within the campesinista faction, however, there was much more theoretical diversity, growing particularly out of disagreement over the nature of the relation between the peasantry and the state; and this point of contention had as a natural corollary the voicing of different opinions concerning the validity of supposing that the state might take meaningful action to sustain and support a revitalized group of direct producers in the Mexican countryside.

On the side of those who argued not only for the necessary survival of a sector of smallholding rural families, but also for the political capacity of the Mexican state to carry out programs which would ensure adequate levels of living among those families, was Gustavo Esteva, founder and director of the Commission for Rural Development (COPIDER). Esteva was trained as an industrial sociologist, and perhaps partly for that reason developed a theory of the place of the peasantry within capitalist society (as a noncapitalist form subordinated, or 'subsumed,' entirely by the logic of capital) which was broadly circulationist in nature. At the same time, Esteva formed part of the group of Mexican social scientists, including a number of dependentistas and cultural ecologists, who were engaged in a search for 'another development,' of a less centralized nature than that epitomized in either industrial capitalism or industrial socialism. And as a long-time participant in the formulation of food policy, through work in the National Commission for Popular Subsistence (CONASUPO), he was well acquainted with the intricate functioning of the state.

Esteva, like Armando Bartra and many other Marxist students of the peasantry, saw most direct rural producers as the domestic laborers of capitalist investors who preferred to 'assume the direction of the productive process without transforming it.'[31] But he differed from the former in insisting that such a structural position could be taken as a starting point for organization in defense of peasant interests, without the necessity for destroying the entire capitalist formation in the process. The peasantry, like industrial workers, could organize and bargain, in a process of 'collective mercantile contracting,' which was similar in some respects to cooperativism. Such a strategy was made possible by the fact that capitalists were no longer interested in owning land directly, and therefore represented less and less of a threat to the peasantry in terms of the kind of agrarian struggle which had so long and tragically characterized the history of rural Mexico.

Esteva's proposition thus foresaw the indefinite coexistence of peasant and capitalist agriculture within the agrarian structure of the country – the latter operating capital-intensive enterprises for which few laborers were required, and the former developing, with official assistance and the support of their own interest groups, a kind of labor-intensive technology which would raise productivity without destroying the familial and communal base of peasant society. In the maintenance of such a structure, the strength of independent peasant organization was obviously vital.[32]

This argument for a strategic alliance between peasantry and state grew out of the conviction that the state was integrated by a heterogeneous group of powerholders, not all of whom were dedicated to the promotion of the interests of the bourgeoisie. The institutionalization of power relations which followed upon the Mexican Revolution, in this view, included groups who represented the interests of the (rural and urban) proletariat, as well as those of capital; and the strength of popular representatives could be made felt in official circles if grassroots organization were sufficiently promoted. The distance between such a position and that of campesinistas like Armando Bartra need hardly be dwelled upon further.

Arturo Warman on the ultimate contradiction between state and peasantry

To say that campesinistas were divisible into groups whose political strategies varied according to their estimation of the possibility of an eventual alliance between the peasantry and the state did not, however, exhaust the range of difference within the school. Even among those who saw promotion of radical change in the nature of Mexican society as the only option of the peasantry, there was considerable disagreement over where political support might be sought and what kind of new society should be promoted. The majority, it would seem, looked forward to an alliance of the peasantry (as a semi-proletariat) with the rural and urban proletariat, and to the construction of a socialist society in which industrial development would continue to be of primary importance. Others, in contrast, were more doubtful of the ultimate affinity of peasantry and urban proletariat, and more skeptical concerning the interest of the peasantry in contributing to the formation of an industrial socialist state. To understand the position of the latter within the campesinista school, it is useful to look at the work of Arturo Warman.

Warman shared with Roger Bartra, Luisa Paré, and a number of other protagonists in the campesinista-descampesinista debate a period of training at the National School of Anthropology during the mid-1960s, which included a careful review of the classical works of Marx.

His academic acquaintance with the structural problems of the peasantry was, however, supplemented in a particular way by long experience as an employee of various government agencies which formed the institutional interface between the peasantry and the wider society. Warman therefore not only analysed the role of the state in the countryside, but participated in it; and the conclusion he drew from his association with official programs lent no support to the hypothesis that an alliance between peasantry and state could constitute a valid alternative for the future.

For Warman, the Mexican state, 'the carrier and guardian . . . of the industrial capitalist mode of production,' 'established the general conditions for the exploitation of the peasantry.'[33] This it did not as a monolithic 'committee for the protection of the interests of the bourgeoisie,' as some orthodox Marxists insisted, but as a dependent link in a heterogeneous world capitalist system. Through the activities of the state, the disadvantages suffered by national capitalists in the international market (including high prices for inputs and low prices for outputs) were compensated by passing the burden of unequal exchange backward toward the peasantry. And in the process, the state became 'the principal promoter and executor of an economic policy which drained resources from the countryside in order to accumulate and reproduce them' in capitalist agriculture and industry at both national and international levels.[34]

From the end of the Revolution onward, and particularly in the postwar period, 'almost all [forms] of public investment in the countryside — irrigation, credit, scientific investigation, agricultural extension, guaranteed prices — [had] operated as subsidies to capitalist production' and as a consequence had strengthened the ability of large private farmers to encroach upon the peasantry.[35] At the same time, manipulation of the constitutionally granted monopoly of the state over title to land, combined with considerable control over the supply of credit to land reform beneficiaries, permitted government agencies to engage in parallel forms of surplus appropriation, not necessarily controlled directly by the private sector, but ultimately congruent with the needs of the latter. As Warman was one of the first to note, the fact that the revolution had ended with the establishment by the state of a kind of protectorate over the peasantry (in which the latter supposedly became the 'favored sons of the [postrevolutionary] regime') signified not the liberation of direct rural producers, but their exploitation at the hands of a new group, the bureaucracy; and the interests of those employees of the state, like the interests of the ruling factions they represented, were as indissolubly linked to the ideal of individual enrichment as those of the most ardent champion of free enterprise within the private sector.[36]

To make such a statement was not, however, in Warman's work, to justify drawing clear lines of conflict between the urban and rural exploited, on the one hand, and a capitalist class (in direction of the state), on the other. The policy of the state reflected promotion of a style of modernization, an illusory form of urban industrial development, which premised the economic advance of the entire nonpeasant population of the country on the exploitation of direct agricultural producers, just as earlier dependentistas and cultural ecologists had long suggested.

> Not only [did] agricultural entrepreneurs and the state participate in these processes, but the entire social grouping created in pursuit of capitalist industrial development. Bankers, industrialists, and bureaucrats to a great extent, but also the middle classes and even marginal [urban dwellers] as a block, divide up the wealth of the peasantry ... In different ways, we are all part of the peasant problem, and the peasantry knows it.[37]

Therefore it was not likely that there could be an easy alliance between direct agricultural producers and members of the urban working class as long as there was no fundamental change in the style of development pursued.

The consolidation of cultural ecology and its contribution to an alternative form of campesinismo

In sum, then, the peasantry was in Warman's view caught up in a struggle to defend itself not only from a capitalist system of production but also from an urban industrial way of life. And the only way in which one could hope to understand the societal implications of this struggle — once the broad outlines of the macrostructural confrontation between capitalist and noncapitalist forms of organization, within a dependent setting, had been traced — was to listen to the voices of rural people themselves. Warman thus stood for a kind of campesinismo which stressed seeing Mexican society as the peasants saw it, and for a kind of anthropology which retreated from the high road of macrostructuralism toward a return to regional and local studies, without losing sight of conditioning national and international factors in the process.

The school within historical structuralism most congenial to this kind of analysis was cultural ecology, which with the return of Angel Palerm to Mexico in 1967 had begun to assume long-delayed importance in the general theoretical arsenal of Mexican anthropology. From a tradition guiding the work of only a small number of ethnohistorians and archeologists in the 1960s (for reasons discussed at length in Chapter 3), cultural ecology grew by the mid-1970s to represent a significant alternative to a strict Marxist-Leninist treatment of the peasantry, and to orient a considerable part of all field work undertaken in the Mexican countryside. Its early institutional base at the Iberoamerican University, where Palerm established headquarters in the Department of Social Sciences and where Warman also taught, was soon broadened by the founding in 1973 of a Center for Higher Studies of the National Institute of Anthropology and History (CISINAH), over which Palerm immediately presided, and by the founding in 1978 of a Department of Anthropology at the Metropolitan University (Ixtapalapa), staffed and directed by students of Palerm.

Such rapid growth in the influence exercised by cultural ecologists within Mexican anthropology was encouraged by a coincidence of scholarly and practical interests between cultural ecologists and dependentistas, and therefore by a pooling of effort oriented toward the promotion of studies in which regional and ethnic differences (always a primary concern of dependentistas) were considered as part of a broader attempt to understand varying forms of adaptation and response by the peasantry to the structural constraints of insertion within a wider capitalist framework (always of importance to cultural ecologists). The emphasis which both schools placed upon the possible diversity of social mechanisms serving to encourage unequal access to opportunity and resources within Mexican society set them somewhat apart from those within the classical Marxist-Leninist tradition who were concerned almost exclusively with analysing class conflict.[38] In addition, while the classical tradition tended (through its emphasis on the need to go beyond appearances, or perceptions of reality, and to ferret out the real significance of social phenomena) to give more importance to the analytical acumen of the scientist than to the outlook of social actors themselves, Mexican cultural ecology and anthropological dependentismo were very concerned with the latter.

When the interest in finding paths toward 'another development' of a noncentralized nature, shown both by cultural ecologists and by that part of the dependentista school characterized in Chapter 4 as 'probabilistic,' was added to previously mentioned points of affinity, the reason for the gradual fusion of research efforts within these two groups should be clear. After 1972, in which Guillermo Bonfil assumed direction of the National Institute of Anthropology and History, seminars and projects financed by the Institute, and dealing with structural constraints upon the peasantry, generated material for the presentation of a distinctive form of campesinismo within the ongoing policy debate of the 1970s.

Cultural ecologists and the 'peasant mode of production'

At the center of the web of propositions which made up this final form of campesinismo lay a commitment to the likelihood of multilineal evolution. Bonfil, Palerm, Warman, Stavenhagen and others among cultural ecologists and dependentistas were simply not convinced of the inevitability of a single, unilinear progression of human history, through capitalism toward industrial socialism, nor of the concomitant necessity for a homogenization of social relations throughout the entire social system. They left more room for variation, both through positing the possible continued existence of an alternative, locally shaped, peasant substratum or subculture, and through suggesting that one of the keys to the survival of the latter was precisely the increasing heterogeneity, rather than homogeneity, of the response made by rural people to the pressures imposed by industrial capitalism.

In order to assert the importance of the peasantry in the future conformation of Mexican society, not simply as an ally of the urban working class in the struggle for control over the productive resources of capitalism, but as the bearers of an alternative way of life, campesinistas of this school tended (with considerable variation in degree of emphasis) to treat the peasantry as part of a separate mode of production, and thus to have recourse to the same theoretical tools employed by their opposite numbers at the relatively most orthodox pole of historical structuralism. Such a surprising coincidence of concepts among the most convinced of campesinistas and descampesinistas was related, no doubt, to the potential for exclusivity of the construct: the rigid structural boundaries inherent in an isolable 'mode of production' could as well be utilized (in the hands of campesinistas) to strengthen a claim for the survival capacity of the peasantry, whatever the future of the capitalist system, as they could be utilized (in the hands of descampesinistas) to emphasize the anachronistic nature of peasant life and therefore its imminent demise.

Nevertheless, the way in which cultural ecologists-cum-dependentistas handled the idea of a 'peasant economy' or 'mode of production' was obviously at odds with that of more orthodox Marxist-Leninist colleagues on a number of counts. While Roger Bartra, for example, presented the 'simple mercantile mode of production' as a construct specifically utilized by Marx for dealing with the structural position of the peasantry, Palerm and others within his school were less concerned to prove the parentage of what they called the 'peasant mode of production,' and were content to justify it as an ideal type of use in understanding a specific and well-documented social phenomenon. Similarly, while Bartra considered the 'simple mercantile mode' a remnant of the precapitalist past, cultural ecologists and dependentistas were convinced of the extraordinary contemporary relevance of the 'peasant mode.'

These differences were in turn related to a more profound divergence of the two schools in their handling of the articulation of peasant and capitalist modes. Bartra envisioned the subordination of the simple mercantile mode as a process of progressive penetration by the socioeconomic organization of capitalism, and therefore of disintegration and transformation. Palerm, Warman and others insisted, on the other hand, that although the constant necessity to interact with representatives of capitalist society forced continuous changes in the livelihood strategies of the peasantry, the basic structural characteristics of the 'peasant mode,' including particular forms of family and communal cooperation as well as particular subjection to exploitative outsiders, remained unchanged.

Such a distinction between adaptive strategies (utilized by peasant families to assure a living under conditions of declining access to physical resources and increasing exploitation) on the one hand, and fundamental systemic requirements of a peasant mode of production, on the other, allowed cultural ecologists like Palerm and Warman to look at the growing involvement of rural people in wage labor without necessarily seeing a process of proletarianization. Thus Palerm argued in his well-known article on 'peasant-capitalist articulation: the M-D-M formula' that the peasantry continuously shuffled three forms of sustenance — self-provisioning, sale of goods on the market, and wage labor — in an attempt to obtain a minimum family income. And in practice, the latter of these alternatives was coming to assume predominant importance throughout most areas of the Mexican countryside. Yet this did not proletarianize the peasantry 'as long as it continued to obtain from self-provisioning an indispensable part of its subsistence.'[39]

Warman made the same point on a number of occasions, most particularly bringing into question the validity of utilizing census statistics on the increase in 'landless laborers' to support the argument that capitalist wage relations were rapidly reducing the peasantry to a proletariat. Aside from the notorious unreliability of those statistics, Warman criticized their shallowness: his own field experience suggested that formal lack of title to land, or 'landlessness,' had little to do with limiting real access to that resource, both because the perversities of bureaucratic practice in the Mexican countryside had prevented many cultivators from obtaining formal title, and because the pervasive reciprocal relationships within peasant communities assured almost all long-term residents *de facto* access to a small plot of some kind, whether they were legally entitled to it or not. The fact that most rural people could therefore be registered as participating frequently in wage labor merely indicated a turn taken in the constant search for means of survival; it said nothing about 'from whom the wage was received or what it implied as a social relation.'[40]

There were, in the opinion of campesinistas of the cultural ecology-cum-dependentismo school, not only microsociological but also macrosociological reasons why the kind of complete disintegration of the peasant mode foreseen by more orthodox Marxist colleagues was in practice very unlikely to come about. At the first level stood the formidable resiliency of communal organization upon which the peasant mode ultimately rested, and which served as the final defense of rural people under siege by the forces of capitalism. And at the second level stood the macrosystemic requirements of the world capitalist system itself, shored up by constant recourse to cheap peasant labor or produce and therefore constantly torn between a tendency to destroy that source of wealth through overappropriation and a tendency to protect it in order to preserve the possibility of future exploitation. Here cultural ecologists like Palerm and Warman followed the logic of Rosa Luxemburg to the conclusion that the extinction of noncapitalist modes of production must also perforce imply the extinction of capitalism itself.

At this point, neither Palerm nor Warman fell into the neofunctionalist posture of supposing that since capitalist society needed the peasantry, it would 'recreate' the latter indefinitely. On the contrary,

Historical structuralism and the fate of the peasantry, 1970-80

both noted the increasing harshness of exploitation to which peasant families were subject and the astonishing ingenuity required of rural people in their constant re-elaboration of survival strategies. Their difference with Roger Bartra and others lay not in a diverging assessment of the seriousness of conflict between peasant and capitalist modes, but rather in a dissenting opinion on the structural place occupied by the peasantry at the moment of final battle and the ability of the peasantry to emerge victorious. The fact that anthropologists working within the classical Marxist-Leninist tradition supposed the peasantry to be gradually absorbed into the wage labor force of capitalism in the process of proletarianization in effect left no organizational common front in existence around which a qualitatively separate peasantry could rally and fight. The simple mercantile mode disappeared in pieces, and quietly. If rural people were not generally proletarianized, however, but simply engaged in a desperate effort to preserve a distinctive form of existence, they reached the definitive point of confrontation as a group with a common cause to defend, and that cause lay outside the rationale of capitalism. To the extent that the awesome contradictions within the world capitalist system — and between it and what Palerm often called 'state capitalism' or industrial socialism — created the real possibility of a breakdown in the apparently unilinear course of modern industrial society, the 'peasant mode' might indeed provide a viable alternative to humanity. As Arturo Warman once put it, 'modernity [might have] less probability for survival than peasant antiquarianism.'[41]

The diversification of peasant adaptive strategies: a case study of agricultural involution in eastern Morelos

Without doubt, the most comprehensive effort to illustrate the tenets of cultural ecology through analysis of the historical experience of the peasantry in a single, well-defined region of Mexico was that directed by Warman during his stay at the Center for Advanced Studies of the National Institute of Anthropology and History (CISINAH) during 1972 and 1973, and published in a book entitled *Y venimos a contradecir* in 1976.[42] The fact that Warman chose such a title, taken from colonial documents in which the indigenous population of the region under study, eastern Morelos, appeared time and time again before Spanish officials to 'contradict' the right of the conquerors to appropriate communal lands, constituted symbolic testimony to his position on the side of a beleaguered peasant society. And the fact that the book was written as a doctoral thesis supervised by Clifford Geertz at Princeton suggested Warman's interest in a phenomenon first discussed by Geertz — agricultural involution.

What Warman and his team of researchers found in the history of the peasantry of eastern Morelos was a continuous long-term process of intensifying exploitation, broken or weakened at times by temporary economic crises in the wider capitalist system or by explosions of peasant protest exemplified in the Mexican Revolution of 1910, but tending nevertheless toward an ever-greater exaction of surplus value from the majority of the rural population of the region. This exaction took varying forms during different historical periods: the encroachment of haciendas upon communal land and a consequent requirement for peasant families to work for a low wage on the latifundia in order to survive, before the revolution; the maintenance of low prices for agricultural goods once the peasantry had recovered its lands and entered the national market as small producers; the manipulation of credit when most peasant families had come to depend upon manufactured goods both for agricultural production and household consumption.

In response to their constant inability to make ends meet, the smallholders of eastern Morelos gradually modernized and diversified their farming activities, incorporating new crops, new manufactured inputs, selling to ever more distant urban markets. At the same time, they brought formerly idle land under cultivation, even when its marginal productivity was low; they rented and sharecropped land, belonging to other peasants and to large landholders; they stopped rotating fields. All of these measures required an increasing investment of unpaid family labor, both to substitute for capital the families did not have and to pay the price for increasing amounts of capital they had at any rate to borrow. Therefore over the years the peasantry worked harder and harder, and produced more and more, while experiencing proportionally very much less substantive improvements in levels of living, when there were any improvements at all.[43]

The two most important elements permitting most smallholders of eastern Morelos to meet the increasingly onerous terms of incorporation within the national and international market without being displaced altogether were their ties to a variety of intermediaries, or brokers, whose interests lay in maintaining an economic or political clientele; and their ability to make use of the range of traditional social relations which regulated mutual assistance within kin groups and community.

Paradoxically, Warman noted, 'to be more modern..., the peasants [had] to reinforce their traditionalism.'[44] Their survival depended upon strong families, trustworthy *compadres*, landless neighbors willing to exchange their unpaid labor for access to a garden plot, community solidarity. Without the contribution of nonmonetized labor to the task of production, as well as the contribution of nonmonetized tools, implements and animals, the cost of farming would have been prohibitive.[45]

In consequence, then, Warman concluded that 'it [was] possible for a peasant to plant onions, tomatoes or sorghum for the market, emigrate as a *bracero* or tranquilly convert to protestantism – all little "traditional" no doubt – without ceasing to be a peasant.'[46] As long as his livelihood depended upon a noncapitalist use of land and labor, and upon manipulation of the possibilities for reciprocity inherent in the traditional social structure of small farming communities in order to satisfy the exploitative demands of the wider society, he was to be found within a distinctive 'peasant mode of production.' And the surplus which he created in the company of millions of fellows, a surplus 'which [could] be measured only with difficulty but which could nevertheless be clearly perceived and analysed, [was] the real and effective support of industrial capitalism,' to be eliminated only at the risk of collapse of the latter.[47]

The assignment of temporary urban roles within peasant families: Lourdes Arizpe on 'migration in shifts' and the changing place of women

With the passage of time, one of the increasingly important elements in the adaptive strategies of peasant families throughout Mexico became migration toward cities, whether of a permanent or a temporary nature. It might be noted that permanent migration from peasant villages was not a subject which captured the attention of historical-structuralist anthropologists during the 1970s. Pioneering work on peasant adaptation to city life had in fact been done by Oscar Lewis in the early 1950s; and the few anthropologists who continued that tradition in the 1960s and 1970s tended also to base their work upon a functionalist heritage. The best-known of these efforts was no doubt that of Robert V. Kemper, who systematically followed migrants from Tzintzuntzan to Mexico City, and utilized information previously gathered in conjunction with George Foster to permit an extremely well-documented analysis of how villagers were absorbed into the fabric of everyday life in the capital.[48]

Historical structuralists were, however, very much interested in the phenomenon of periodic 'raiding' of urban employment opportunities by temporary migrants, and in the corollary tactic of producing as many children as possible within peasant families, so that a maximum number of wage earners could be deployed outside villages beleaguered by the approaching limits of agricultural involution, as well as by the disappearance of many traditional nonagricultural sources of livelihood. 'Faced with increasing exploitation and decreasing productivity,' Warman noted, 'the ultimate solution consisted in augmenting the size of the labor force.'[49]

In understanding the dynamics of this process, in which a wide variety of temporary urban roles were assigned to different members of peasant households, and the resources of all members subsequently pooled to ensure continuation of the basic agricultural activity which defined community membership, the analytical framework first proposed by Chayanov was obviously extremely useful. Needless to say, cultural ecologists had recourse to the latter with regularity, for the periodic redistribution of work according to the demographic composition of peasant households had for years been among the principal concerns of their school. Interestingly enough, however, as the decade of the 1970s drew to a close social scientists at all points along the spectrum of historical structuralism turned with insistence to the question of demographic adaptation to the pressures of capitalism[50] – often related to the phenomenon of migration – and virtually without exception drew heavily upon the insights of Chayanov.

A pioneer in this field was Lourdes Arizpe, whose early interest in the interrelationship between economic environment and kinship patterns at the local level (presented in a master's thesis for the National School of Anthropology entitled *Parentesco y economia en una sociedad nahua*[51] and heightened during a period of study under Julian Pitt-Rivers at the London School of Economics) evolved through the mid-1970s toward a broader concern with urban-based elements in the livelihood strategies of rural families, including the internal composition of the latter. Work among the Mazahua of the state of Mexico, located some three hundred kilometers northwest of Mexico City, in particular suggested to Arizpe the possibility of elaborating a model of 'relay migration' which seemed to provide a convincing explanation for survival of pauperized peasant families otherwise physically unable to make a living in a degraded and divided rural setting. As she concluded in a recent publication of the Colegio de México, with which she was associated,

If resources had become centralized in the city, it was necessary [for Mazahua families] to send representatives to reclaim some of those resources. Through migrating in shifts, they channelled back to the rural domestic grouping some of the riches which the city had extracted from it through a process of unequal development. The city managed the circulation of capital, in goods and money. The peasants, on atomized lands, managed the circulation of a capital peculiar to them: their children.[52]

The profile of migration from Mazahua families, Arizpe found, was intimately related to their demographic structure, and therefore to the relation of dependents to able-bodied workers, defined in terms set by the requirements of the wider society. Plotting the periodicity of emigration by members of different ages and sexes seemed in fact to suggest that investing in children who could work in urban areas for a time before returning home to marry constituted a rational — indeed vital — adaptive strategy of the land-poor Mazahua. They thus escaped the passive suffering of macrostructural change, and 'took measures to strengthen their own position' which could 'change or slow down [broader] structural processes' and help them assert their role as active participants in shaping the society of the future.[53]

In this complex attempt by peasant families to provide an urban labor market with the kind of human input for which the latter seemed to exhibit greatest demand, the question of gender of peasant migrants was obviously of considerable relevance. Certain industries and services were more likely to be open to women than to men, and therefore to exert a particular kind of 'pull' on the female population of the countryside at the same time that they established institutional limits on the nature of opportunity available to migrating peasant women. Arizpe devoted special attention to this issue in a separate piece of research on Mazahua women who transferred themselves and their entire families to Mexico City during certain periods of each year in order to sell fruits and candies on downtown street corners and thus to raise the capital with which subsistence agriculture could be financed.[54] And in the process, she laid the groundwork for a new field of women's studies within Mexican anthropology, concomitant with the growing presence of women within the profession itself and the sudden irruption of feminism upon the stage of social thought at both national and international levels.[55]

Distinguishing ethnicity and class

The definition of an area of research within historical structuralism which was ultimately bounded by gender, rather than by class, opened an intellectual door leading toward further revision of the fundamental principles of Marxism. What part of the structural determinants of the life chances of women could be attributed to their place in the economy, and what part only to their sex, was indeed to become the subject of intense debate. And the same could be said of another research area in which Arizpe took a leading interest during the 1970s – that of ethnicity.

With the ascendancy of a Marxist approach to the study of the peasantry, whether as mode of production or as class, the subject of the relation between ethnicity and class, so fruitfully explored by indigenistas and dependentistas during the 1950s and 1960s, had been temporarily relegated to a secondary plane or frankly disdained. The distinction which Bonfil and Stavenhagen had made between the negative elements of ethnic discrimination, in which domination of culturally distinct human groupings was justified through reference to depreciatory stereotypes, and the positive elements of ethnic identity, was discarded, to be replaced with a virtually unanimous emphasis on the first of the two phenomena. Thus Henri Favre could write, in his extremely detailed analysis of 'continuity and change among the Mexican Maya,' that Indian culture 'enclose[d] [those involved] in an artificial universe ever more disconnected from reality – in an almost pathological world which reflected the real one only marginally ... It alienated [the Indian] to the extent of making him participate in his own oppression.'[56] And Judith Friedlander summarized her view of being Indian in Hueyapan with the statement that

> To be Indian in Hueyapan is to have a primarily negative identity. Indian-ness is more a measure of what the villagers are not or do not have vis-à-vis the Hispanic elite than it is of what they are or have. To complicate matters, the standard by which the Hueyapeños are evaluated is always changing. For over 400 years, while Hueyapeños have been filling the void of their Indian-ness by accumulating symbols identified with the Hispanic elite, the Mexican upper classes have been continuously acquiring new symbols and rejecting many of the old ones. As the elite redefines its own identity, it demotes characteristics previously associated with its prestigious high status to the low level of *nonculture or Indian-ness*. Consequently, despite the fact that the 'content' of Hueyapan culture is always changing,

the 'structural' relationship of Indian to Hispanic remains the same. The villagers are still Indians by virtue of the fact that they continue to lack what the elite continues to acquire.[57]

The most frequent position taken in the 1970s by Marxist students of the Mexican peasantry, concerning the question of ethnicity, was simply that it did not exist outside the confines of class analysis. It was a cultural manifestation of economic domination which would be cast off in a process of class struggle,[58] and therefore hardly worthy of consideration. This view was, however, challenged by Arizpe, who (like Bonfil and Stavenhagen) saw in ethnic identity not only a mechanism of defense and a form of response to threatened social disorganization, but also an element around which indigenous groups of Mexico could organize politically. It might be true that once the latter were no longer exploited economically, they would cease to find it useful to maintain a separate identity. But in the meantime, their political impotence – based upon the stigma of 'Indianness' – made them even more exploitable than mestizo compatriots of the same peasant class.

To illustrate the point that social stigma, based upon an entirely subjective evaluation by mestizos of unlike cultures, served to 'maintain the benefits of economic development within the limits of their own group,' whatever the concomitant effects of class, Arizpe compared the history of two neighboring peasant communities – one Mazahua, one mestizo – which received equal amounts of land during the Cárdenas period and therefore began the postwar period upon a relatively equal economic footing.[59] By the 1970s, the non-Indian group was clearly much better off than the Indian one; and differentiation could not be traced to immediately unequal access to the means of production. It could be traced, however, to the forms of social organization and types of interaction with the wider society permitted by ethnicity. Mestizo families were not forced by ethnic barriers to depend entirely for their livelihood upon the limited resources contained within their own community; their sons or daughters obtained some education, participated in politics and commerce, brought home the wages of bureaucrats or industrial workers, and in the process reduced the absolute pressure of population on agricultural land. Mazahua families, in contrast, could not participate in politics except through the medium of Indian caciques; language barriers kept their children out of school; and lack of alternative sources of income contributed to a fragmentation of family holdings which in the end made farming, without the supplementary income obtained from seasonal migration, an untenable enterprise. Clearly, the life chances of the latter were affected by a peculiar form of 'institutionalized exclusion' which students of the peasantry would do well not to ignore.

The eclipse and revival of the concept of culture

In the last analysis, the concept of ethnicity, with its immediate connotation of exclusivity or 'otherness' and its intimate relation to mechanisms of domination and exploitation, was of all the relatively traditional concerns of Mexican anthropology the one least incompatible with those of historical structuralism in the 1970s. The concept of culture, however, enjoyed an almost total rejection.[60] Most Marxists considered it a 'mystification' of reality unworthy of serious scholarly attention; and even cultural ecologists preferred to talk in terms of immediate forms of socioeconomic adaptation than to use the word 'culture.'

Such a tactic, it might be added, was perhaps more an element of weakness than of strength in the general argument of cultural ecology, because proof of the assertion made by members of the school for a separate, resilient 'peasant mode of producton' obviously lay in the last analysis in a demonstration of the vitality of an identifiable system of values and beliefs which gave meaning distinct from that prevailing in urban industrial capitalism to peasant society. A precapitalist mode of production without a vital 'ideological superstructure' which others might associate with culture could only disintegrate into a complex of precapitalist work relations for which a new set of connotations had been provided.[61]

In part, the infrequency with which cultural ecologists referred directly to culture during the 1970s in Mexico was attributable to the fact that they used the concept as a virtual synonym for 'adaptive mechanisms,'[62] and therefore assumed its presence in all discussions of the latter. Yet in practice, the 'adaptive mechanisms' of which they spoke were almost always presented in the relatively short-term framework of specific challenges and responses, and did not fully touch upon broader elements of behavioral continuity which might have contributed to the maintenance of a particular way of life. The existence of 'peasant culture' was mentioned only in passing, as when Palerm admitted, in his discussion of the likelihood of the dissolution of the peasantry, the possibility that loss of all sources of self-provisioning could bring about complete proletarianization, 'except from the cultural point of view.'[63]

Historical structuralism and the fate of the peasantry, 1970-80   173

There was no elaboration on that point. To the extent that culture had constituted a central concern of anthropology from the time of its consolidation as an academic discipline onward, its virtual abandonment by many historical structuralists engaged in the study of the peasantry implied a concomitant weakening of their identity as anthropologists. If the debate on the future of the peasantry required almost exclusive concern with the issues of political economy, what contribution could an anthropologist make which an economist or sociologist could not make better? Was it not more realistic to speak in terms of the tasks confronting Marxism than to dwell upon the possible utility of anthropology?

These issues were raised with increasing frequency in new professional publications which appeared in the latter 1970s in Mexico, most particularly *Nueva Antropología* and *Marxismo y Antropología*. And the current of discussion which flowed through the pages of both was more favorable to the strengthening of a universal science of Marxism than to the revitalization of anthropology as such. Héctor Díaz Polanco put forward perhaps the most radical position when he argued that 'Marxist theory suppose[d] the scientific definition of objects of investigation totally different from those proposed within anthropology' and found the suggestion of simply 'applying Marxism to anthropology' 'a brake upon Marxist scientific research.' Marxism should stand by itself; and anthropology, in the absence of association with Marxism a completely bourgeois science, should disappear.[64]

Cultural ecologists and dependentistas presented the most coherent common front against such a position, for their research strategies had always been premised upon a revisionist application of Marxist theory to selected areas of a much broader anthropological practice. They objected not only to what they considered Marxist determinism, but also to the recurring suggestion that all social phenomena could be studied from the perspective of class. Bonfil, for example, insisted that 'the over-all analysis of Mexican society . . . [could] not be reduced to class analysis';[65] and Stavenhagen clearly stated that

> human cultures [had] a dynamic of their own which widely surpassed the economic structures with which they might be associated at different stages of their evolution . . . Of course, there [were] cultural elements closely linked to the class position of a worker and his family . . . , but there [were] also cultural elements which outdistanced any class position.'[66]

There was, in other words, something of fundamental positive value in the study of culture − a stance which both Stavenhagen and Bonfil had upheld through years of practical efforts in defense of a pluricultural Mexican society, but which the great majority of historical structuralists had rejected in fear of association with earlier 'culturalist' schools. If anthropology were not entirely to disappear within the sphere of Marxism, if it were to assert a separate identity which gave its practice meaning, an object of study to some extent distinguishable from that of Marxism had once again to be put forward. That object, still imprecisely defined and probably subject to intense revision and debate, was most likely to be culture.[67]

Historical structuralism and public policy in the 1970s

Before closing this discussion of the development of various currents within historical structuralism during the past decade, it is important to turn, however summarily, to the question of the influence of paradigmatic boundaries on the public understanding of rural problems, and most particularly on the formulation of policy. This is especially the case because the 1970s seem clearly to have been, in retrospect, the years when the hold of earlier 'culturalist' explanations of rural poverty upon the imagination of policymakers was definitively broken and a number of premises associated with the general tenets of historical structuralism were absorbed sufficiently to influence the course of public programming in a way unthinkable at any time since the end of the Cárdenas administration in 1940.

The most basic thesis of historical structuralism accepted in official circles during the 1970s was that which ascribed the deepening poverty of the countryside primarily to the working of exploitative mechanisms linking local people to the wider society, rather than primarily to the cultural idiosyncrasies of any particular rural setting. Such a reversal, which could be noted even within traditional strongholds of 'culturalism', like the National Indian Institute, implied the progressive assignment of ever-larger proportions of the federal budget to programs designed to redress an acknowledged disequilibrium in rural-urban exchange. Thus between 1970 and 1976, during the presidential term of Luis Echeverría, the real federal expenditure on low-interest rural credit increased spectacularly; guaranteed prices for farm products doubled, on an average, and shortly trebled; federally financed crop reception centers, local warehouses and silos, and outlets for low-cost inputs like fertilizers and insecticides were built in rural areas never before directly linked to assistential programs of the state, in the avowed hope of reducing the monopolistic control of long-entrenched regional intermediaries. All were means suggested by the conclusions of the ICAD study (with its dependentista focus) and repeatedly emphasized in any number of subsequent discussions of unequal exchange dwelling upon such exploitative mechanisms as usury, commercial chicanery, and monopolistic control over the product of captive credit recipients.

Policymakers' perception of rural problems was also gradually influenced by repeated public reference to the concept of a 'peasant economy,' and thus to the catastrophic effects of increased risk-taking which were likely to accompany the increasing involvement of peasant families in production for a capitalist market. Therefore within the package of new programs instituted in 1980 under the aegis of the presidential coordinating agency known as the Mexican Food System (*Sistema Alimentario Mexicano*, or SAM), an important place was given to subsidized crop insurance, as well as to increasing federally financed subsidies to peasant production begun in the preceding half of the decade. It became legitimate, in policy circles, to maintain that the semi-subsistence sector of Mexican agriculture, long a net contributor to the rest of the economy, should enjoy the benefits of becoming a net recipient — and more to the point, that a redirection of national resources toward the peasantry was essential if a livelihood disaster of major proportions were to be averted in the countryside.

At the same time, policymakers began to see the peasantry not only as producers, but also as consumers, and to channel toward it some of the social welfare benefits previously reserved only for organized urban sectors of the population. Rural families in depressed agricultural areas were affiliated in significant numbers with the national Social Security System and a massive effort to construct rural clinics and hospitals begun; government-sponsored food stores (under the control of the *Compañia Nacional de Subsistencias Populares*, or CONASUPO) were opened by the thousands in rural villages in an attempt to lower the cost of eating in the countryside; official support was offered for the establishment of rural transport cooperatives. The fact that these programs were often entrusted to a Coordinating Office for Marginal Areas (*Comisión de Planeación para Zonas Marginadas*, or COPLAMAR), under which the National Indian Institute was placed as a specialized agency, illustrated both that the wider problems of the peasantry as a whole had taken precedence over the particular problems of culturally distinct groups, and that the concept of 'marginality' as first proposed in the 1960s (involving a lack of participation in the benefits of development) had come to form part of standard official usage.

It would be illusory to think that such changes in policy were only, or even primarily, the result of enlightenment provided by the intellectual effort of historical structuralists. They were a necessary response to an extremely critical turn of events in the countryside, including some which threatened the economic and political viability of the nation as a whole. From the late 1960s onward, per capita agricultural production began to decline continuously; urban food prices rose concomitantly, as did food imports. A part of the problem could be traced to the terminal impoverishment of semi-subsistence agriculture, implying an inevitable reduction in the volume of surplus staples available for sale on the regional or national market. Another part seemed related to the abandonment of production by members of small-farming families convinced that they could make a better living in the city than in the countryside. Many rural areas, in other words, had ceased to provide the minimum prerequisites for a stable farming population. And the result was a kind of saturation of urban centers, accompanied by food scarcity and rising prices, which could only be reversed by making family farming an attractive alternative to migration.

Thus a tangible crisis, affecting centers of urban power, forced the need to understand problems of rural livelihood upon those charged with policy elaboration, and they turned to the work of historical structuralists in search of answers. It should be emphasized, however, that (virtually by definition) only a part of the historical structuralist definition of the problem at hand could be accepted. The unjust, and ultimately untenable, exploitation of peasant labor through the working of a vitiated commercial circuit, in which the manipulation of credit was of central importance, could be challenged through the creation of alternative state-controlled channels. But the equally vitiated network of group relations underlying the apparatus of the state itself, much analysed by historical structuralists, could not be replaced. And there lay a dilemma of perhaps insurmountable dimensions. It was epitomized in the consistency with which programs to reverse the flow of benefits from countryside to city, and to subsidize peasant production, were financed by international borrowing and the investment of new oil revenues rather than by any structural challenge either to the landholdings or the income of the capitalist sector.

Peasant organization was, of course, one step supported by all

Historical structuralism and the fate of the peasantry, 1970-80

factions of the historical structuralist camp as a necessary element in bringing about a fundamental redistribution of power, and hence of material goods, within Mexican society. And during the Echeverría administration, official support was given to the collectivization of ejido agriculture: agrarian communities which would agree to join individual parcels into a single block, to be worked by the collectivity, received special credit incentives and were scheduled to form the basis for a pyramid of secondary processing and industrial activities also under the control of the peasantry. The effort, induced from above by government promoters, was approved by a minority of historical structuralist social scientists with faith in the effectiveness of an alliance between the peasantry and the state. The majority of those whose vision of rural problems was oriented by the paradigm, however, predicted inevitable failure, both because the venture was directed from above and because it was impossible for an enclave of socialized agricultural enterprises to survive within a predominantly capitalist socioeconomic formation. Cultural ecologists like Warman emphasized the element of imposition in yet another state-directed reorganization of peasant resources. Revisionist Marxists saw it primarily in terms of an attempt by representatives of capital to exploit peasant labor more rationally; and relatively more orthodox Marxists denounced it out of hand as an economic impossibility promoted only to heighten the capacity of the ruling coalition to manipulate the peasantry politically.

In fact the program was suspended in 1977, under pressure from the right. But grass-roots peasant mobilization, impelled by the deteriorating livelihood situation in the countryside, continued to increase, and to this widening movement of protest historical structuralists gave their full support. Through the national organization of the Mexican Communist Party, orthodox Marxists concentrated upon assisting landless agricultural workers to form unions and to strike; revisionist Marxists joined cultural ecologists and dependentistas in allying themselves with agrarian organizations seeking to gain or protect a right to land; and all denounced a rising tide of repression carried out at the behest of both traditional and modern agrarian interests.

6 Conclusions

At the end of this long, and sometimes difficult, examination of the changing ways in which anthropologists have approached the question of rural otherness in postrevolutionary Mexico, what can one conclude concerning the utility of the exercise? Have changing explanatory frameworks reflected fundamental changes in rural society? Or can they more aptly be said to have mirrored a broader range of mental stimuli, making particular ways of looking at rural life more intellectually satisfying, or more useful in terms of policy, for urban-based observers at given historical moments than others might conceivably have been?

The first response which comes to mind, when one turns back over the material discussed in the preceding pages, is that the way anthropologists have approached the countryside at any particular time has been above all a function of the intellectual structure of schools in which they have been trained and not of a random confrontation with life in rural Mexico. Both foreign academics and Mexican colleagues have gone into rural areas in search of situations which fit their preconceived images of adequate field sites, and have done their best to see local reality in terms validated by a previously adopted set of assumptions. The work of early ethnographic particularists provides perhaps the most outstanding proof of this assertion: armed with the belief that anthropologists could only study primitive peoples, the former were capable of travelling long distances through an unacceptably non-primitive countryside before finding field sites sufficiently isolated to warrant attention. Later, functionalists tended to look at community integration within areas with a strong communal tradition, and indigenistas to find cultural impediments to national participation in mountainous 'refuge regions.' The turn toward carrying out research in mestizo communities or among landless agricultural workers came only with the substitution of assumptions drawn from historical structuralism for earlier ones associated with culturalism.

Anthropologists, then, have in general chosen a kind of social milieu

Conclusions

which seemed to offer the objective conditions of support for intellectual concerns central to their own world view. In so doing, they have not behaved unscientifically, if one adopts the definition of scientific endeavor put forward by Kuhn. Drawing a series of boundaries around areas of relevant enquiry, and accepting certain hypotheses concerning the interrelation of elements within those boundaries, students of rural life have simply set out to 'solve puzzles' within the mental framework at their disposal. It would indeed have been unscientific if they had attempted such a feat in environments patently unsuited to the paradigm employed.

This congruence of social setting and paradigmatic concern has, however, implied a necessarily very partial and selective advance over time in the cumulative picture of rural Mexico available to those who would attempt to gain a broad view of livelihood from the literature at hand. If one looks, for example, at the Mexican countryside as it appeared on the mental map provided by members of the anthropological profession who wrote about it in the immediate postrevolutionary period, one sees only those points which correspond to what were at the moment the few lingering remnants of isolated primitive groups, or communities which observers chose unrealistically to designate as such. Yet the countryside as a whole could hardly have been characterized in that way at any time in its post-Conquest history. With the synthesizing effort of an increasingly institutionalized ethnography, the picture began quickly to change: isolated groups of culturally distinct people were grouped together in 'culture areas,' and it became clear that there were regions of Nahuas, Purépechas, Otomíes, and so forth. But were all rural people 'Indian,' in the sense of 'primitive,' as such intellectual categories quite clearly implied? A negative response to that query did not begin to emerge until the 1930s, when Robert Redfield and others within the structural-functionalist school suggested that most people in the Mexican countryside could best be seen not as primitives but as 'folk,' sharing a common cultural heritage with both pre-Conquest and post-Conquest society. And in consequence, the anthropological map of rural Mexico was to be systematically populated from the end of that decade onward with 'folk communities,' scattered throughout the central and southern part of the national territory both within and without previously designated culture areas.

The expansion of the social field within which anthropologists could pursue intellectual interests legitimated by their world view or paradigm was, even if analysed only in geographical terms, quite clearly of remarkable proportions between 1910 and 1940. Not only could functionalists settle in Spanish-speaking villages sustaining occasional contact with the wider society (a paradigmatic impossibility for academic particularists), but they could also consider the ways in which local culture had been molded by that contact through a process which came to be known as 'acculturation.' They could not, however, escape the boundaries of the community, any more than earlier ethnographers had been able to look beyond the limits of the village or tribe.

To see the Mexican countryside as more than an aggregate of virtually self-contained human settlements, one must work one's way into the literature of indigenismo, and even there one is confronted with a persistent tendency to emphasize sociocultural phenomena at the community level above all other considerations. In the early postwar period, indigenistas placed the study of local livelihood within a regional framework, determined not only by cultural characteristics but also by the nature of socioeconomic relations obtaining between single rural villages and a dominant regional urban center. Thus they extended the paradigmatic boundaries of relevant 'systemness' outward to the borders of geographical units including many indigenous communities and at least one exploitative mestizo city. Nevertheless the greatest part of both their academic and practical effort was in fact directed toward single indigenous communities, where they tended to concentrate on localized cultural impediments to modernization.

It was only with the development, during the 1950s, of the alternative paradigms of cultural ecology and dependentismo that the single community was definitively superseded as privileged unit of analysis by the socioeconomic region, and the latter in turn placed within the framework of a world capitalist system. The picture of the Mexican countryside painted by anthropologists then began to take on the conceptual form of levels of interaction, in which groups of people within villages were linked through various mechanisms to others in both rural and urban settings, and the latter to still others to be found at the apices of national and international networks of power. Within cultural ecology, this shift was epitomized by Julian Steward's concepts of 'levels of integration' and Eric Wolf's concern with 'group relations in complex society'; within dependentismo, by the concept of a chain of exploitation extending from metropolitan centers of capitalist accumulation to the most remote areas of the Third World. That there were differences in emphasis in these separately developed intellectual traditions has been shown in preceding chapters; but with

Conclusions 181

the passage of time, a single distinguishable area of paradigmatic agreement could be increasingly identified.

The discontinuity in both geographical and thematic boundaries of anthropological concern concomitant upon paradigmatic shifts from functionalism to historical structuralism, from the 1950s onward, entered a new and far more critical stage at the turn of the 1970s, when the world view associated with classical Marxism-Leninism was applied to the Mexican countryside with ever greater frequency by anthropologists and other social scientists so opposed to localism and empiricism that they preferred to consider rural livelihood only in terms of the generic laws of capitalist development, without necessarily submitting those laws to proof in any concrete situation at all. In such a situation, the question of appropriate geographical units of analysis became irrelevant. Practitioners of the discipline had reached the final limits of universality, from which they could begin retreating — as in fact a strong current of revisionist Marxism quite clearly did — toward a reconstruction of more finite boundaries by the end of the decade.

A second point which must immediately be made concerning the general development of the anthropological treatment of rural Mexico in the postrevolutonary period is that just as the nature and extent of social settings within which members of the profession worked were determined by paradigmatic conviction, rather than random experience, so too the initial formation of one set of theoretical assumptions, rather than another, grew out of considerations originally far removed from day-to-day existence to the Mexican countryside. A common characteristic of all paradigms discussed herein has been their elaboration around issues debated within what might usefully be called a world philosophical subculture, of scant immediate concern to rural people.

In essence, this subculture has been characterized by a long-standing preoccupation with the direction of human development — with questions of 'evolution' or 'progress.' And each of the paradigms under analysis has been so structured as to offer a particular commentary on that topic. Thus ethnographic particularists, fundamentally influenced by Franz Boas, hoped to contribute field material to a worldwide catalogue of cultural variation, illustrating in the process the extraordinary variety of human society and providing scholarly ammunition with which to refute contemporary arguments for the necessary unilinear evolution of mankind. Functionalists, associated with Redfield, were oriented toward an application, within the Mexican countryside, of theories concerning the transition from rural to urban civilization requiring, as an initial contribution, the characterization of generically 'urban' and 'rural' community. Indigenistas, formed in the philosophical tradition of nineteenth-century European liberalism, absorbed within Mexican intellectual circles in decades preceding the revolution and surviving the latter relatively intact, fervently believed in the inevitability of progress from a backward, isolated, Indian society to a modern mestizo, national one. Orthodox Marxists and deterministic dependentistas were similarly convinced of the unilinear advance of man toward liberation from oppression of all kinds. And between the two extremes of denial and affirmation of unilineal evolutionary development were cultural ecologists and probabilistic dependentistas, who held firmly to the theory of multilineal evolution, through which separate groups of people would devise distinguishable paths toward a more satisfactory form of existence.

These philosophical positions, apparently so intellectually distant from the concrete task of deciphering local arrangements of livelihood, lie behind much of what can be considered the systematic biases of anthropologists associated with each paradigm. Both particularists and functionalists of the Redfield school, for example, could not see poverty: in the case of the former, because they had been prepared by their relativist heritage to consider all ways of living equally valid; and in the case of the latter, because it was their task to search out the positive or 'functional' elements of rural community. Indigenistas, as well as applied functionalist anthropologists who shared the liberal philosophical heritage of indigenismo could, on the other hand, see no aspect of daily life in 'backward' or 'traditional' villages quite so clearly as poverty and interpersonal conflict. For 'progress' to have meaning, the existential moment had to be unacceptable. The same observation applied equally to orthodox Marxists. It was only in the intellectual world of anti-incorporationist indigenismo, revisionist Marxism, cultural ecology and probabilistic dependentismo that a real space was maintained for simultaneous consideration of both positive and negative elements in concrete rural situations, since some elements in contemporary designs for living were proposed as useful in mitigating or changing others considered harmful.

It should perhaps be explicitly noted that persistent biases toward branding life in rural villages as either inherently good or inherently bad were entirely independent of position on a political spectrum: 'conservative' functionalists (of the applied school), 'nationalistic' indigenistas like Gamio and Aguirre Beltrán, and 'radical' orthodox Marxists joined

Conclusions

forces in labelling prevailing designs for living throughout much of the Mexican countryside as 'backward'; just as other 'conservative' or 'liberal' functionalists (associated with Redfield), 'nationalistic' indigenistas of the anti-incorporationist vein epitomized by Moisés Sáenz, and 'radical' cultural ecologists or dependentistas were broadly united by their positive evaluation of the sociocultural resources of the countryside. The fact that several of the major paradigms under discussion (most obviously functionalism and indigenismo) were themselves split on the issue is an indication of the complexity of their ideological components: thus functionalists might all agree on the inevitability of unilinear evolution, but be either pessimistic or optimistic concerning the outcome of the process; and indigenistas, while united in the belief that the formation of an integrated nation state must be fostered, could entertain differing opinions concerning the contribution which indigenous cultures might make to the new conformation. Even within the framework of Marxism, it will be remembered that the distinction between orthodoxy and revisionism ran roughly parallel to that between 'descampesinistas' and 'campesinistas,' implying disagreement concerning the importance of an organized peasantry in an eventual challenge to capitalism.

As those associated with each major anthropological school took an intellectual position concerning the central question of the direction of social change in human history, then, they concomitantly excluded from consideration those aspects of rural life which might not have conformed to their belief. In the same way, they were likely to find their view of local reality molded by implicit or explicit assumptions formed in response to a second central concern of the philosophical subculture of the social sciences, that of the relative importance of mental or material elements in determining the nature of society. And here the division along paradigmatic lines was generally quite clearcut: particularists, functionalists and indigenistas were concerned above all with the mental, or cultural aspects of human existence; cultural ecologists, dependentistas, orthodox and revisionist Marxists with the material. Nevertheless, a peculiar element of subtlety was added to indigenista, cultural ecological, and dependenista thought by the tendency of all three to stray from the extremes of the mental-material spectrum and, while maintaining an identifiable emphasis on one explanatory area or another, to consider to some extent the necessary interrelation between the two. Indigenistas were perhaps the first to do so in the specific context of the Mexican countryside, as they began to develop theories linking ethnic stereotypes with exploitation; dependentistas took up the same issue and refined the anthropological discussion of it; and cultural ecologists joined dependentistas in insisting upon analysis of the specifically mental component of capitalist expansion, implying a process of cultural disorganization in a rapidly modernizing countryside.

These attempts at a synthesis of mental and material considerations offered tangible proof that there need be no necessary restriction of the study of cultural phenomena to paradigms structured exclusively around analysis of the harmonious elements of rural life, any more than an emphasis on changing material conditions need be automatically associated with the study of conflict. In taking a paradigmatic stand on the relative importance of conflict and harmony in human existence, however, anthropologists did deal with a third general question within the philosophical realm of the social sciences in a way which tended further to restrict the scope of their vision. And in fact, the stereotyped equation of 'culturalism' with a blindness to conflict, like that of Marxism with total emphasis on conflict, came to characterize any simplified discussion of the history of Mexican anthropology, the complexity of real intellectual activity notwithstanding.

By the time anthropologist observers established themselves in the rural social settings where they were to carry out their studies, then, the way in which they were likely to perceive their surroundings had already been determined to a considerable extent by the placement of paradigms in relation to the central issues of a worldwide philosophical subculture. Whether salient characteristics of rural life were to constitute a hindrance to local, national, or universal 'progress,' whether the harmonious or the conflictive elements of social interaction were to be given analytical priority, whether the mental or the material aspects of life were of greatest explanatory utility – all were questions resolved without any special necessity to work out answers based upon immediate experience alone. And this most fundamental characteristic of the anthropological endeavor (or indeed of any endeavor developed within a scientific paradigm) contributed to a certain probable divorce between what one anthropologist wrote about and what another would have seen had he been oriented by a different set of intellectual coordinates.

If such an affirmation is basically sound, however – if anthropologists are likely to engage above all in what might be called generic commentary – what can be said for the importance of contact with real sociocultural situations in providing the groundwork for empirical testing

Conclusions

of hypotheses suggested by accepted paradigms? Has not repeated contact with an intractable reality contributed fundamentally to the series of shifts in paradigmatic allegiance which has formed the central thread of disciplinary practice during the past half century? The answer to these questions seems to be both yes and no. On the one hand, there can be no doubt that the most basic reorientation of anthropological thought in twentieth-century Mexico, occurring from the late 1940s through the early 1960s, and involving the virtual abandonment of a broadly functionalist position in favor of a broadly historical structural one, was very much facilitated by the inability of traditional functionalism to explain the way in which local people were integrated into the wider socioeconomic system. Significantly, those who most often came into contact with phenomena like caciquismo, brokerage, exploitative mechanisms of regional trade or outright violence were indigenistas, whose primary task was as much practical development work as academic investigation; and it was indigenismo which constituted the first national challenge to functionalism. In the same vein, it is clear that the abandonment of a rigidly orthodox Marxist interpretation of rural change during the 1970s was made necessary by an embarrassingly persistent failure of the peasantry to disappear.

There have been, in other words, factual challenges to existing paradigms so basic that they have spelled the virtual rejection of particular intellectual traditions. Nevertheless, any supposition that the trajectory of changing anthropological explanation can be plotted along a line closely congruent at all points with observed changes in rural reality, or that empirical observation has been the primary factor leading in most cases to the adoption of particular paradigms, would be unfounded. The most that can be said, perhaps, is that changes in anthropological world views have occurred in relative congruence with broader trends in the development of the wider society as a whole, and that to the extent that such trends have enveloped the countryside as well as the city, they have been relevant by definition to alterations in the environment of rural livelihood.

To bring this point into sharper focus, let us look for a moment at elements in specific cases of paradigmatic elaboration relatively unrelated to any direct interest in explaining a perplexing concrete situation in rural Mexico. The first of these might be Redfieldian functionalism, which was developed in Chicago, through an exchange of ideas not only with American students of rural sociology (including Redfield's own father-in-law, Robert Park), but also with European theorists like Radcliffe-Brown. It was an international intellectual construct, and the fact that it was introduced in Mexico as an alternative to ethnographic particularism had little indeed to do with previous *factual* failures of the latter. Similarly, the first appearance of cultural ecology within the social setting of Mexico grew out of the intellectual dissatisfaction of Julian Steward, and then of Eric Wolf, with the interpretive power of functionalism. The concrete experience of both which supported such dissatisfaction had not been in Mexico, but in Puerto Rico; and Steward's conclusion that rural communities were being increasingly integrated into ever-wider spheres of interaction thus constituted a general commentary on world development, which could be, and was, eventually, applied in any number of concrete situations, including some in Mexico.

Particular concern with the socioeconomic and cultural characteristics of what came, during the 1950s, to be called the 'peasantry,' as well as the special interest shown during the 1960s and 1970s by all paradigms within the broad field of historical structuralism in the impact of capitalist development upon rural society, can as plausibly be attributed to the postwar facilitation of communication between European and American social scientists, and to the consequent adoption of long-held European concepts concerning the subordination of small rural producers, as to any necessarily immediate change in the basic characteristics of the rural socioeconomic and cultural field which anthropologists might observe in Mexico. Were the near-subsistence cultivators of the Mexican countryside any more of a 'peasantry' in 1960 than they had been, adopting the terminology of historical structuralism, in 1860? Most probably not. But new concepts reaching Mexico from Europe, through the medium of European social scientists working in American universities (Eric Wolf), European political refugees resident from the late 1930s in Mexico (Angel Palerm), the experiences of Mexican and other Latin American students in European universities (Stavenhagen, González Casanova, Cardoso), as well as the appearance in Mexico of previously untranslated works of Marx, permitted them to be seen as such.

The process through which alternative paradigms made their appearance in anthropological circles and were successively applied to the Mexican countryside in the six decades following the revolution, then, was often as much a reflection of an attempt by members of the profession to interpret old facts more satisfactorily as it was a response to new or contradictory data. When Oscar Lewis challenged Redfield

Conclusions

through a searching restudy of Tepoztlán, or young indigenista field workers clashed with the established functionalist doctrine of their teachers, insisting upon the registration of concrete mechanisms of domination and exploitation in field notes of the latter (as was the case, for example, with Julio de la Fuente and Malinowski), one can say that observed reality was impinging upon paradigmatic points of reference in a way which could only encourage change. But for the most part, the first arguments of new schools appeared to be based directly upon the field work of earlier ones, and to accept the factual material gathered by intellectual predecessors virtually without empirical challenge. What distinguished the written works of ethnographic particularists and functionalists, to take an early case in point, was not the kind of livelihood data which was collected, but the interpretative framework in which it was presented. Similarly, once the turn toward an examination of interethnic conflict had been taken by indigenistas, field studies produced by the latter served as perhaps the single most important reservoir of (unchallenged) empirical data from which dependentistas drew their information. And when orthodox Marxists re-entered the field of peasant studies at the turn of the 1970s, it was in large part with statistics produced by the dependentista-directed ICAD report that they fleshed in the empirical areas of their discourse.

The production of new kinds of information seems, in other words, generally to have followed, rather than preceded, paradigmatic change. Proponents of most intellectual strategies for approaching the countryside have accepted the data base of predecessors, reinterpreted it, and then gone on to open up new areas requiring a kind of empirical quest not previously given priority within the discipline. Once a static ethnographic description of village life in certain regions had been obtained, functionalist anthropologists surpassed the data of particularists by giving special attention to the integrative institutions of folk communities, as well as by carrying out psychological studies of interpersonal relations in village contexts. Indigenistas added the dynamic element of historical research, and the first paradigmatically defined need to study exploitative interethnic relations in a regional context. Cultural ecologists required not only the most carefully conducted historical research yet undertaken by anthropologists, but also the study of ecological aspects of rural life, as well as the specific consideration of the impact of capitalist incorporation upon village livelihood, in which such adaptive strategies as the formation of informal networks of interpersonal relations transcending the local level were to be specifically taken into account. Dependentistas found the clarification of the nature of the agrarian structure of special relevance, and generated the first national statistical picture of the socioeconomic stratification of the Mexican countryside, combined with detailed qualitative pictures of such groups as landless laborers, large landowners and the commercial agricultural bourgeoisie. Orthodox Marxists who recognized the importance of studying the peasantry concentrated especially upon the role of the political manipulation of rural people in maintaining the authority of the state; and revisionist Marxists began to conduct original research on the way in which the surplus generated by peasant labor passed through, and interacted with, a national and international circuit of capital. That such a sustained expansion in the scope of anthropological enquiry has been congruent with the general evolution of an ever more closely knit world system need hardly be added.

The cumulative — and in certain respects, dialectical — nature of this half-century-long encounter with the Mexican countryside is, then, one of its most outstanding characteristics. Proponents of each successive theoretical framework have been engaged in an intellectual argument with predecessors, constructing new forms of explanation by disagreeing with existing ones and thus engaging in a dialectical exercise. At the same time, the cumulation of empirical data, with great frequency not challenged by succeeding paradigms, had made it possible for later observers to take for granted a knowledge of certain basic elements of rural life already commented upon by others, and to dedicate themselves to the search for new material, involving new themes or areas of concern, most probably in new geographical settings. The communality of the endeavor over the years should not be forgotten, irreconcilable world views notwithstanding.

Another equally salient characteristic of the kind of scientific work carried out by anthropologists in rural Mexico during the past sixty years has been what might be called its interpretive core. As the preceding discussion has amply illustrated, social anthropologists have generally been unable to approach the countryside as natural scientists might come to terms with their subject matter, by elaborating concrete hypotheses which could be definitively proved or disproved in the course of research — and from which laws of confiable predictive power would ultimately emerge.

This is not, quite obviously, to say that hypotheses have not been regularly formulated and ways inevitably found to test them: Redfield sustained the likelihood of a particular kind of sociocultural

Conclusions 189

disorganization and reorganization in the course of the urbanization of national society and carried out a synchronic comparison involving four points on a rural-urban continuum which approximated as nearly as his environment permitted the requirements of a scientific experiment. Foster, Lewis and Cancian collected an impressive amount of survey data with which to sustain their hypotheses concerning the personal correlates of modernizing behavior in Tzintzuntzan, Tepoztlán and Zinacantan. Historical material of considerable complexity was gathered by indigenistas, cultural ecologists and dependentistas, and applied to an hypothesis concerning the colonial roots of particular patterns of exploitation and domination in the Latin American countryside. An increasing amount of both micro and macroeconomic information is now being generated by all members of the historical structuralist current preoccupied with proving the hypothesis that within a dependent capitalist system, semi-subsistence cultivators will always be systematically despoiled of the fruits of their labor in the process of commodity exchange. The lists of examples could be extended indefinitely.

But these are not unequivocal proofs sustaining inviolable causal laws, nor can they ever be so, given the complexity of the human subject matter at hand. They are, as Theodore Abel recently put it in a general discussion of the future of sociological theory, interpretations serving rather 'to provide orientations in important and fateful areas of human living and to offer new and generalized comprehensions of the human condition.'[1] As long as they are recognized as such, they are of immense importance in affecting the way in which men themselves reshape their destiny; if taken mistakenly for laws, they are likely to be degraded to the level of dogma.

The peculiarity of interpretive intellectual activity in the social sciences, however, especially when compared with the apparently far more rigorous application of laws in the physical ones, is that the former, while not being able to lay claim to any complete certainty in its *prediction* of the future, has the great advantage of being in a position to attempt to *influence* the future. Each way of explaining the salient aspects of rural life at any given moment, and of relating the latter to the general nature of rural-urban interaction, contains within it an implicit or explicit prescription for policy, inherent in the characterization of positive and negative elements of prevailing situations. And when one looks back over the course of anthropological interpretation of parameters surrounding rural livelihood in Mexico, it would seem that such prescription can be rather clearly differentiated along two lines: one which has emphasized the urgency of eliminating all barriers (whether cultural, physical, economic or social) still separating the rural population of the nation from full participation in a modern, national, capitalist industrial society; and one which has, in contrast, suggested the advisability of reinforcing such barriers at strategic points, in order to assure local control over or participation in certain aspects of livelihood likely to suffer when entrusted entirely to the vicissitudes of the broader system. Proponents of the first line of action have included applied functionalists, incorporationist indigenistas, and orthodox Marxists, all of whom have worked unstintingly toward the creation of a single national society; and of the second, anti-incorporationist indigenistas, cultural ecologists and probabilistic dependentistas, whose efforts to support local identity have been equally noteworthy.

It should be stressed that in this discussion there has been, for at least three decades, no real pretense to establish the original isolation or 'closedness' of the vast majority of the rural communities of the Mexican countryside. The existence of some degree of long interaction with the wider society is granted by virtually all schools as an historically verifiable fact. Nor has there been much disagreement concerning the presence of a broad trend toward ever-greater integration of rural people into a national, and international, system. Populations once only marginally dependent upon the goods and services available outside their own locality have grown visibly more so in the postwar period, often to the extent of forming a transient society entirely viable in neither a rural nor an urban setting.

The debate has not been tabled, then, between those who would romantically advocate the maintenance or re-establishment of some ideal form of rural autarchy, on the one hand, and those who question the practicality of such a model on the other – although it has been frequently misrepresented as such. It has been conducted around the question of whether it is or is not advisable, both from the standpoint of reinforcing the livelihood options of the rural population and from that of contributing to the quality of life in the wider society, to work toward an inversion of the present trend toward urban centralization, returning to the local or regional level as great a part of the socio-economic and cultural capacity to meet basic needs as possible.

Historical experience does not support the assertion that such a turn of events occurs naturally, except in the aftermath of a fundamental

Conclusions

disorganization of the wider society. It did occur, to a considerable extent, following the revolution of 1910, to take a not so distant Mexican example; and it is likely to become feasible once more — barring a worldwide economic collapse or wartime disaster — only as a response to an extraordinary political organization of beleaguered peasants, allied with growing masses of 'marginal' people, finding no adequate means of survival in either urban or rural settings. The nature of future Mexican society has thus become inextricably related to the fate of 'peasants in cities'[2] and the latter to the capacity of the national socioeconomic system to provide a place for nonagricultural labor. If sufficient remunerative employment can be generated by a modernizing, but dependent, industrial economy to offset the negative effects of the progressive elimination of local bases for rural livelihood, the Mexican peasantry (both in the negative sense of an exploited semi-subsistence farming sector and in the positive sense of a group of family enterprises operating within the context of strongly integrated local communities) may in all likelihood disappear. And with it will go the legacy of an era in the history of Mexican anthropology. If such alternative sources of livelihood are not forthcoming, however, the peasantry cannot disappear, for it has no place to go. There can be little doubt in such a case that rural people, whether at home or squatting on the outskirts of cities, will provide impetus for the decentralization of an unviable urban society, about which anthropologists have debated so long.

Notes

Preface

1 See Cynthia Hewitt de Alcántara, 'The process of change in rural Mexico: a bibliographical appraisal,' in United Nations Research Institute for Social Development, *Measurement and Analysis of Progress at the Local Level*, vol. III, Geneva: 1979, pp. 1-54.

Introduction

1 The first major statement of Kuhn's position will be found in *The Structure of Scientific Revolutions*, Chicago: University of Chicago Press, 1962; and the second in *The Essential Tension*, published by the same press in 1977.
2 Kuhn, *The Structure of Scientific Revolutions, op. cit.*, pp. 15, 21, 37.
3 Margaret Masterman, 'The nature of a paradigm,' in Imre Lakatos and Alan Musgrave (eds), *Criticism and the Growth of Knowledge*, Cambridge: Cambridge University Press, 1970, p. 74.
4 Thomas Kuhn, 'Reflections on my critics,' in Lakatos and Musgrave, *op. cit.*, pp. 276-7. Paul Feyerabend presents the most extreme case for linguistic sources of incomparability among paradigms; see his 'Consolations for the specialist' in the same volume, pp. 197-230.
5 Feyerabend, *op. cit.*, p. 228.

1 Particularism, Marxism and functionalism in Mexican anthropology, 1920-50

1 The inability of perhaps the greatest social thinker of the period to escape racial stereotypes when talking of the situation in the countryside can be observed in Andrés Molina Enríquez, *Los grandes problemas nacionales*, Mexico City: Editorial Era, 1978 (first published in 1909).
2 Manuel Gamio, *Forjando patria (pro-nacionalismo)*, Mexico City: Porrua, 1916.
3 See Frederick Starr, 'The Mexican situation: Manuel Gamio's program,' *American Journal of Sociology*, vol. 24, no. 2, September 1918.
4 Manuel Gamio, *La población del Valle de Teotihuacan*, Mexico City: Talleres Gráficos de la Nación, 1922, p. 52.
5 See Vasconcelos's argument in favor of the formation of a worldwide 'cosmic race' in his *La raza cósmica*, Mexico City: Espasa-Calpe, 1948.
6 For biographical data on Sáenz, see Isidro Castillo, 'Prólogo,' in Moisés Sáenz, *Carapan*, Morelia: Gobierno del Estado de Michoacán, 1966.
7 Frank Tannenbaum, *Peace by Revolution: Mexico after 1910*, New York: Columbia University Press, 1933.
8 Moisés, Sáenz, *Caparan, Bosquejo de una experiencia*, Lima: 1936, p. 175.

9 Moisés Sáenz, *México íntegro*, Lima: Imprenta Torres Aguirre, 1939, p. 219.
10 *Ibid.*, p. 220.
11 *Ibid.*, pp. xi—xii and 232.
12 See Gonzalo Aguirre Beltrán, 'Introducción,' in Vicente Lombardo Toledano, *El problema del indio*, Mexico City: SEP Setentas, 1973, p. 25.
13 The program of the Institute, later to be harshly criticized, is discussed in William Townsend, *They Found a Common Language*, New York: Harper & Row, 1972.
14 Gonzalo Aguirre Beltrán in Lombardo Toledano, *op. cit.*, p. 27.
15 Alfred Kroeber, *Anthropology: Culture Patterns and Processes*, New York: Harcourt Brace, 1963 (selected chapters from *Anthropology*, 1923).
16 See Howard Cline, 'Mexican community studies,' *Hispanic American Historical Review*, vol. 32, no. 2, 1952, pp. 212—42, for mention of Radcliffe-Brown's early influence on Redfield. Both men shared a period of time together on the faculty of the University of Chicago.
17 Redfield himself noted that strong conflict within Chan Kom tended to be resolved through the migration of a dissident group, leaving the remaining society in general agreement on principles. For a relatively recent treatment of growing conflict in Chan Kom, see Victor Goldkind, 'Class conflict and cacique in Chan Kom,' *Southwestern Journal of Anthropology*, vol. 22, no. 4, 1966, pp. 325—44.
18 A particularly interesting comment on this trend is made by Guillermo Bonfil Batalla in 'El campo de investigación de la antropología social en México: un ensayo sobre sus neuvas perspectivas,' *Anales de Antropología*, UNAM, Instituto de Investigaciones Históricas, vol. VII, 1970.

In fact, the community was usually defined as the principal settlement of a small county, or *municipio*, and the hamlets surrounding it. The case for taking the *municipio* as the basic unit of anthropological analysis was made first by Sol Tax (an associate of Redfield) in 'The municipios of the Midwestern Highlands of Guatemala,' *American Anthropologist*, vol. 39, 1937, pp. 423—33. It was repeated in Ralph Beals, Robert Redfield and Sol Tax, 'Anthropological research problems with reference to the contemporary peoples of Mexico and Guatemala,' *American Anthropologist*, vol. 45, no. 1, 1943, pp. 1—21, as follows: 'in much of [Guatemala and Chiapas], the natural unit for study is a village with a dependent rural area the boundaries of which mark off local cultural differences as well as delimit administrative units. (For practical study purposes, this is true of many groups in Mexico even though local cultural differences are less marked)' (p. 12).
19 Robert Redfield, *Tepoztlán: A Mexican Village*, Chicago: University of Chicago Press, 1973, p. 13 (first edition, 1930). Elsie Clews Parsons carried out a similar exercise, also concerned with Spanish-Indian 'acculturation,' in *Mitla: Town of the Souls*, Chicago: University of Chicago Press, 1936. In addition, specialized articles on particular aspects of European culture found in Mexican Indian communities appear with relative frequency in *Revista Mexicana de Geografía e Historia*, *American Anthropologist* and other professional journals of the 1930s and 1940s.
20 Redfield, *Tepoztlán: A Mexican Village*, *op. cit.*, p. 218: 'if the interest is not in depiction, but in studying social change as it takes place — in social anthropology as contrasted with ethnology, in the terminology of Radcliffe-Brown — then Tepoztlán presents an excellent opportunity. This opportunity is for the study of the change whereby a folk community is slowly

becoming more like the city. This change is a case of diffusion, occurring in an easily observed situation, so slowly as not to accomplish the disorganization of the community, and under practical circumstances which liberate the student from responsibility to record the fragmentary vestiges of a disappearing culture.'

21 Robert Redfield, Ralph Linton and Melville Herskovits, 'Memorandum on Acculturation,' *American Anthropologist*, vol. 38, 1936, pp. 149-52.

22 Ralph Beals, 'Acculturation,' in Sol Tax (ed.), *Anthropology Today: Selections*, Chicago: University of Chicago Press, 1962, p. 377.

23 This account is taken from Alfonso Villa Rojas, 'Fieldwork in the Mayan region of Mexico,' in George Foster, Thayer Scudder, Elizabeth Colson and Robert V. Kemper (eds), *Long-term Field Research in Social Anthropology*, New York: Academic Press, 1979, pp. 46-7.

24 See the introduction and conclusion of Redfield, *Tepoztlán: A Mexican Village, op. cit.*

25 Redfield, 'The little community,' p. 110, in *The Little Community and Peasant Society and Culture*, Chicago: University of Chicago Press, 1965, p. 110. The essay was written in 1953.

26 See pp. 105-7 of 'The little community,' *op. cit.*, and Robert Redfield, *Chan Kom: A Village that Chose Progress*, Chicago: University of Chicago Press, 1949.

27 Looking back on his work in Chan Kom, Redfield noted in 1953 that the 'central subject matter' was 'the collective mentality of the community.' 'The little community,' *op. cit.*, p. 105.

28 A particularly perceptive study of this kind, commissioned by Redfield in 1952, was Calixta Guiteras Holmes, *Perils of the Soul: The World View of a Tzotzil Indian*, New York: Free Press of Glencoe, 1961.

29 See the introduction to Oscar Lewis, *Life in a Mexican Village: Tepoztlán Restudied*, Urbana: University of Illinois Press, 1951; George Foster, 'What is folk culture?', *American Anthropologist*, vol. 55, 1953, pp. 159-72; Ralph Beals, 'Community typologies in Latin America,' *Anthropological Linguistics*, vol. 3, no. 1, 1961, pp. 8-15; and for Redfield's reply, 'The little community,' *op. cit.*

30 For a fuller discussion of the Pátzcuaro Conference and the founding of the Interamerican Indian Institute, see Gonzalo Aguirre Beltrán, *Teoría y práctica de la educación indígena*, Mexico City: SEP Setentas, 1973.

31 *América Indígena*, vol. 3, 1943, p. 85.

32 See Sol Tax, 'Anthropology and administration,' *América Indígena*, vol. 5, no. 1, 1945, pp. 21-33, where an extremely strong case is made for treating anthropology as a science, not an applied program. One might argue, however, that the kind of teaching in which Tax engaged – involving a large number of students at the National School of Anthropology – could not help but have implications for the practice of applied anthropology in Mexico.

33 Daniel Rubín de la Borbolla and Ralph Beals, 'The Tarasca [sic] Project,' *American Anthropologist*, vol. 42, no. 4, 1940, pp. 708-12. The fact that a group of Mexican and American linguists were currently working on a second 'Tarascan Project' – the promotion of literacy in the native language – lent added force to the applied nature of the Rubín-Beals program.

34 Ralph Beals, Pedro Carrasco and Thomas McCorkle, *Houses and House Use of the Sierra Tarascans*, Washington: Smithsonian Institute of Social Anthropology, publication no. 1, 1944, p. 1.

35 *Ibid.*, and Ralph Beals, 'The diet of a Sierra Tarascan community,' *América*

	Indígena, vol. 3, no. 4, 1943, pp. 295-304.
36	Ralph Beals, *Cherán: A Sierra Tarascan Village* first edition, 1946. New edition 1973, Cooper Square Publishers, New York.
37	*Ibid.*, pp. 12 and 58.
38	See Eric Wolf, 'Levels of communal relations,' in Robert Wauchope and Manning Nash (eds), *Handbook of Middle American Indians*, vol. 6, Austin: University of Texas Press, 1967, pp. 299-316; and Paul Friedrich, 'A Tarascan cacicazgo: structure, function,' in *Proceedings of the American Ethnological Society*, 1958, pp. 23-9. In his treatment of 'The Tarascans,' in the *Handbook of Middle American Indians*, vol. 8, 1969, Beals made brief reference to the fact that 'The Tarascan territory was long the center of conflict between agraristas and cristeros' but did not elaborate further (p. 728).
39	Beals reported in his *Ethnology of the Western Mixe*, Berkeley and Los Angeles: University of California Press, 1945, that his best informant and firm friend was a cacique. This was also true of a number of other anthropologists of the period, for the familiarity of caciques with Spanish and the mestizo world made it possible for them to communicate well with outsiders. The problem lay not in the frequency with which caciques were trusted informants of anthropologists, but in the failure of the latter to understand fully the role of the former. The extremes of political naivety to which uncritical functionalism could lead are displayed in Calixta Guiteras Holmes, *Sayula*, Mexico City: Sociedad Mexicana de Geografía y Estadística, 1952, where the birthplace and home territory of one of the politically most influential families of Mexico (that of President Miguel Alemán) is portrayed as a sleepy Indian village being developed through the altruism of the president.
40	Robert C. West, *Cultural Geography of the Modern Tarascan Area*, Washington: Smithsonian Insitute of Social Anthropology, publication no. 7, 1948; and Donald Brand, assisted by José Corona Núñez, *Quiroga: A Mexican Municipio*, Washington: Smithsonian Institute of Social Anthropology, publication no. 11, 1951.
41	George Foster, assisted by Gabriel Ospina, *Empire's Children: The People of Tzintzuntzan*, Washington: Smithsonian Institute of Social Anthropology, publication no. 6, 1948.
42	*Ibid.*, p. 287.
43	*Ibid.*, p. 288.
44	*Ibid.*, pp. 288-90.
45	George Foster, *Tzintzuntzan: Mexican Peasants in a Changing World*, Boston: Little, Brown & Company, 1967, p. 4. In the same paragraph, Foster reminds his readers that the peasant 'problem' has not arisen out of 'neglect and unconcern on the part of more fortunate peoples, but because the combination of factors which simultaneously motivate people to change, which loosen the fetters of traditional social organization ... have only partially been determined'.
46	See James Acheson, 'Limited good or limited goods? Response to economic opportunity in a Tarascan Pueblo,' *American Anthropologist*, vol. 74, no. 5, 1972, pp. 1151-69.
47	This is not to suggest that Foster himself abandoned his professional commitment to cultural pluralism. In fact, he continued to insist upon looking for 'the elements of culture which [could] be modified or eliminated without doing violence to the total configuration.' (Foster, *Empire's Children: The People of Tzintzuntzan, op. cit.*, p. 291.)

48 Among these studies are May Díaz, *Tonalá: Conservatism, Responsibility and Authority in a Mexican Town*, Berkeley: University of California Press, 1970; Cynthia Nelson, *The Waiting Village: Social Change in Rural Mexico*, Boston: Little, Brown & Company, 1971; and Lola Romanucci-Ross, *Conflict, Violence and Morality in a Mexican Village*, Palo Alto: National Press Books, 1973.
49 See Oscar Lewis, *Life in a Mexican Village: Tepoztlán Restudied*, Urbana: University of Illinois Press, 1963, p. ix. First edition, 1951.
50 For a discussion by a sociologist of the problems of anthropological field work, see Robert Bierstedt, 'The limitations of anthropological methods in sociology,' *American Sociological Review*, vol. 54, 1948, pp. 22-30.
51 Lewis, *op. cit.*, 1963 edn, p. 250.
52 *Ibid.*, p. 430.
53 *Ibid.*, pp. 174-7.
54 *Ibid.*, pp. 177.
55 *Ibid.*, p. 170.
56 *Ibid.*, p. xxiv.
57 *Ibid.*, p. 440.
58 Oscar Lewis, 'Urbanization without breakdown,' *Scientific Monthly*, vol. 75, 1952, pp. 31-41.
59 See Lewis, *Life in a Mexican Village: Tepotzlán Restudied*, *op. cit.*, pp. 446-8, in which he stresses the fact that 'Tepoztecans do not have many of the problems which beset our own modern industrial civilization' (including exploitation and the lust for power and prestige), and complains of the 'unplanned and haphazard nature of social change due to urban influence.'
60 *Ibid.*, pp. 428-9.
61 *Ibid.*, p. 294.
62 *Ibid.*, p. 292.
63 *Ibid.*, p. 296.
64 *Ibid.*, p. 292.
65 For a closely related attempt to analyse culture and personality in a Mexican village through recourse to the concept of 'Social Character,' see Erich Fromm and Michael Maccoby, *The Social Character of a Mexican Village*, New York: Praeger, 1970. The book is based upon field work carried out in Morelos between 1957 and 1963.
66 See Oscar Lewis, 'The culture of poverty,' in Dwight Heath (ed.), *Contemporary Cultures and Societies of Latin America*, 2nd edition, New York: Random House, 1974, pp. 469-79.
67 Oscar Lewis, *Pedro Martínez: A Mexican Peasant and His Family*, New York: Vintage Books, 1967, Introduction.
68 Lewis in Heath, *op. cit.*, p. 477. The difference between Foster and Lewis is clearly reflected in their treatment of the political role of the peasantry. Foster constantly stresses the passivity and impotence of peasants, and almost entirely omits discussion of the Mexican Revolution in both his books on Tzintzuntzan. Lewis deals with the Revolution in much greater detail and places peasants like Pedro Martínez squarely at the center stage of history.
69 Participants included Tax, Foster, Beals, Guiteras Holmes, Wagley, Camara, Villa Rojas, Jimenez Moreno, Kirchhoff, de la Fuente, Betty Starr, Isabel Kelly, Gillin, Whetten, and June Helms, among others. Redfield presented a paper with Tax, but was never recorded as speaking during the discussion. In institutional terms, members of the seminar could be divided into three groups: the independent investigators; associates of the Redfield-Carnegie

Foundation projects, first in Yucatán and later in the highlands of Chiapas; and representatives of the congeries of universities and foundations collaborating in various stages of the Tarascan Project. The papers and edited discussion of the seminar were published in 1952 in a book entitled *Heritage of Conquest*, reissued in 1968 by Cooper Square Publishers, New York. Howard Cline, *op. cit.*, provides a very helpful discussion of the institutional background of the seminar.

70 The completed table, drawn up by the seminar, was as follows (100 equals 'complete retention of pre-Columbian traits'): (*Heritage of Conquest, op. cit.*, pp. 263-4)

Group	Total points	Language	Technology	Social Organization	Religion
Lacandón	400	100	100	100	100
Tzeltal	330	70	90	90	80
Quintana Roo	270	100	90	40	40
Soteapan	265	65	50	60	90
Chinantec	260	70	90	70	30
Mazatec	250	80	40	70	60
Mixe	230	75	55	50	50
Sayula	215	80	60	50	25
Totonaca	205	60	70	50	25
Mixteca	190	60	40	40	50
Otomí	190	60	60	40	30
Huasteca	170	60	40	50	20
Zapotec	155	70	30	30	25
Maya of Yucatán	140	40	40	30	30
Tepoztlán	100	10	20	40	30
Tarascan	45	25	10	0	10

71 Manuel Gamio, 'Las características culturales y los censos indígenas,' *América Indígena*, vol. 2, no. 3, 1942, pp. 15-20.
72 Alfonso Caso, 'Definicion del indio y lo indio,' *América Indígena*, vol. 8, 1948, pp. 239-47.

2 A dialogue on ethnic conflict: indigenismo and functionalism, 1950-70

1 Bronislaw Malinowski and Julio de la Fuente, *La economía de un sistema de mercados en México*, Escuela Nacional de Antropología e Historia, 1957, p. 19.
2 Marvin Harris, *The Rise of Anthropological Theory*, New York: Crowell, 1968, pp. 562-7.
3 Biographical data is taken from the Introduction, by Gonzalo Aguirre Beltrán, to Julio de la Fuente, *Educación, antropología y desarrollo de la comunidad*, Mexico City: INI, 1964, pp. 2-3.
4 *Yalálag: Una villa zapoteca serrana*, Mexico City: Museo Nacional de Antropología, 1949. Field work, 1937-9.
5 See Gonzalo Aguirre Beltrán, *Teoria y práctica de la educación indigena*, Mexico City, SEP Setentas, 1973, p. 184, for a brief treatment of Malinowski's trip to Mexico.
6 Malinowski and de la Fuente, *op. cit.*, p. 174.
7 *Ibid.*
8 *Ibid.*, p. 118.

9 See particularly a paper written by de la Fuente in 1944, 'Relaciones étnicas en la sierra norte de Oaxaca,' republished in *Relaciones interétnicas*, Mexico City: INI, 1965, pp. 33-47.
10 John Gillin, *The Culture of Security in San Carlos*, New Orleans: Tulane, 1951; and Melvin Tumin, *Caste in a Peasant Society*, Princeton: Princeton University Press, 1952.
11 Julio de la Fuente, 'Ethnic and Communal Relations,' in Sol Tax, *Heritage of Conquest*, New York: Cooper Square Publishers, 1968. First edition 1952.
12 Gonzalo Aguirre Beltrán, Introduction to Julio de la Fuente, *Relaciones Interétnicas, op. cit.*, p. 11.
13 Aguirre Beltrán's classic summary of his work on African elements in Mexican culture will be found in *Cuijla: Esbozo etnográfico de un pueblo negro*, Mexico City: Fondo de Cultura Económica, 1958.
14 See Aguirre Beltrán, *Teoría y práctica de la educación indígena, op. cit.*, pp. 185-9.
15 All were published by the Instituto Nacional Indigenista as *Memorias del INI*: that of Moisés T. de la Peña (*Problemas sociales y económicos de las mixtecas*) in 1950; that of Gonzalo Aguirre Beltrán (*Problemas de la población indígena de la Cuenca del Tepalcatepec*) in 1952; that of Francisco Plancarte (*El problema indígena tarahumara*) in 1954; and that of Alfonso Villa Rojas (*Los mazatecos y el problema indígena de la Cuenca del Papaloapan*) in 1955.
16 Plancarte did provide ample information on the way of life of mestizos in the Tarahumara region, as well as on patterns of exploitation by mestizos of the Indian population.
17 Aguirre Beltrán, *Teoria y práctica de la educación indígena, op. cit.*, pp. 187-8.
18 Gonzalo Aguirre Beltrán, *Formas de gobierno indígena*, Mexico City: Imprenta Universitaria, 1953; *Programas de salud en la situación intercultural*, Mexico City: Instituto Indigenista Interamericano, 1955; and Gonzalo Aguirre Beltrán, *El proceso de aculturación y el cambio sociocultural en México*, Mexico City: Universidad Iberoamericana, 1970. First edition, UNAM, 1957.
19 This summary of Aguirre Beltrán's historical position is taken from *El proceso de aculturación . . . , op. cit.*, pp. 134-5.
20 *Ibid.*, pp. 135-6.
21 As Alejandro Marroquín put it in his study of the market system of the mestizo city of Tlaxiaco, Oaxaca, commissioned by Aguirre Beltrán in 1953, Tlaxiaco had 'a parasitic economy, without its own bases of production, resting on the exploitation of an Indian labor force.' Alejandro Marroquín, *La cuidad mercado (Tlaxiaco)*, Mexico City: UNAM, Imprenta Universitaria, 1957, p. 241.
22 The reader should compare this definition of an Indian with the definition of a peasant concomitantly being worked out by Eric Wolf, and discussed in Chapter 3. Andrew Pearse was later to draw upon such a comparison in order to conclude that an Indian might most clearly be characterized as a subcategory of the peasantry: a '*colonial* peasant.' (see Andrew Pearse, *The Latin American Peasant*, London: Frank Cass & Company, 1975, p. 61.) And George Collier summed up his understanding of the two positions by saying that 'Where more centrally situated rural groups became peasants, dominated *peripheral* groups became ethnic [Indian].' (George Collier, *Fields of the Tzotzil*, Austin: University of Texas Press,

1975, p. 212.)
23 'We are not interested in discussing the convenience or inconvenience of industrialization as a means of resolving national economic problems, nor are we interested in measuring the positive and negative effects which that process might have on Indian communities. We are presented with a fact, an irreversible process, which for good or for bad we must accept, because we do not have the possibility to change the path which has been imposed upon us by the general course of Western culture in the orbit of which we live.' Aguirre Beltrán, *Teoria y práctica de la educación indígena, op. cit.,* p. 245.
24 See Gonzalo Aguirre Beltrán, *Antropología social: 1950-75*, mimeo, 1977, Library of the Instituto de Investigaciones Antropológicas, UNAM, p. 117; and 'El indigenismo y la antropología comprometida' (privately published booklet, without date), in which Aguirre Beltrán answers his critics by saying,

> Policy in general, and indigenista policy in particular, are not generated at the whim of a person or an institution which impose their unfettered will; they are influenced by the permanent conflict between prevailing points of view sustained within very different segments of the government. (p. 14)

25 Aguirre Beltrán, *El proceso de aculturación* . . . , *op. cit.*, p. 143.
26 For a discussion of this point with specific reference to Chiapas, see Robert Wasserstrom and Jan Rus, 'Civil religious hierarchies in central Chiapas: a critical perspective,' *American Ethnologist*, vol. 7, no. 2, 1980.
27 Aguirre Beltrán, *El proceso de aculturación* . . . , *op. cit.*, p. 143.
28 This is the argument presented in Aguirre Beltrán, *Formas de gobierno indígena, op. cit.*
29 The paragraph is based on Aguirre Beltrán, *El proceso de aculturación* . . . , *op. cit.*, pp. 143-5.
30 Aguirre Beltrán, *Teoría y práctica de la educación indígena, op. cit.*, p. 268.
31 R.A.M. van Zantwijk noted at the end of his study of ethnic identity in Ihuatzio (Michoacán), for example, that

> If the government could . . . strengthen . . . certain elements of the identity [of Indian minorities], individuals of indigenous communities would conserve their own cultural dignity and would make a much more valuable contribution to the national culture than if they lost their own identity and fell within the lowest stratum of national society, becoming mestizos without culture and without roots . . . *While an Indian minority is economically weak, cultural differences are a favorable factor*, and therefore those who direct development programs should not try to destroy the identity of the community as rapidly as possible.

> R. A. M. van Zantwijk, *Los servidores de los santos: La identidad social y cultural de una comunidad tarasca en México*, Mexico City: Instituto Nacional Indigenista, 1974, pp. 286-7. First published in Dutch in 1965.

32 Information on the history of the Harvard Chiapas Project is taken primarily from Evon Vogt, 'The Harvard Chiapas Project: 1957-1975,' in George Foster, Thayer Scudder, Elizabeth Colson and Robert V. Kemper (eds), *Long-Term Field Research in Social Anthropology*, New York: Academic Press, 1979, pp. 279-301.

33 *Ibid.*, p. 283.
34 *Ibid.*
35 See Clifford Geertz, 'Studies in peasant life: community and society,' in Bernard Siegel and Ralph Beals (eds), *Biennial Review of Anthropology*, 1961, Palo Alto: Stanford University Press, 1962, pp. 1-41, for an excellent discussion of doubts centering on the community-study method.
36 Sol Tax, *Notas sobre Zincantan, Chiapas.* University of Chicago Library microfilm collection, 1943; and Ricardo Pozas, *Chamula: Un pueblo indio de los altos de Chiapas*, Mexico City: Memorias de Instituto Nacional Indigenista, no. 8, 1958.
37 Evon Vogt, *Zinacantan: A Maya Community in the Highlands of Chiapas*, Cambridge: Belknap Press of Harvard University, 1969.
38 Vogt, 'The Harvard Chiapas Project: 1957-1975,' *op. cit.*, p. 295.
39 Evon Vogt, *The Zinacantecos of Mexico: A Modern Way of Life*, New York: Holt, Rinehart & Winston, 1970, p. 100. Emphasis on ritual and beliefs can be illustrated by a glance at some of the titles in the Harvard Chiapas Project Bibliography: Richard Shweder, 'Aspects of Cognition in Zinacanteco Shamans,' in W. A. Lessa and Evon Vogt (eds), *Reader in Comparative Religion: An Anthropological Approach*, New York: Harper & Row, 1972; Sarah Blaffer, *The Black Man of Zinacantan: A Central American Legend*, Austin: University of Texas Press, 1972; Victoria Bricker, *Ritual Humor in Highland Chiapas*, Austin: University of Texas Press, 1973; Francesca Cancian, *What are Norms? A Study of Belief and Action in a Maya Community*, Cambridge: Cambridge University Press, 1975; Evon Vogt, *Tortillas for the Gods: A Symbolic Analysis of Zinacanteco Rituals*, Cambridge: Harvard University Press, 1976.
40 Ricardo Pozas, talking of the history of social research in the Chiapas highlands, noted that most research

> pushed the real problems to one side ... and became lost in a multitude of irrelevant facts ... The brief investigations carried out by members of a Cultural Mission before beginning their work are more useful, even with all their deficiencies, than exhaustive studies undertaken with the most modern research techniques. (*El Desarrollo de la Comunidad: Técnicas de investigación social*, Mexico City: UNAM, 1964, p. 34. First edition, 1961)

41 Frank Cancian, *Change and Uncertainty in a Peasant Economy: The Maya Corn Farmers of Zinacantan*, Palo Alto: Stanford University Press, 1972, p. 131.
42 *Ibid.*, p. 129.
43 *Ibid.*, pp. 34 and 38.
44 This position was most clearly stated by Manning Nash in 'Political relations in Guatemala,' *Social and Economic Studies*, vol. 7, 1958, pp. 65-75.
45 Frank Cancian, 'Political and religious organizations,' in Manning Nash (ed.), *Handbook of Middle American Indians*, op. cit., vol. 6, p. 293.
46 Frank Cancian, *Economics and Prestige in a Maya Community: The Religious Cargo System in Zinacantan*, Palo Alto: Stanford University Press, 1965.
47 The 'Man-In-Nature Project' of the University of Chicago, headed by Norman McQuown and Julian Pitt-Rivers, began in 1957 and ended in 1962. During that time, geographers, botanists, linguists, archeologists and ethnographers explored various aspects of ethnic variation in Chiapas. The somewhat sketchy results of the project have been published in

Norman McQuown, *Report on the Man-In-Nature Project*, University of Chicago, mimeo, 1959, 3 volumes; and Norman McQuown and Julian Pitt-Rivers, *Ensayos de antropología en la zona central de Chiapas*, Mexico City: Instituto Nacional Indigenista, 1970.
48 Sol Tax, 'Ethnic relations in Guatemala,' *América Indígena*, vol. 2, no. 4, 1942, pp. 43-8; and J.S. Furnivall, *Netherlands India*, Cambridge: Cambridge University Press, 1944.
49 See Sol Tax, 'Los indios en la economía de Guatemala,' in Jorge Luis Arriola (ed.), *Integración social en Guatemala*, Guatemala City: Seminario de Integración Social Guatemalteca, 1956, pp. 107-28; Manning Nash, 'Ralaciones políticas en Guatemala,' *ibid.*, pp. 139-56; and Manning Nash, 'The multiple society in economic development: Mexico and Guatemala,' *American Anthropologist*, vol. 59, no. 5, 1957, pp. 825-33. All quotes in the paragraph are taken from Nash, *Primitive and Peasant Economic Systems*, San Francisco: Chandler, 1966, pp. 126-7.
50 See Foster's supporting commentary on Tax's position, presented in Arriola (ed.), *Integración social en Guatemala*, *op. cit.*, p. 129. Also Tax, *ibid.*, p. 116.
51 Nash, 'The multiple society in economic development: Mexico and Guatemala,' *op. cit.*, p. 827.
52 Manning Nash, *Primitive and Peasant Economic Systems*, *op. cit.*, p. 122. Nash was for many years editor of the journal *Economic Development and Cultural Change*, published at the University of Chicago, which was dedicated to the study of modernization.
53 Tax, 'Los indios en la economía de Guatemala,' *op. cit.*, p. 125.
54 *Ibid.*, p. 126. Manning Nash's study of industrialization in Cantel, Guatemala (*Machine Age Maya*, American Anthropological Association Memoir 87, 1958) made this point forcefully.
55 For a functionalist picture of relations among Indians and mestizos, see Robert Redfield, 'Primitive merchants of Guatemala,' *Quarterly Journal of Inter-American Relations*, vol. 1, no. 4, 1939, pp. 42-56; and Sol Tax, 'World view and social relations in Guatemala,' *American Anthropologist*, vo. 43, 1941.
56 See discussion of the work of Leach and Gluckman in Adam Kuper, *Antropologia y antropólogos: La escuela británica, 1922-1972*, Barcelona: Editorial Anagrama, 1973, chapter VI.
57 George Collier, *Fields of the Tzotzil: The Ecological Bases of Tradition in Highland Chiapas*, Austin: University of Texas Press, 1975, p. 212. Collier utilized the concept of 'ecology' not in the way Harvard or Chicago functionalists were accustomed to understand it (as local physical niches), but as a synonym for the entire physical and social environment impinging upon a community. That environment included patterns of regional domination.
58 *Ibid.*, p. 190.
59 Benjamin Colby and Pierre van den Berghe, 'Ethnic relations in Southeastern Mexico,' *American Anthropologist*, vol. 63, 1961, pp. 772-92; and Pierre van den Berghe, *South Africa: A Study in Conflict*, Middletown: Wesleyan University Press, 1965.
60 Benjamin Colby and Pierre van den Berghe, *Ixil Country: A Plural Society in Highland Guatemala*, Berkeley: University of California Press, 1969, p. 4.
61 *Ibid.*, pp. 20, 184.
62 Fredrick Barth (ed.), *Ethnic Groups and Boundaries: The Social Organiza-*

tion of Culture Difference, Oslo: Universitetsforlaget, 1970.
63 Henning Siverts, 'Estabilidad étnica y dinámica de límites en el sur de México,' in Barth, *Ethnic Groups and Boundaries, op. cit.*, pp. 131-51; and Henning Siverts, *Oxchuc: Una comunidad maya en México*, Mexico City: Instituto Nacional Indigenista, 1969.
64 Barth, *Ethnic Groups and Boundaries, op. cit.*, p. 41.
65 Julian Pitt-Rivers, 'Los ladinos,' in McQuown and Pitt-Rivers, *Ensayos de antropología* . . . , *op. cit.*, and Julian Pitt-Rivers, 'Race in Latin America,' *Archives of European Sociology*, vol. 19, 1973, pp. 3-31.

3 Cultural ecology, Marxism, and the development of a theory of the peasantry, 1950-70

1 This he justified by noting that 'communities are, with better communications, increasingly merging into regions, and regions into a world picture.' See Julian Steward, 'Acculturation studies in Latin America: some needs and problems,' *American Anthropologist*, vol. 45, no. 2, 1943, pp. 198-204, p. 201.
2 Julian Steward, 'Levels of sociocultural integration: an operational concept,' reprinted as Chapter 3 in Steward, *Theory of Culture Change*, Urbana: University of Illinois Press, 1963, pp. 43-63, p. 44.
3 Territorially based subgroups, such as the community, were called 'vertical,' and occupational or status groups, crosscutting geographical boundaries, were called 'horizontal.' Redfield characterized Steward's conception as a kind of lattice, with horizontal and vertical groups forming the framework, through which suprapersonal institutions wound like a vine. See Robert Redfield, *The Little Community and Peasant Society and Culture*, Chicago: University of Chicago Press, 1965, p. 25.
4 Steward, *Theory of Culture Change, op. cit.*, p. 47.
5 *Ibid.*, p. 51.
6 See Julian Steward, 'Culture area and cultural type in aboriginal America: methodological considerations,' first presented as a paper to the 1952 meeting of the American Anthropological Association and reprinted in Steward, *Theory of Culture Change, op. cit.*, pp. 78-97, p. 87.
7 'Classes are sociocultural groups, or segments arranged in an hierarchical order. But the hierarchy functions principally in the locality. It does not always follow that segments having the same relative status in different localities will be equivalent if the local or regional subcultures are unlike.' (Steward, *Theory of Culture Change, op. cit.*, p. 67.)
8 See Eric Wolf, *The Mexican Bajio in the Eighteenth Century*, Baton Rouge: Middle American Research Institute of Tulane University, Publication no. 18, 1955; and Eric Wolf, *Sons of the Shaking Earth*, Chicago: University of Chicago Press, 1959.
9 Wolf, *Sons of the Shaking Earth, op. cit.*, p. 203.
10 *Ibid.*, p. 214.
11 *Ibid.*, p. 218.
12 Eric Wolf, 'Types of Latin American peasantry: a preliminary discussion,' *American Anthropologist*, vol. 57, 1955, pp. 452-71; and Eric Wolf, 'Closed corporate peasant communities in Mesoamerica and central Java,' *Southwestern Journal of Anthropology*, vol. 13, 1957, pp. 1-18.
13 Frank Tannenbaum's classic work on *The Mexican Agrarian Revolution*, published in 1930 by the Brookings Institution, is a case in point. Tannen-

Notes to pages 76-80

baum taught at Columbia for almost half a century.
14 Wolf, *Sons of the Shaking Earth, op. cit.*, p. 230.
15 Wolf, 'Types of Latin American peasantry,' *op. cit.*, p. 457. The congruence of this observation with later elaboration of the concept of 'refuge region' by Aguirre Beltrán, already disccussed in Chapter 2, is noteworthy.
16 Eric Wolf, 'Levels of communal relations,' in Robert Wauchope and Manning Nash (eds), *Handbook of Middle American Indians*, vol. 6, Austin: University of Texas Press, 1967, pp. 299-316, p.299.
17 *Ibid.*, pp. 313-16.
18 The 'open' community was by definition non-Indian, since it had lost the principal structural requisites of Indianness. See Wolf, *Sons of the Shaking Earth, op. cit.*, p. 287.
19 Robert Rhodes (*Conflict, Solidarity and Social Change in Mesoamerican Peasant Communities: An Exploratory Analysis*, PhD thesis, Princeton University, 1972) has compared the two models and pointed out their similarities. See the summary table, p. 19.
20 'As in the corporate peasant community, land tends to be marginal and technology primitive. Yet functionally both land and technology are elements in a different complex of relationships. The buyers of peasant produce have an interest in the continued 'backwardness' of the peasant. Reorganization of his productive apparatus would absorb capital and credit which can be spent better in expanding the market by buying means of transportation, engaging middlemen, etc. Moreover, by keeping the productive apparatus unchanged, the buyer can reduce the risk of having his capital tied up in the means of production . . . , if and when the bottom drops out of the market. The buyers of peasant produce thus trade increased productivity per man-hour for the lessened risks of investment.' 'Types of Latin American peasantry,' *op. cit.*, p. 464.
21 *Ibid.*, p. 468.
22 Redfield, 'Peasant society and culture,' *op. cit.*, p. 25.
23 *Ibid.*, p. 24.
24 Julian Steward, 'Levels of sociocultural integration,' in *Theory of Culture Change, op. cit.*, p. 52.
25 'The diagnostic criteria pertaining to folk culture and folk society are structural, and have to do with relationships. Content is a useful but nonetheless incidental criterion in defining folk.' Foster, 'What is folk culture?', *American Anthropologist*, vol. 55, 1953, pp. 159-72, p. 171.
26 Wolf, 'Types of Latin American peasantry,' *op. cit.*, p. 469.
27 Redfield, Peasant society and culture,' *op. cit.*, p. 20. Redfield said (on p. 17 of the same work) that 'the possibility of clarifying the typical characteristics of peasantry [had first] occurred to [him] when Horace Miner published his account of a French-Canadian parish' in 1939. Nevertheless, he acknowledged his debt to Wolf for the definition he eventually adopted in 1955.
28 In 'Peasant society and culture,' Redfield defines a peasant community as 'a dependent community,' p. 3.
29 The most complete statement of this position is to be found in Eric Wolf, *Peasants*, Englewood Cliffs: Prentice Hall, 1966, pp. 9-11. For an earlier formulation, see Eric Wolf, 'Aspects of group relations . . . ,' in Dwight Heath (ed.), *Contemporary Cultures and Societies of Latin America*, 2nd edn, New York: Random House, 1974, p. 70.
30 Alvin W. Gouldner, *For Sociology: Renewal and Critique in Sociology Today*, Harmondsworth: Penguin Books, 1975, p. 236.

31 Redfield, 'Peasant society and culture,' *op. cit.*, pp. 38-9.
32 Foster discusses the 'dubious creativity of the peasantry' in his article entitled 'What is a peasant,' Jack Potter, May Díaz and George Foster (eds), *Peasant Society: A Reader*, Boston: Little, Brown, 1967, pp. 2-14.
33 Wolf, *Peasants, op. cit.*, p. 11.
34 Wolf, *Peasants, op. cit.*
35 Gordon Childe, *What Happened in History*, Harmondsworth: Penguin, 1964, p. 30. First published in 1942.
36 Angel Palerm, 'Ensayo de critica al desarrollo regional en Mexico,' in David Barkin (ed.), *Los beneficiarios del desarrollo regional*, Mexico: SEP Setentas, 1972, p. 21.
37 Wolf, *Peasants, op. cit.*, pp. 3-4.
38 See Harry Pearson, 'The economy has no surplus: a critique of a theory of development,' in Karl Polanyi, Conrad M. Arensberg and Harry W. Pearson (eds), *Trade and Market in Early Empires*, Glencoe: The Free Press, 1957.
39 Marvin Harris, 'The economy has no surplus?', *American Anthropologist*, vol. 61, no. 2, 1959, pp. 185-9.
40 See particularly Eric Wolf and Sidney Mintz, 'Haciendas y plantaciones en Mesoamerica y las Antillas,' in Enrique Florescano (ed.), *Haciendas, plantaciones y latifundios en América Latina*, Mexico: Siglo XXI, 1975, pp. 493-531. First written in 1957 and published in *Social and Economic Studies* (University of the West Indies), vol. 6.
41 See Gonzalo Aguirre Beltrán, 'Angel Palerm Vich,' *América Indígena*, vol. 41, no. 1, enero-marzo, 1981, pp. 151-62.
42 An excellent discussion of the asiatic mode of production can be found in Maurice Godelier, 'El pensamiento de Marx y Engels sobre las sociedades primitivas: Intento de balance crítico,' in *Economía, fetichismo y religión en las sociedades primitivas*, Mexico: Siglo XXI, 1978. For the history of Palerm's interest in the concept, see Angel Palerm, *Agricultura y sociedad en Mesoamérica*, Mexico: SEP Setentas, 1972.
43 See Angel Palerm, 'The agricultural basis of urban civilization in Mesoamerica,' in Julian Steward (ed.), *Irrigation Civilizations*, Washington: Pan American Union, 1955; and Eric Wolf and Angel Palerm, 'Irrigation in the old Acolhua Domain,' *Southwestern Journal of Anthropology*, vol. 11, no. 3, 1955, pp. 265-81.
44 George Foster, *A Primitive Mexican Economy*, New York: American Ethnological Society, vol. V, 1942.
45 Sol Tax, *Penny Capitalism: A Guatemalan Indian Economy*, Washington: Smithsonian Institute of Social Anthropology, Publication no. 16, 1953.
46 Most particularly J.H. Boeke, *Economics and Economical Policy of Dual Societies*, New York: Institute of Pacific Relations, 1953.
47 Sahlins's classic discussion of the domestic mode of production is to be found in Marshall Sahlins, *Stone Age Economics*, Chicago: Aldine, 1972.
48 The phrase is Sahlins's. *Ibid.*, p. 82.
49 Wolf, *Peasants, op. cit.*, pp. 14-15.
50 This was a direct reference to Marx's distinction between systems of exchange for use (typified by the formula C-M-C, or commodities exchanged for money in order to buy more commodities) and for profit (M-C-M, or money given for commodities destined to make more money). In Wolf's words, 'a considerable share of the peasant's replacement fund may become somebody else's fund of profit.' *Ibid.*, p. 9.
51 Clifford Geertz, *Agricultural Involution: The Processes of Ecological Change in Indonesia*, Berkeley: University of California Press, 1963; and

Angel Palerm, *Sobre la fórmula M-D-M y la articulación del modo campesino de producción al sistema capitalista dominante*, Mexico City: Centro de Estudios Superiores del INAH, Cuadernos de la Casa Chata, no. 5, 1977.

52 Thus, for example, Wolf noted that

although the form of domain as such is relevant to the way a peasant ecosystem is organized, providing the pattern for social relations, it is the way the pattern is utilized by the powerholders which is decisive in shaping the profile of the total system.' *Peasants, op. cit.*, p. 56.

53 Raymond Firth, *Elements of Social Organization*, Boston: Beacon Press, 1963, p. ix. First edition, 1951.
54 Eric Wolf, 'Kindship, friendship, and patron-client relations in complex societies,' in Michael Banton (ed.), *The Social Anthropology of Complex Societies*, Edinburgh: Tavistock, 1966. Product of a conference held in 1963.
55 J.A. Barnes, 'Class and committees in a Norwegian parish island,' *Human Relations*, vol. 7, 1954, pp. 39-58.
56 See Wolf, *Peasants, op. cit.*, pp. 77-81.
57 The term is Michael Kenney's.
58 Sydney Mintz and Eric Wolf, 'An analysis of ritual co-parenthood,' in Jack Potter, George Foster, and May N. Diaz (ed), *Peasant Society: A Reader*, Boston: Little Brown, 1967, p. 190. The article was first published in 1950.
59 Wolf, 'Aspects of group relations . . . ,' *op. cit.*, pp. 78-9.
60 *Ibid.*, p. 79. It is interesting to compare this definition of the broker with the somewhat similar concept of the 'hinge,' proposed by Redfield during the mid-1950s. Upon reading Barnes, Redfield also began to think in terms of a 'nation-wide network' of relations binding members of peasant communities to the wider society; and he also suggested the need to characterize the kinds of people who serve as links between local and national levels. There is, however, no suggestion in his treatment of the problem that the maintenance of conflict is a condition for the functioning of the 'hinge.' (See Redfield, 'Peasant Society and Culture', *op. cit.*, p. 27 *passim*.) Wolf's broker is a kind of entrepreneur in the field of conflict management. Redfield's is a selfless administrator, teacher or priest.
61 Hamza Alavi, 'Peasant classes and primordial loyalties,' *Journal of Peasant Studies*, vol. I, no. 1, October, 1973, p. 42.
62 George Foster, 'The dyadic contract: a model for the social structure of a Mexican peasant village,' in Potter, Foster, and Díaz (eds), *op. cit.*, p. 215.
63 See Eric Wolf, *Peasant Wars of the Twentieth Century*, New York: Harper & Row, 1969.
64 They have done so, however, in the 1970s. See Eric Wolf, 'Encounter with Norbert Elias,' in *Human Figurations: Essays for Norbert Elias, Amsterdams Sociologisch Tijdschrift*, 1977, pp. 28-35; and Angel Palerm, *Sobre la formula M-D-M . . . , op. cit.*
65 For an example of Palerm's critique of dogmatism in Marx, see Angel Palerm, *Agricultura y sociedad en Mesoamérica, op. cit.*, as well as his 'Antropología y marxismo en crisis,' *Nueva Antropología*, vol. 3, no. 11, 1979, pp. 41-60.
66 A discussion of the evolutionary/ecological approach to the concept of culture can be found in Roger Keesing, 'Theories of culture,' in Bernard Siegal *et al.* (eds), *Annual Review of Anthropology*, vol. 3, 1974, (Palo Alto: Annual Reviews, Inc.), pp. 73-97.

67 Eric Wolf, *Peasant Wars of the Twentieth Century, op. cit.*, pp. 276-9.
68 Karl Polanyi noted in *The Great Transformation*, New York: Rinehart, 1944, p. 157, that 'not economic exploitation [in itself] ... but the disintegration of the cultural environment of the victim is then the cause of degradation.' See also Wolf, *Peasant Wars of the Twentieth Century, op. cit.*, p. 279.
69 Wolf, *Peasant Wars of the Twentieth Century, op. cit.*, p. 280.
70 *Ibid.*, p. xv.
71 'The peasant's role is thus essentially tragic: his efforts to undo a grievous present only usher in a vaster, more uncertain future.' *Ibid.*, p. 301.
72 Among recent discussions of the incorporative process which draw upon Wolf's insights, Joel Migdal's, *Peasants, Politics, and Revolution: Pressures toward Political and Social Change in the Third World*, Princeton: Princeton University Press, 1974, would seem to be particularly perceptive. Two excellent doctoral theses written by Americans during the 1950s and 1960s, which were based upon Mexican materials and broadly informed by the paradigm of cultural ecology, are John Kunkel, *Nation and Peasant Communities in Mexico*, University of Michigan, 1959; and Janet Moone, *Desarrollo Tarasco*, Mexico City: Instituto Interamericano and Janet Moone, *Desarrollo Tarasco*, Mexico City: Instituto Interamericano Indigenista, special edition no. 67, 1973 (field work in 1967). Kunkel's advisors included Marshall Sahlins and Elman Service.
73 Angel Palerm, 'La disputa de los antropólogos mexicanos,' *América Indígena*, vol. 35, 1975, p. 168.
74 A number of cultural ecologists and Marxists grouped themselves around the figure of Paul Kirchhoff, a German archeologist and teacher at the National School of Anthropology whose international standing not only permitted him constant access to new materials, but also provided defense for an interest in historical materialism. For a discussion of Kirchhoff's work, see Barbro Dahlgren (ed.), *Mesoamérica: Homenaje al Doctor Paul Kirchhoff*, Mexico City: SEP-INAH, 1979.
75 Palerm, 'La antropología aplicada y el desarrollo de la comunidad,' *Anuario Indigenista*, vol. 29, 1969, p. 158.
76 *Ibid.*, p. 157.

4 Anthropology and the dependency paradigm in Mexico, 1960-75

1 V.I. Lenin, *Selected Works*, Moscow: Progress Publishers, 1967, vol. I, pp. 742-3; cited by Ronald Chilcote, 'Dependency: a critical synthesis of the literature,' *Latin American Perspectives*, vol. I, no. 1, Spring, 1974, p. 8. For a discussion of the relation between theories of imperialism and dependency, see Suzanne Bodenheimer, 'Dependency and imperialism,' *NACLA* Newsletter, vol. IV, May-June, 1970, pp. 18-27.
2 See Theotonio dos Santos, 'The crisis of development theory and the problem of dependence in Latin America,' in Harry Bernstein (ed.), *Underdevelopment and Development: The Third World Today*, Harmondsworth: Penguin Books, 1973, pp. 72-3; and Pablo González Casanova, *La democracia en México*, Mexico City: Editorial Era, 3rd edition, 1969, p. 19.
3 Hobson's book, *Imperialism*, was published in 1902. The first Marxist treatment was Rudolf Hilferding's in 1910. See Angel Palerm, *Modos de Producción y formaciones socioeconómicas*, Mexico City: Editorial Edicol, 1976, p. 77.

4   An excellent new treatment of the development of economic theory in ECLA is Octavio Rodríguez, *La teoría del subdesarrollo de la CEPAL*, Mexico City: Siglo XXI, 1980. See also José Serra and Fernando Cardoso, 'Las desventuras de la dialéctica de la dependencia,' *Revista Mexicana de Sociología*, vol. 40, special edition, 1978, pp. 9-55.
5   Paul Baran and Paul Sweezy, *Monopoly Capital*, New York: Monthly Review Press, 1966; and Paul Baran, *The Political Economy of Growth*, New York: Monthly Review Press, 1957.
6   André Gunder Frank in fact noted that his interest in historical research on underdevelopment in Latin America was first stimulated through reading Baran and Sweezy. André Gunder Frank, *Capitalism and Underdevelopment in Latin America*, New York: Modern Reader, third edition, 1967, Introduction.
7   Celso Furtado, *El mito del desarrollo*, Mexico City: Siglo XXI, 1975; *Obstacles to Development in Latin America*, New York: Doubleday & Company, 1970; *Desarrollo y subdesarrollo*, Buenos Aires, EUDEBA, 1964 (first published in Portuguese in 1961.)
8   Fernando Henrique Cardoso and Enzo Faletto, *Dependencia y desarrollo en América Latina*, Mexico City: Siglo XXI, sixth edition, 1972, pp. 23-4. First edition, ILPES, 1967.
9   Aníbal Quijano, *Dependencia, cambio social y urbanización en Latinoamérica*, Santiago de Chile: ECLA, 1967, p. 5.
10 Georges Balandier, *Sociologie Actuelle de l'Afrique Noire*, Paris: Presses Universitaires de France, 1963, chapter I.
11 Georges Balandier, 'La sociologia de la dependencia,' in Balandier, *Teoría de la descolonización*, Buenos Aires: Editorial Tiempo Contemporaneo, 1973, pp. 15-32. The essay was first published in 1952 in *Cahiers Internationaux de Sociologie*, vol. 12.
12 This is not to say that Balandier was in agreement with Lévi-Strauss on most elements of anthropological research.
13 Georges Balandier, 'La problemática de las clases sociales en formación,' in *Teoría de la descolonización*, *op. cit.*, p. 102. The article was first published in 1965.
14 Cardoso and Faletto, *op. cit.*, p. 30.
15 For one of the earliest and best statements by a Latin American sociologist of the reasons why class action in dependent countries could not be pressed into molds provided by Marxist analysis of stratification in an earlier European context, see Rodolfo Stavenhagen, 'Siete tesis equivocadas sobre América Latina,' *El Día*, 25 and 26 June, 1965. Reprinted in Stavenhagen, *Sociología y subdesarrollo*, Mexico City: Editorial Nuestro Tiempo, 1972, pp. 15-38.
16 A particular form of alliance to which the dependency paradigm paid much attention was populism. For a good discussion of the various ways in which populism was approached, see Aldo Solari *et al.*, *Teoría, acción social y desarrollo en América Latina*, Mexico City: Siglo XXI, 1976, chapter 12. The book is a text elaborated by the staff of ILPES, and therefore provides an insider's view of the formation of dependency theory in Latin America.
17 André Gunder Frank, *Capitalism and Underdevelopment in Latin America*, New York and London: Modern Reader, 1967, third edition, p. 7.
18 Credit for first use of the term is generally given to Maurice Dobb, in his discussion of *Political Economy and Capitalism*, published in 1937 by George Routledge of London. C. Wright Mills also characterized 'the developed sections in the interior of the underdeveloped world – the

capital and the coast — [as] a curious kind of imperialistic power which has, in its own way, internal colonies' in 1957, at a seminar organized by the Latin American Faculty of Social Sciences. See Solari *et al.*, *Teoría, acción social y desarrollo*, *op. cit.*, p. 410.

19   Pablo González Casanova, 'Sociedad plural, colonialismo interno y desarrolo,' *América Latina*, vol. 6, no. 3, July-September, 1963. The article was presented again in slightly modified form in *La democracia en México*, *op. cit.*

20   André Gunder Frank, 'La democracia en México de Pablo Gónzalez Casanova,' in *Economia politica del subdesarrollo en América Latina*, Buenos Aires: Ediciones Signos, 1970, pp. 215-30.

21   Gunder Frank, *Capitalism and Underdvelopment*..., *op. cit.*, pp. 19-20.

22   'Beyond the more obvious expropriation of producers by owners of capital, we may also distinguish another type of appropriation of capital and surplus by one or a few capitalists from the many ... In the peripheries of the world capitalist system, the essential nature of the metropolis-satellite relation remains commercial.' *Ibid.*

23   Frank's notes were published in 1975 by the Publications Committee of the Students Association of the National School of Anthropology with the title *La agricultura mexicana: Transformación del modo de producción, 1521-1630*. Studies of the history of capitalism in Mexico under way by the late 1960s included Enrique Florescano, *Origen y desarrollo de los problemas agrarios de México, 1500-1821*, Mexico City: Editorial Era, 1976 (first edition 1971); Enrique Semo, *Historia del capitalismo en México: Los orígenes*, Mexico City: Editorial Era, 1973; and Sergio de la Peña, *La formación del capitalismo en México*, Mexico City: Siglo XXI, 1975.

24   Pablo González Casanova, *La sociología de la explotación*, Mexico City: Siglo XXI, 1969, p. 132.

25   This paraphrases the first chapter of *La democracia en Mexico, op. cit.*, first published in 1965.

26   See Pablo González Casanova, 'Sociedad plural y desarrollo: el caso de México,' *América Latina*, vol. 5, no. 4, October-December, 1962, pp. 31-52.

27   Nathan Whetten, *Rural Mexico*, Chicago: University of Chicago Press, 1948.

28   *La democracia en Mexico*, *op. cit.*, p. 92.

29   González Casanova, *La sociologia de la explotación*, *op. cit.*, p. 213.

30   See Aníbal Quijano, 'Redefinición de la dependencia y proceso de marginalización en América Latina,' in F. Weffort and A. Quijano, *Populismo, marginalización y dependencia*, Centroamerica: EDUCA, 1973; and José Nun, 'Superproblación relativa, ejército industrial de reserva y masa marginal,' *Revista Latinoamericana de Sociología*, vol. 5, no. 2, 1969, pp. 178-237. Rodolfo Stavenhagen noted that

> in fact what has come to be called the 'marginal mass' exhibits characteristics of the subproletarian condition. Some would be tempted to identify this population with the classical lumpenproletariat of Marxist literature, but the comparison is not valid because it involves totally different socioeconomic structures ... It is a population integrated into a certain economic system and a certain power structure, but integrated at the lowest levels and suffering the most acute forms of domination and exploitation. ('El futuro de América Latina: entre el subdesarrollo y la revolución,' in Stavenhagen, *Sociología y subdesarrollo*, Editorial Nuestro Tiempo, 1972, pp. 53-4.)

31 Gino Germani, *El concepto de marginalidad*, Buenos Aires: Nueva Visión, 1973, p. 66.
32 *Ibid.*, p. 19.
33 See Pablo González Casanova, 'Sociedad plural, colonialismo interno y desarrollo,' *op. cit.*
34 Rodolfo Stavenhagen has insisted less upon the necessary component of ethnic domination within internal colonialism than González Casanova. Nevertheless he has pointed out that while 'internal colonialism is not a structural relation [found] exclusively in Indian areas, . . . it is in those areas that it appears in its sharpest form.' 'La sociedad plural en América Latina,' *Diálogos* (El Colegio de México), no. 55, January-February, 1974, p. 8.
35 Rodolfo Stavenhagen, *Las clases sociales en las sociedades agrarias*, Mexico City: Siglo XXI, 1969, p. 205. The thesis was completed in the early 1960s.
36 Stavenhagen made this point for peasant communities in general, whether Indian or non-Indian, in 'Changing functions of the community in underdeveloped countries,' *Sociologia Ruralis*, vol. IV, nos. 3/4, 1964, pp. 315-31.
37 Stavenhagen, 'La sociedad plural en América Latina,' *op. cit.*, p. 10.
38 Ricardo Pozas, *Chamula*, Mexico City: Instituto Nacional Indigenista, second edition, 1979, vol. I, p. 216.
39 Guillermo Bonfil, 'El concepto de indio en Amércia: una categoría de la situación colonial,' *Anales de Antropología*, 1972, pp. 110, 115 and 123.
40 For Stavenhagen's challenge to Aguirre Beltrán on this point, see 'Castas, clases y proceso dominical,' in *Homenaje a Gonzalo Aguirre Beltrán*, Mexico City: Instituto Indigenista Interamericano and the University of Veracruz, 1973, vol. II, pp. 239-48.
41 See Arturo Warman, Margarita Nolasco, Guillermo Bonfil, Mercedes Olivera and Enrique Valencia, *De eso que llaman la antropología mexicana*, Mexico City: Nuestro Tiempo, 1970.
42 See Lourdes Arizpe, 'El surgimiento de la conciencia indígena,' part III of *El reto del pluralismo cultural*, Mexico City: Instituto Nacional Indigenista, 1979.
43 A collection of Rodolfo Stavenhagen's essays in the Mexico City newspapers *Excelsior* and *Uno Mas Uno* can be found in *Testimonios*, Mexico City: UNAM, 1978. Bonfil and Arturo Warman contributed frequently to the same newspapers.
44 An account of the work of the Department of Popular Culture and the program of training for Indian linguists will be found in Marina Anguiano, 'La etnología como factor de reforzamiento de la identidad étnica,' *América Indígena*, vol. 39, no. 3, July-September 1979, pp. 573-86.
45 Rodolfo Stavenhagen, '¿Cómo descolonizar las ciencias sociales?', in *Sociología y subdesarrollo*, *op. cit.*, p. 219. These ideas were first presented in a talk to the Society for Applied Anthropology in 1971. See also Guillermo Bonfil, 'Del indigenismo de la revolución a la antropología crítica,' in *De eso que llaman la antropología mexicana*, *op. cit.*, pp. 39-65.
46 Stavenhagen, '¿Cómo descolonizar las ciencias sociales?', *op. cit.*, p. 210.
47 See particularly Guillermo Bonfil, '¿Es aplicable la antropología "aplicada"? Un ensayo de crítica antropológica,' *América Latina*, vol. 6, no. 1, January-March, 1963, pp. 29-52.
48 Guillermo Bonfil, *Cholula: La ciudad sagrada en la era industrial*, Mexico City: UNAM, 1973.
49 Anthropologists who did write on agrarian problems before 1960 include

Miguel Othón de Mendizábal, who worked particularly on La Laguna and the Mezquital Valley during the 1940s (*Obras completas de Miguel Othón de Mendizábal*, Mexico City: Talleres Gráficos de la Nación, 1946); Raymond Wilkie, who studied the ejido of San Miguel in La Laguna during 1953 and again between 1966 and 1967 (*San Miguel: A Mexican Collective Ejido*, Palo Alto: Stanford University Press, 1971); and Paul Friedrich, who did field work in Naranjo, Michoacán, during 1955-6 for his *Agrarian Revolt in a Mexican Village* (Englewood Cliffs: Prentice Hall, 1970).

50 These might be divided into several groups. First, there was a small group of American historians, rural sociologists, and political scientists, often attached to Mexican government ministries during the decades immediately following the revolution, who combined a valuable macrosociological, political and historical discussion of the agrarian reform with case studies of local land tenure developments. (Frank Tannenbaum, *The Mexican Agrarian Revolution*, New York: Macmillan, 1929; Eyler Simpson, *The Ejido: Mexico's Way Out*, Chapel Hill: University of North Carolina Press, 1937; Nathan Whetten, *Rural Mexico*, Chicago: University of Chicago Press, 1948; Clarence Senior, *Land Reform and Democracy*, Gainesville: University of Florida Press, 1954). Then there were a number of excellent appraisals of the social and political implications of agrarian reform at the regional or national level by men intimately involved in carrying out official programs. (Marco Antonio Durán, *Del agrarismo a la revolución agrícola*, Mexico City: Talleres Gráficos de la Nacion, 1947; Manuel Mesa Andraca, 'La situación henequenera en Yucatán,' *Problemas Agrícolas e Industriales de México*, vol. 7, no. 2, April-June, 1955; Liga de Agrónomos Socialistas, *El colectivismo agrario en México: La Comarca Lagunera*, Mexico City: 1940; Emilio Lopez Zamora, articles collected in *El Agua, la tierra*, Mexico City: Fondo de Cultura Económica, 1977, and written from the 1940s onward.) Finally, there were a very large number of studies carried out by historians and agricultural economists, the first tending to concentrate on the minutiae of political contests at the regional or national level and the second on problems of land use and credit. (See particularly Jesús Silva Hérzog, *El agrarismo mexicano y la reforma agraria*, Mexico City: Fondo de Cultura Económica, 1959; and Ramón Fernández y Fernández, *Propiedad privada vs. ejidos*, Chapingo: Escuela Nacional de Agricultura, 1953.)

51 Margaret de Forest Woodbridge found that one-third of the sixty-six community studies she surveyed made no mention at all of land reform or the existence of ejidos. See *Fifty Years of Mexican Community Studies: Perspectives on Land Reform*, master's thesis, University of California at Los Angeles, 1973.

52 Mendieta y Núñez wrote *El problema agrario en México*, published by Porrúa of Mexico City in 1943, and running to nine editions by 1966.

53 For a description of the original plan to conduct a comparative study of ejidos, see Fausto Galván Campos, 'El estudio comparativo del ejido,' *Revista Mexicana de Sociología*, vol. I, no. 2, 1939, pp. 95-110. The outstanding ethnographer of the Institute was Francisco Rojas González, whose work is reviewed by Mendieta y Núñez in the same journal, vol. 24, no. 1, 1963.

54 Mendieta y Nuñez, *Efectos sociales de la reforma agraria en tres comunidades ejidales de la República Mexicana*. Mexico City: UNAM, 1960.

55 On the first congress, see T. Lynn Smith, 'El desarollo de la sociología rural en Latinoamérica,' *Revista Mexicana de Sociología*, vol. 19, nos. 1, 2, 3,

Notes to pages 122-8   211

   1957. The second produced a book of useful essays entitled *Estudios sociológicos sobre la reforma agraria*, Mexico City: UNAM, 1965.
56 For a discussion of various forms of peasant organization and protest against the prevailing modalities of Mexican agrarian reform, see Gerrit Huizer, *La lucha campesina en México*, Mexico City: Centro de Investigaciones Agrarias, 1970.
57 Among early professional theses on mestizo agrarian reform communities were Guillermo Bonfil, *Diagnóstico del hambre en Sudzal, Yucatán*; and Margarita Nolasco, *La tenencia de la tierra en San Juan Teotihuacan*. Both were presented in 1961.
58 For an idea of the position of the directors of the ICAD study at the international level see the articles by Solon Barraclough, Thomas Carroll, Rafael Baraona, Ernest Feder and Marvin Sternberg in Oscar Delgado (ed.), *Reformas agrarias en la América Latina*, Mexico City: Fondo de Cultura Económica, 1965.
59 Andrew Pearse discussed the categories in an article published in *América Latina*, vol. 6, no. 3, 1963, pp. 77-84.
60 A summary of the ICAD findings will be found in Solon Barraclough and Arthur Domike, 'Agrarian structure in seven Latin American countries,' in Rodolfo Stavenhagen (ed.), *Agrarian Problems and Peasant Movements in Latin America*, Garden City, New York: Doubleday, 1970, pp. 41-96.
61 The Commission on Economic History of the Latin American Council on the Social Sciences (CLACSO) published a compendium of such work in Enrique Florescano (ed.), *Haciendas, latifundios y plantaciones en América Latina*, Mexico City: Siglo XXI, 1975. The book includes Wolf and Mintz's classic article on 'Haciendas y plantaciones en Mesoamérica y las Antillas,' pp. 493-531.
62 Monographs and papers produced in the course of field work for the ICAD study in Mexico include the following: Sergio Alcántara Ferrer, *El proceso de cambio económico-social en Taretan, Michoacán*, master's thesis, National School of Anthropology, 1968; and by the same author, *La organización colectivista ejidal en la Comarca Lagunera*, manuscript, Centro de Investigaciones Agrarias, 1967; Silvia Gómez Tagle, *Organización de las sociedades de crédito ejidal en La Laguna*, master's thesis, National School of Anthropology, 1968; Susana Glantz, *El ejido colectivo en Nueva Italia*, Mexico City: SEP-INAH, 1974; Sergio Maturana and Iván Restrepo, *El azúcar: Problema de México (Un estudio regional en Michoacán)*, Mexico City: Centro de Investigaciones Agrarias, 1970; Sergio Maturana and Jose Sanchez, *Las Comunidades de la Meseta Tarasca*, Mexico City: Centro de Investigaciones Agrarias, 1970; Gerrit Huizer, *La lucha campesina en México*, op. cit.; René Barbosa and Sergio Maturana, *El arrendamiento de tierras ejidales*, Mexico City: Centro de Investigaciones Agrarias, 1972; Henry Landsberger and Cynthia Hewitt de Alcántara, *Peasant Organization in La Laguna, Mexico*, Washington, ICAD, 1970; Iván Restrepo and Salomón Eckstein, *La agricultura colectiva en México*, Mexico City: Siglo XXI, 1975.
63 Centro de Investigaciones Agrarias, *Estructura agraria y desarrollo agrícola en México*, Mexico City: Fondo de Cultura Económica, 1974. First mimeographed edition, 1970.
64 Stavenhagen, 'Social aspects of agrarian structure in Mexico,' in *Agrarian Problems and Peasant Movements in Latin America*, op. cit., p. 261.
65 Centro de Investigaciones Agrarias, op. cit., p. xvi.
66 See particularly Rodolfo Stavenhagen, 'Un modelo para el estudio de las

organizaciones políticas en México,' *Revista Mexicana de Sociología*, vol. 29, no. 2, April-June, 1967, pp. 329-36. Among the studies of agrarian politics, not directly associated with the ICAD project, which Stavenhagen encouraged were Raymond Buve, *Boeren-mobilisatie en landhervorming tijdens en na de Mexicaanse revolutie: de Vallei van Nativitas, Tlaxcala, tussen 1910 en 1940*, Amsterdam: CEDLA Incidentele Publicatie Nummer 9, 1977; Frans Schryer, *The Rancheros of Pisaflores*, Toronto: Toronto University Press, 1980; David Ronfeldt, *Atencingo: The Politics of Agrarian Struggle in a Mexican Ejido*, Palo Alto: Stanford University Press, 1973; and Heather Fowler Salamini, *Agrarian Radicalism in Veracruz, 1920-1938*, Lincoln: University of Nebraska Press, 1978.

67 Examples of their work are Ruy Mauro Marini, *La dialéctica de la dependencia*, Mexico City: Editorial Era, 1973; Ernest Feder, 'La nueva penetración de la agricultura de los paises subdesarrollados por los paises industriales y sus empresas multinacionales,' *Trimestre Económico*, vol. 42, no. 169, 1976; and various articles in Ursula Oswald (ed.), *Mercado y dependencia*, Mexico City: Editorial Nueva Imagen, 1979.

68 This point of view is presented in Marc Nerfin (ed.), *Another Development: Approaches and Strategies*, Uppsala: Dag Hammarskjöld Foundation, 1977. For Mexico, the book contains articles by both Stavenhagen and Hewitt de Alcántara.

5 Historical structuralism and the fate of the peasantry, 1970-80

1 See Roger Bartra 'La tipología y la periodificación en el método arqueológico,' written in 1964 and included in Bartra, *Marxismo y sociedades antiguas*, Mexico City: Editorial Grijalbo, 1975; and 'Tributo y tenencia de la tierra en la sociedad azteca,' written in 1970 and included in the same volume.

2 Roger Bartra (ed.), *El modo de producción asiático*, Mexico City: Editorial Era, 1969.

3 Roger Bartra, 'Modos de producción,' in Bartra, *Breve diccionario de sociología marxista*, Mexico City: Grijalbo, 1973, pp. 105-7.

4 Artisans also formed part of the mode. Whether it was appropriate to speak of a 'peasant mode of production,' rather than simply of the peasantry within a 'simple mercantile mode of production,' was a source of some disagreement among Marxists of various persuasions. The most abstract and Althusserian among them were convinced of the utility of the former term (see Héctor Díaz Polanco, *Teoría marxista de la economía campesina*, Mexico City: Juan Pablos, 1977, p. 75); Bartra and his group tended to find it spurious (see Manuel Coello, 'El novísimo ciclo M-D-M transformado y el "modo campesino de producción",' *Antropología y Marxismo*, vol. 1, no. 2, 1979-80, pp. 19-36.

5 Roger Bartra, 'La teoría del valor y la economía campesina: Invitación a la lectura de Chayanov, *Comercio Exterior*, vol. 25, no. 5, May, 1975, p. 518.

6 Roger Bartra, *Estructura agraria y clases sociales en Mexico*, Mexico City: Editorial Era, 1974.

7 Rodolfo Stavenhagen had in fact given early attention to the class structure of the Mexican countryside. His scheme included four categories: the rural (commercial) bourgeoisie; medium and large landholders; minifundistas; and the agricultural proletariat. See Stavenhagen, *Las clases sociales en las sociedades agrarias, op. cit.*, pp. 265 ff.

8 See Mario Margulis, *Contradicciones en la estructura agraria y transferencias de valor*, Mexico City: El Colegio de Mexico, Jornadas 90, 1979, pp. 36-7; Roger Bartra, 'La teoría del valor...,' *op. cit.*, p. 520.
9 Roger Bartra, *El poder despótico burgués*, Mexico City: Editorial Era, 1978, p. 51; and Roger Bartra, *Caciquismo y poder político en el México rural*, Mexico City: Siglo XXI, 1975, p. 24.
10 Roger Bartra, 'Y si los campesinos se extinguen: reflexiones sobre la coyuntura política de 1976 en México,' *Historia y Sociedad*, segunda época, no. 8, 1975, p. 77.
11 See Fernando Rello, 'Modo de producción y classes sociales,' *Cuadernos Políticos*, no. 8, 1976.
12 Bartra, *El poder despótico burgues*, *op. cit.*, pp. 70-1.
13 Sergio de la Peña, 'Acumulación originaria y el fin de los modos de producción no-capitalistas en América Latina,' *Historia y Sociedad*, segunda época, no. 5, Spring, 1975, p. 73.
14 The best statement of Wasserstrom's position will be found in *Class and Society in Central Chiapas*, Berkeley and Los Angeles: University of California Press, 1983. See also Robert Wasserstrom, 'Land and labour in central Chiapas: a regional analysis,' *Development and Change*, vol. 8, 1977, pp. 441-63. The debate between Wasserstrom and Bartra took place in the journal *Historia y Sociedad*, segunda época, nos. 9 and 10, 1976, under the heading of 'La Polémica.'
15 Margulis, *op. cit.*, p. 5.
16 Héctor Díaz Polanco, 'En torno al carácter social del campesino,' in Luisa Paré (ed.), *Polémica sobre las clases sociales en el campo mexicano*, Mexico City: Editorial Macehual, 1979, p. 76.
17 Kostas Vergopoulos, 'Capitalismo disforme: el caso de la agricultura en el capitalismo,' in S. Amin and K. Vergopoulos, *La cuestión campesina y el capitalismo*, Mexico City: Editorial Nuestro Tiempo, 1975, p. 215.
18 *Ibid.*, p. 220.
19 Roger Bartra, 'Modos de producción y estructura agraria subcapitalista en México,' *Historia y Sociedad*, segunda época, no. 1, 1974, pp. 23-30.
20 Armando Bartra, 'La renta capitalista de la tierra,' *Cuadernos Agrarios*, vol. 1, no. 2, April-June 1976, pp. 5-78.
21 Armando Bartra, *La explotación del trabajo campesino por el capital*, Mexico City: Editorial Macehual, 1979.
22 See Luisa Paré, *Los endrogados. Ensayo sobre la organización de una cooperativa agrícola en la región de la desembocadura del Rio Balsas*, master's thesis, ENAH, 1968; Luisa Paré, 'Tianguis y economía capitalista,' *Nueva Antropología*, vol. I, no. 2, 1975, pp. 85-93; and Luisa Paré *et al.*, *Ensayos sobre el problema cañero*, Mexico City: Instituto de Investigaciones Sociales, UNAM, 1979.
23 Luisa Paré, *El proletariado agrícola en México*, Mexico City: Siglo XXI, 1977, p. 51.
24 Armando Bartra, *La explotación del trabajo campesino...*, *op. cit.*, pp. 120-1.
25 *Ibid.*, p. 97.
26 *Ibid.*, p. 45.
27 See Armando Bartra, *Notas sobre la cuestión campesina (México 1970-1976)*, Mexico City: Editorial Macehual, 1979; and Gustavo Gordillo, 'Pasado y presente del movimiento campesina en México,' *Cuadernos Políticos*, no. 23, January-March 1980; Rosa Elena Montes de Oca, 'La cuestión agraria y el movimiento campesino: 1970-1976,' *Cuadernos*

	Políticos, no. 14, October-December 1977.
28	Armando Bartra, *La explotación del trabajo campesino* . . . , *op. cit.*, p. 26.
29	For the earliest attempt to draw the boundaries between campesinistas and descampesinistas, see Ernest Feder, 'Campesinistas y descampesinistas. Tres enfoques divergentes (y no incompatibles) sobre la destrucción del campesinado,' *Comercio Exterior*, vol. 27, no. 12, 1977; and vol. 28, no. 1, 1978, pp. 42-51.
30	Roger Bartra, 'Y si los campesinos se extinguen: reflexiones sobre la conyuntura política de 1976 en México,' *Historia y Sociedad*, segunda época, no. 8, 1975, pp. 79-80; and 'La teoría del valor y la economía campesina,' *op. cit.*, p. 524.
31	Gustavo Esteva, 'La economía campesina actual como opción de desarrollo,' *Investigacion Económica*, vol. 38, no. 147, January-March 1979, p. 237.
32	See especially Gustavo Esteva, '¿Y si los campesinos existen?', *Comercio Exterior*, vol. 28, no. 6, June 1978, pp. 699-713, as well as his more recent book *La batalla en el México rural*, Mexico City: Siglo XXI, 1980.
33	Arturo Warman, *Y venimos a contradecir*, Mexico City: Ediciones de la Casa Chata, 1976, pp. 334 and 336.
34	Arturo Warman, *Ensayos sobre el campesinado en México*, Mexico City: Nueva Imagen, 1980, p. 199.
35	*Ibid.*, p. 200.
36	Warman's *Los campesinos: Hijos predilectos del regimen*, published by Editorial Nuestro Tiempo in 1972, contains scathing denunciations of capital accumulation by bureaucrats at the expense of the peasantry.
37	*Ibid.*, p. 130.
38	One of the most frequent criticisms by orthodox Marxists of the dependentista research strategy was, in fact, that it 'obstructed class analysis.' See Agustín Cueva, 'Problemas y perspectivas de la teoría de la dependencia,' *Historia y Sociedad*, segunda época, no. 3, Fall 1974, p. 57.
39	Angel Palerm, 'Articulación campesinado-capitalismo: sobre la fórmula M-D-M,' in Palerm, *Antropología y marxismo*, Mexico City: Editorial Nueva Imagen, 1980, pp. 199-224.
40	Arturo Warman, 'El problema del proletariado agrícola,' in Paré (ed.), *Polémica sobre las clases sociales en el campo mexicano*, *op. cit.*, p. 86.
41	Arturo Warman, *Los campesinos: Hijos predilectos del régimen*, *op. cit.*, p. 129. Palerm made a similar point in 'Antropólogos y campesinos: los limites del capitalismo' (*Antropología y marxismo*, p. 187):

> [A]nthropologists consider the diversity of forms of life within the peasantry as potential reserves for the survival of the human race. No one can predict the crises which may arise, nor anticipate to what extent the historical and actual experiences of the peasants may contribute to confronting and solving them.

42	Arturo Warman, *Y venimos a contradecir*, *op. cit.*
43	*Ibid.*, p. 303.
44	*Ibid.*, p. 15.
45	'If the remuneration of peasant labor had been calculated in terms of the value of the product produced, it would have equalled less than one-half of the prevailing minimum wage.' *Ibid.*, p. 310. For a series of detailed discussions of the internal accounting of peasant production units in eastern Morelos, see the reports of members of Warman's team published in Alonso, Corcuera Garza and Melville, *Los campesinos de la tierra de*

	Zapata, vol. II, Mexico City: SEPINAH, 1974.
46	Arturo Warman, *Y venimos a contradecir, op. cit.*, p. 15.
47	*Ibid.*
48	See Oscar Lewis, 'Urbanization without breakdown: a case study,' *Scientific Monthly*, vol. 75, 1952, pp. 31-41; and Robert V. Kemper, *Migration and Adaptation: Tzintzuntzan Peasants in Mexico City*, Beverley Hills: Sage Publications, 1977; as well as Douglas Butterworth, 'A study of the urbanization process among Mixtec migrants from Tilantongo to Mexico City,' *América Indígena*, vol. 22, no. 3, 1966, pp. 257-74.
49	Arturo Warman, *Y venimos a contradecir, op cit.*
50	See particularly Mario Margulis, 'Reproducción social de la vida y reproducción del capital,' *Nueva Antropología*, vol. 4, nos. 13-14, May 1980, pp. 47-64; Marielle Martínez and Teresa Rendón, 'Fuerza de trabajo y reproducción campesina,' *Comercio Exterior*, vol. 28, no. 6, 1978, pp. 663-74; and Marielle Martínez, 'Comunidad y familia en la dinámica social campesina,' *Nueva Antropología, op. cit.*, pp. 243-59.
51	Lourdes Arizpe, *Parentesco y economía en una sociedad nahua*, Mexico City, SEP-INI, no. 22, 1973.
52	Lourdes Arizpe, *La migración por relevos y la reproducción social del campesinado*, Mexico City, El Colegio de México, Cuadernos del CES, no. 28, 1980, p. 38. The same argument can be found in English in Lourdes Arizpe, 'Relay migration and the survival of the peasant household,' in Jorge Balán (ed.), *Why People Move*, Paris: UNESCO, 1981.
53	*Ibid.*, p. 11.
54	Lourdes Arizpe, *Indígenas en la Ciudad de México: El caso de las 'Marías'*, Mexico City: SEP Setentas, 1975.
55	The nature of the small but rapidly growing body of literature on peasant women is still too heterogeneous to permit adequate characterization. For a representative selection of published material, the reader is referred to vol. 4, no. 9 (September 1979) of *Cuadernos Agrarios*, dedicated to 'la mujer campesina'; and to vol. 38, no. 4 (April-June, 1978) of *América Indígena* on the same topic.
56	Henri Favre, *Cambio y continuidad entre los mayas de México*, Mexico City: Siglo XXI, 1973, p. 370.
57	Judith Friedlander, *Being Indian in Hueyapan: A Study of Forced Identity in Contemporary Mexico*, New York: St Martins Press, 1975, p. 71.
58	A reconsideration of 'the ethnic question' will be found in vol. 3, no. 9 (October 1978) of *Nueva Antropología*.
59	Lourdes Arizpe, *Migración, etnicismo y cambio económico*, Mexico City: El Colegio de México, 1978, p. 238. Barbara Margolies also carried out field work in the Mazahua area on the question of why 'ethnicity obscured class relations,' and came to a similar analysis of 'institutionalized exclusion.' See Margolies, *Princes of the Earth: Subcultural Diversity in a Mexican Municipality*, Washington: AAA Special Publication no. 2, 1975.
60	Lourdes Arizpe, for example, was careful to point out that 'The key point [in her analysis] . . . [was] not to evaluate indigenous or Mazahua culture in themselves, but to look at the reason why there should be an ideology which ascribed to the latter inferiority.' *Migración, etnicismo y cambio económico, op. cit.*, p. 223.
61	An interesting discussion of this point will be found in Heleieth Saffioti, 'Women, mode of production, and social formations,' *Latin American Perspectives*, vol. 4, nos. 1-2, Winter-Spring 1977, p. 30.

62 See Angel Palerm, 'Antropólogos y campesinos: los límites del capitalismo,' in the collection of essays *Antropología y marxismo, op. cit.*, p. 186, for his statement on the 'superiority of culture, considered as an adaptive mechanism.'
63 Palerm, 'Articulación campesinado-capitalismo...,' *op. cit.*, p. 215.
64 Héctor Díaz Polanco, 'Comentario,' in *Mesa Redonda sobre Marxismo y Antropología*, special issue of *Nueva Antropología*, vol. 3, no. 11, August 1979, p. 34. The round table took place in July 1978.
65 Guillermo Bonfil, 'El objeto de estudio de la antropología,' in *ibid.*, p. 24.
66 Rodolfo Stavenhagen, 'Clase, etnia, y comunidad,' in Stavenhagen, *Problemas étnicos y campesinos: Ensayos*, Mexico City: INI, 1980, p. 16. The article was written in 1978.
67 In fact, by 1980 a number of anthropologists broadly associated with Marxism, and originally loath to consider 'superstructural' aspects of peasant life, had begun to conduct field work on problems of culture change. The re-establishment of a specialization in 'ethnology' in the National School of Anthropology, in 1978, as an alternative election to the more rigorously economic focus of its Marxist studies program, presaged such a change.

6 Conclusions

1 Theodore Abel, 'On the future of sociological theory,' *International Social Science Journal*, vol. 33, no. 2, 1981, p. 220.
2 The term is Bryan Roberts's. See his *Los campesinos en la ciudad*, Mexico City: Siglo XXI, 1980.

Index

Numbers in brackets after a page reference indicate notes.

Abel, Theodore, 189
Acheson, James, 195 (46)
acculturation, 22-7, 55-6
adaptive strategy, 165-9, 172
administrative domain, 83
agrarian problems, 8, 120-5
agricultural involution, 165-7
agriculture, *see* rural
Aguirre Beltrán, Gonzalo, 48-57, 63-9 *passim*, 75, 112, 116
Alcántara Ferrer, Sergio, 211 (62)
Alonso, Jorge, 214 (45)
Althusser, Louis, 133-4
Amin, Samir, 147-8
Anguiano, Marina, 209 (44)
anthropological perspectives on rural Mexico: cultural ecology and Marxism, 70-96; dependency paradigm, 97-130; ethnic conflict, indigenismo and functionalism, 42-6; historical structuralism and fate of peasantry, 131-77; paradigms, importance of, 2-5, 178-91 *passim*; particularism, Marxism and functionalism, 8-41
anthropology and knowledge, redistribution of, 119-20
anti-incorporationist indigenismo, 14-16, 117, 182-3
anti-Marxism, 73
anti-surplus system, 87
applied anthropology, formalism in, 29-32
archaeology, 11
Argentina, 106
Arizpe, Lourdes, 167-9, 171
articulated modes of production, 136-46
asiatic mode of production, 83-5, 133-4
Autonomous Department of Indian Affairs, 15, 18

backwardness concept, 9-10, 12, 182-3
Balandier, Georges, 101-3, 114, 129
Balibar, E., 134
Baran, Paul, 100
Baraona, Rafael, 211 (58)
Barbosa, Reni, 211 (62)
Barnes, J. A., 89
Barraclough, Solon, 211 (58), 211 (60)
Barth, Fredrik, 68-9
Bartra, Roger, 133-65 *passim*; on exploitation of peasantry, 151-4
Basauri, Carlos, 19
Beals, Ralph, 19, 23, 27-32, 36-7, 195 (39), 196 (69)
Biersted, Robert, 196 (50)
Blaffer, Sarah, 200 (39)
Boas, Franz, 9-10, 14, 93, 95, 181
Bonfil, Guillermo, 116-20, 130, 162, 170, 174, 209 (41, 43), 211 (57)
Brand, Donald, 32
Brazil, 106
Bricker, Victoria, 200 (39)
broker concept, 90
Bureau of Indian Affairs, 40, 48, 57
Burma, 64
Butterworth, Douglas, 215 (48)
Buve, Raymond, 212 (66)

caciquismo, 31-2, 90
Calles, P. E., 142
Camara, Fernando, 75, 196 (69)
campesinismo, 156-64, 160-2, 164, 183
Cancian, Francesca, 200 (39)
Cancian, Frank, 60-3, 189
capital, exploitation of peasant labor by, 151-4
capitalism, 65, 68, 97-100, 109, 130; as culture, 93; modes of production, 136-9, 146-51; state, 165
Carapan, 15

Cárdenas, Lázaro, 16-17, 34, 47, 117, 174
Cardoso, Fernando Henrique, 100, 104, 186
cargo system, 62
Carnegie Foundation, see Yucatán Project
Carroll, Thomas, 211 (58)
Caso, Alfonso, 27, 40, 46, 49, 57
caste, see class
Center for Agrarian Research, 123-5, 128
Center for Higher Studies of National Institute for Anthropology and History, 161-2, 165
Chamula, 58-61, 116
Chan Kom, 20-1, 24, 26
change, cultural, 22-7, 43
Chávez Orozco, Luis, 16-18
Chayanov, A. V., 86-7, 131, 135, 168
Cherán, 30-1
Chiapas highlands, 39-40, 49, 57-60, 63-7, 69, 114, 145
Chicago School, 44
Chichen Itzá, 24
Childe, Gordon, 81, 133
Chile, 106
circulationist argument, see Marxism, revisionist
city, see urban
civil-religious hierarchy, 55, 60-3
class and caste, 8; action and peasantry, 154-6; analysis, 137; distinguishing, 170-2; in ethnic relations, 113-16, 170-2; system, 89; subordinate, peasantry as, 146-9
Cline, Howard, 196 (69)
closed corporate community, 73-8
coalitions, 88-91
Coello, Manuel, 212 (4)
Colby, Benjamin, 67-9
Collier, George, 67, 198 (22)
colonial: past, metropolis-satellite relations in isolated reducts of, 50-2; situation in dependency paradigm, 101-4, 112-13
Comas, Juan, 19
Commission for Rural Development, 157
communication, 90
Communist Party, 177
community: closed corporate, 73-8; development, 11-12, 55, 95

compradrazgo, 90
CONASUPO, see National Commission for Popular Subsistence
Confederation of Mexican Workers, 17
conflict, 39; ethnic (1950-70), 42-69, 197-202; social and psychological dimensions of, 35-9
Coordinating Office for Marginal Areas, 175
COPIDER, see Commission for Rural etc.
COPLAMAR, see Coordinating Office etc.
Corcuera Garza, A., 214 (45)
corporate community, closed, 73-8
Coser, L., 66
crisis, symptoms of, in functionalism, 39-41
cultural differentiation, 64
cultural diversity, 116-19
cultural ecology, 6, 178-91 passim; campesinismo, alternative form of, 160-2; development of, 71-3; functionalism and, 71; Marxism and development of theory of peasantry (1950-70), 70-96, 202-6; modes of production, 162-5
Cultural Missions, 14
cultural pluralism, 16-19, 22
culturalism, 174, 184
culture: areas, 11, 179; change, 22-7, 43; concept of, 20-1, 172-4

de la Fuente, Julio, 35, 44-9, 51, 67, 69, 112, 116, 187, 196 (69)
de la Peña, Moisés, 49
de la Peña, Sergio, 145, 208 (23)
decolonization of ethnic relations, 116-19
defence, 74-5
Department of Popular Culture, 118
dependentismo, 6, 178-91 passim; anthropology and (1960-75), 97-130, 206-12; concept of, 98-101; in colonial situation, 101-4; contradictory currents within, 128-30; cultural diversity and, 116-19; and indigenismo, 111-16; probabilistic, 129-30
descampesinistas, 156-8, 183
Dewey, John, 14
Díaz, May, 196 (48)

Index

Díaz, Porfirio, 8, 10
Díaz Polanco, Héctor, 147, 173, 212 (4)
differential rent, 149-51
differentiation, cultural, 64
diffusion, *see* acculturation
diffusion of innovation, 61
disadvantaged, *see* marginality
disorganization after urban contact, 25
diversity, cultural, 116-19
Dobb, Maurice, 207 (18)
domain and surplus concepts, 83-5
domestic mode of production, 85-8
Domike, Arthur, 211 (60)
domination: mechanisms of, 83-5; regional and ethnic stereotypes, 46-8
dual societies, 47, 97, 105
Durán, Marco Antonio, 210 (50)
Durkheim, E., 21
dyadic contract, 88-91
Dzitas, 24

Echeverría, Luis, 117, 174
Eckstein, Salomón, 211 (62)
ECLA, *see* Economic Commission for Latin America
ecology, *see* cultural ecology
Economic Commission for Latin America, 98-101, 123
economic: development, 12, 19, 61-2, 66, 99-100; view of postrevolutionary countryside, 125-8
education, 12, 14-15, 18, 33, 43, 56
Engels, F., 132
Escuela de Arquelogí a y Etnografía, 9
Esteva, Gustavo, 157
ethnic relations: class and caste in, 113-16, 170-2; conflict, indigenismo and functionalism, 42-69, 197-202; decolonization of, 116-19; stereotypes and regional domination, 46-8
ethnicity concept, 171-2
ethnographic particularism, *see* particularism

Fabila, Alfonso, 19
families, urban roles in, 67-9
Fanon, F., 116
Favre, Henri, 170

Fernández y Fernández, Ramón, 210 (50)
Feder, Ernest, 211 (58), 212 (67), 214 (29)
Firth, Raymond, 89
FLACSO, *see* Latin American Faculty etc.
Florescano, Enrique, 208 (23), 211 (61)
folk: becomes peasantry, 78-80; communities, theoretical justification for study of, 19-22, 179; culture, 12, 20; -urban continuum, 22-7, 40, 77; *see also* peasantry
foreign colonists, 78
formalism in functionalism, 29-32
Foster, George, 27, 32-9, 88-91, 167, 189
Friedlander, Judith, 170
Friedrich, Paul, 195 (38), 210 (49)
friendship, 91
Fromm, Erich, 196 (65)
functionalism, 6, 178-91 *passim*; crisis in, symptoms of, 39-41; cultural ecology and, 71; culture change theories, 22-7; in formalism, 29-32; and indigenismo, dialogue on ethnic conflict, 42-69, 197-202; inter-ethnic relations, 63-9; and particularism and Marxism, 8-41, 192-7; structural, 19-22
Furnivall, J. S., 64
Furtado, Celso, 100

Gamio, Manuel, 10-15, 19-20, 24, 27-9, 33-6, 40, 44-6, 57, 182
Geertz, Clifford, 59, 88, 166, 200 (35)
Germani, Gino, 111
Gillin, John, 196 (69)
Glantz, Susana, 211 (62)
Gluckman, Max, 66-8, 101
Godelier, M., 133-4, 204 (42)
Goldkind, Victor, 193 (17)
Gómez Tagle, Silvia, 211 (62)
González Casanova, Pablo, 186; dependency, 112-13; exploitative mechanisms, 104-7; marginality, 107-11; political impotence of peasantry, 128
good, limited, image of, 32-5
Gordillo, Gustavo, 213 (27)
Gouldner, Alvin, 80
Guatemala, 67, 86

Guerrero, 137
Guiteras Holmes, Calixta, 194 (28), 195 (39), 196 (69)
Gunder Frank, André, 104-7, 110, 112
Gurvitch, Georges, 105
Gutelman, M., 135

hacienda system, 12-13, 74, 76, 78, 83
Hallowell, Irving, 48
harmony, social, 21
Harris, Marvin, 45, 82
Harvard Chiapas Project, see Chiapas
Helms, June, 196 (69)
Herskovitz, Melville, 48
hierarchy, civil-religious, 55, 60-3
historical structuralism, 6, 178-91 passim; and fate of peasantry, 131-77, 212-16; and public policy, 174-7; see also cultural ecology; dependentismo; Marxism
Hobson, John, 99
household, peasant, 85-8
Hueyapan, 170-1
Huizer, Gerrit, 211 (56)

Iberoamerican University, 93, 161
ICAD, see Inter-American Committee etc.
III, see Interamerican Indian Institute
ILPES, see Latin American Institute etc.
image of limited good, 32-5
INAH, see National Institute of Anthropology
incorporation, 10-13, 94
Index of Acculturation, 40
Indian Coalition, 117
Indian languages, 20
Indianness, 8, 40-2, 46-8, 170
indigenismo, 10-13, 178-91 passim; anti-incorporationist, 14-16; dependency and, 111-16; functionalism, 42-69, 197-202; modernization and, 17-18, 28; postwar problems, 52-4
individualism, 33, 90-1
individualization, 25
industrialism, 12, 66, 99-100
inefficiency within modes of production, 139-41
INI, see National Indian Institute
innovation, diffusion of, 61
integration, 8-19; pilot projects for regional, 48-50; sociocultural, 71-3, 180
Inter-American Committee for Agricultural Development, 123, 125-8, 137-9, 175, 187
Inter-American Development Bank, 123
Interamerican Indian conferences, 45, 48
Interamerican Indian Institute, 28, 35
interethnic relations, see ethnic
internal colonies, 111-13
investment, state, 158-60
involution, 88, 165-7
isolation, 16, 19
Ixil, 67

Jiménez Moreno, Wigberto, 19, 196 (69)

Kemper, Robert, 167
Kelly, Isabel, 196 (69)
kinship, 91
Kirchhoff, Paul, 196 (69), 206 (74)
knowledge, redistribution of, 119-20
Kroeber, Alfred, 20-1, 29, 78
Kuhn, Thomas, 2-4, 179
Kunkel, John, 206 (72)

labor: exploitation, 151-4; theory of value, 138
Lacandones, 40, 72
ladino, 40
land: control over, 75; holding size, 126; importance of, 132; struggle for, 154-6
Landsberger, Henry, 211 (62)
languages, 18, 20, 24, 58
latifundia, 62
Latin American Faculty of Social Sciences, 105
Latin American Institute for Socioeconomic Planning, 101, 123, 207 (16)
Leach, Edmund, 66
Lenin, V. I., and Leninism, 181; dependency, 98-9, 127; historical structuralism, 132, 137-47 passim, 161-3, 165; national self-determination, 17
Lévi-Strauss, Claude, 103
Lewis, Oscar, 27, 35-40, 50, 71, 115, 167, 186, 189
liberal reinterpretation of ethnographic

Index

particularism, 10-13
limited good, image of, 32-5
Lombardo Toledano, Vicente, 16-19, 32, 117
Lopez Mateos, A., 142
Lopez Zamora, Emilio, 210 (50)
Luxemburg, Rosa, 99, 131, 135, 164

Maccoby, Michael, 196 (65)
macrosociological and macroeconomic view of postrevolutionary countryside, 125-8
Maine, H., 23
Malinowski, Bronislaw, 21, 29, 44-6, 187
Manchester School, 101
marginality, 107-11
Margolies, Barbara, 215 (59)
Margulis, Mario, 213 (8), 215 (50)
Marroquín, Alejandro, 198 (21)
Martínez, Marielle P. L. de, 215 (50)
Martínez, Pedro, 39
Marx, Karl and Marxism: cultural ecology and theory of peasantry, 70-96, 202-6; dependency, 97-110, 122, 127, 129; *Grundrisse*, 81, 133; historical structuralism, 131-77 *passim*; indigenismo and functionalism, 43, 47, 50; orthodox, 6, 93, 131-77 *passim*, 188, 190; particularism and functionalism, 8-41, 192-7; pluralism, 16-19; revisionism, 6, 131, 134, 146-9, 154, 188
Masterman, Margaret, 3
Maturana, Sergio, 211 (62)
Maya language, 24, 58
Mayo, 29
Mazahua, 118, 168-9, 171
Mazatecs, 49
McQuown, Norman, 200 (47)
medical services, 12, 14, 43, 56
Meillasoux, Claude, 76, 147, 153
Melville, Roberto, 214 (45)
Mendieta y Núñez, Lucio, 19, 27, 121-2, 125
mercantile domain, 83
Mérida, 24
Merton, Robert, 66
Mesa Andraca, Manuel, 210 (50)
mestizos, 8, 40, 47, 78, 171, 178; Indianness as invention of, 46-8; interdependence with Indians, 75-6; as intermediaries, 56; satellite communities and, 54-7
methodological individualism, 90-1
Metropolitan University, 161
metropolis-satellite relations, 50-2, 104-7; *see also* urban
Mexican Food System, 175
Mexican Revolution, 8, 50, 77, 159, 166
Mexico, *see* anthropological perspectives
Mexico City, 38, 167, 169
Mezquital Valley, 137, 153
Michoacán, 32, 137, 153
Migdal, Joel, 206 (72)
migration, 67-9
Mills, C. Wright, 102, 207 (18)
Miner, Horace, 203 (27)
minifundia, 62, 126
Ministry of Agriculture, 10-11, 13-14
Ministry of Education, 13-14
Mintz, S., 124
Mixe, 29
modernization, 8-41 *passim*, 54, 60-3
modes of production: articulated, 136-46; asiatic, 83-5, 133-4; capitalist, 136-9, 146-51; cultural ecology and, 162-5; domestic, 85-8; exploitation and, 139-41; inefficiency in, 139-41; noncapitalist, 135-9; precapitalist, 133-6; secondary, 141-2
Molina Enriquez, Andrés, 192 (1)
Montes de Oca, Rosa Elena, 213 (27)
Moone, Janet, 206 (72)
Morelos, 165-7
Morgan, Lewis, 73
Morley, Sylvanus, 24
Myrdal, Gunnar, 102

Nahua, 44, 118
Nash, Manning, 64-8, 200 (44)
National Commission for Popular Subsistence, 157, 175
national culture, 71-2
National Indian Institute (earlier Bureau of Indian Affairs), 45, 48-50, 54, 56-9, 118, 174
National Institute for Anthropology and History, 45-6, 95, 161-2, 165
National Peasant Confederation, 117
National Polytechnic Institute, 28
National School of Anthropology, 28, 32, 123

National Science Foundation, 58
national self-determination, 17
National Sociological Congress, 121
national unity, 32-5
National University, 27, 121
negative: identity, 170; view of rural life, 12, 33
Nelson, Cynthia, 196 (48)
Nolasco, Margarita, 209 (41), 211 (57)
non-capitalist modes of production, 135-9
Nun, José, 208 (30)

Oaxaca area, 29, 45-6
Obrégon, A., 142
Ogburn, C., 111
open peasant communities, 77
Organization of American States, 123-4
Oswald, Ursula, 212 (67)
Othón de Mendizábal, Miguel, 19, 210 (49)
overdevelopment, 127

Palerm, Angel, 88, 92-3, 95, 124, 130, 133, 162-5, 172, 186; on asiatic mode of production, 83-5
Panajachel, 86
paradigms, 2-5, 178-91 *passim*; *see also* cultural ecology; dependentismo; functionalism; historical structuralism; indigenismo; Marxism; particularism
Paré, Luisa, 151-4, 158
Park, Robert, 185
Parsons, Elsie Clews, 193 (19)
Parsons, Talcott, 26
particularism, ethnographic, 6, 178-91 *passim*; liberal reinterpretation of, 10-13; and Marxism and functionalism, 8-41, 192-7
patrimonial domain, 83
patron-client relations, 91
Pátzcuaro, 33, 45
Pearse, Andrew, 198 (22), 211 (59)
peasantry: adaptive strategy, 165-7, 172; capital, exploitation by, 151-4; and class action, 154-6; concept of, 146-9, 186; cultural ecology and, 162-5; fate of, and historical structuralism, 131-77, 212-16; folk becomes, 78-80; future, 156-8; household, economic behaviour, 85-8; political subordination of, 141-2; social organization, 88-91; state and, 158-60; theory of, 70-96, 202-6; types of, 78; urban roles, 67-9, 186; utility of, 149-51; *see also* exploitation
Pitt-Rivers, Julian, 69, 168, 200 (47)
Plancarte, Francisco, 49
pluralism, 16-19, 22, 63-9
Polanyi, Karl, 93
policy, public, 174-7
political: behaviour, 132; organization, 118; process, 30-1, 33, 36-7; subordination, 141-2
polyadic coalitions, 89, 91
Popoluca, 86
postrevolutionary period, 125-8
postwar problems, 52-4
poverty, 182
power in communities, 30-1, 33, 36-7
Pozas, Ricardo, 59, 75, 116, 122, 200 (40)
pre-capitalist modes of production, 133-6
prebendal domain, 83
Prebisch, Paul, 99
Preobrazensky, E. A., 131
probabilistic dependentistas, 129-30
production, *see* modes of production
progress, 182
psychological: dimensions of conflict, 35-9; requisites of national unity, 32-5; testing, 36, 38
Puebla, 12, 153
Puerto Rico, 71, 186
puzzle-solving, 2, 179

quantification of rural marginality, 107-9
Quijano, Aníbal, 100, 208 (30)

Radcliffe-Brown, Alfred, 21, 45, 186, 193 (16)
Redfield, Robert, 19-39 *passim*, 45, 49, 72, 75, 80, 179, 181-8, 196 (69), 201 (55), 202 (3), 205 (60)
reform, agrarian, 120-3
refuge regions, 50-2, 70, 111-13
Regional Coordinating Centers, 54-7
regional integration, pilot projects for, 48-50
religious hierarchy, civil-, 55, 60-3

Index

Rello, Fernando, 213 (11)
Rendón, Teresa, 215 (50)
rent, 83; differential, 149-51
rented land, 61-2
research limits, Marxism and cultural ecology, 91-6
resiliency, 129
resistance to change, 43
Restrepo, Iván, 211 (62)
Reyes Osorio, Sergio, 125, 128
Rhodes, Robert, 203 (19)
ritual coparenthood, 90
roads, 61
Roberts, Bryan, 216 (2)
Rojas González, Francisco, 210 (53)
Romanucci-Ross, Lola, 196 (48)
Ronfeldt, David, 212 (66)
Rubín de la Borbolla, Daniel, 30, 32, 35
rural areas, agrarian problems, 8, 120-5; agricultural involution, 165-7; marginality, 107-9; -urban contact and interdependence, 22-7, 40, 71, 81; see also metropolis; urban
Rus, Jan, 199 (26)

Sáenz, Moisés, 14-16, 18-19, 28, 116-17, 183
Sahlins, Marshall, 86
Salamini, Heather Fowler, 212 (66)
SAM, see Mexican Food System
San Cristóbal de las Casas, 49, 61, 63, 69
Sánchez, José, 211 (62)
satellite: communication, 54-7; -metropolis relations, 104-7
Schryer, Frans, 212 (66)
Schweder, Richard, 200 (39)
science, 179
secularization, 25
self: determination, national, 17; exploitation, 87-8
semi-proletariat, 154
Semo, Enrique, 208 (23)
Senior, Clarence, 210 (50)
sharecropping, 83
shifting cultivators, 78
Silva Herzog, Jesús, 210 (50)
Simmel, G., 66
Simpson, Eyler, 210 (50)
Siverts, Henning, 68-9
Smith, T. Lynn, 210 (55)
social: organization of peasantry, 88-91; and psychological dimensions of conflict, 35-9
Solari, Aldo, 207 (16)
Sonora, 29
Spanish: Conquest, 50, 74; language, 18
state and peasantry, 158-60, 165
Stavenhagen, Rodolfo, 130, 162, 170, 173-4, 186; class and caste, interethnic relations, 113-16; decolonization of ethnic relations, 117-18, 120; ICAD studies, 125; rural bourgeoisie, 128, 207 (18), 208 (30), 209 (34), 212 (7)
stereotypes, ethnic, 46-8
Steward, Julian, 29, 32, 71-4, 78, 81, 83-4, 89, 180, 186
structural functionalism, see functionalism
structuralism, see historical structuralism
subordination of peasantry, political, 141-2
subsistence agriculture, 85-6
Summer Language Institute, 18
surpluses, 83-5, 87
Sweezy, Paul, 100

Talavera pottery technique, 12
Tannenbaum, Frank, 202 (13)
Tantoyuca, 48-9
Tarahumara, 49
Tarascan area, 15, 30-3, 49, 72, 118
Tax, Sol, 27-9, 44, 49, 59, 65-6, 68, 75, 86, 193 (18), 194 (32), 196 (69)
Teotihuacan, 11-12, 27
Tepoztlán, 12, 189; Lewis in, 35-9, 186-7; Redfield in, 20, 22
Terray, E., 76
time and sociology paradigms, 4-5
Townsend, William, 18
Tumin, Melvin, 198 (10)
Tusik, 24
Tylor, E., 21
Tzeltal, 58, 64
Tzintzuntzan, 33-4, 36, 38-9, 91, 167, 189
Tzotzil, 39, 58-9, 64

underdevelopment, 127
UNESCO, 105

United Nations: Economic Commission for Latin America, 98-101, 123; Food and Agriculture Organization, 123; Latin American Institute for Socioeconomic Planning, 101, 123
United States, 23, 31, 35
unity, national, 32-5
urban: dimension, folk-, 40, 77; elites, 80; exploitation, 79; -folk continuum, 22-7, 40, 77; power, 176; roles of peasants, 67-9, 186; -rural interdependence, 71, 81; seniorial city, 51; *see also* metropolis; rural

value, labor theory of, 138
van den Berghe, Pierre, 67-8
van Zantwijk, R. A. M., 199 (31)
Vasconcelos, José, 13, 15, 192
Venezuela, 137
Veracruz, 48-9, 86
Vergopoulos, Kostas, 147
Viking Fund Seminar, 39-41
Villa Rojas, Alfonso, 19-20, 24, 28, 49, 75, 196 (69)
Vogt, Evon, 57-9, 64
Warman, Arturo, 130, 158-67, 177, 209 (41), 209 (43)
wartime unity, 32-5
Wasserstrom, Robert, 145, 199 (26)
Weber, Max, 81, 83-4
Weitlaner, Roberto, 19
Wenner-Gren Foundation, 39
Whetten, Nathan, 40, 109, 196 (69), 210 (50)
White, Leslie, 81
Wilkie, Raymond, 210 (49)
Wittfogel, Karl, 81, 84, 131
Wolf, Eric, xiii, 50, 71-94 *passim*, 133, 180; asiatic mode of production, 83-5; capitalist penetration, 115-16; closed corporate community, 73-8; coalitions, 88-91; domain and surplus concepts, 83-5; haciendas and latifundias, 124
women, changing place of, 67-9
Woodbridge, Margaret de Forest, 210 (51)
world view, 2, 26; *see also* paradigms

Yaqui, 29
Yucatán Project, 21, 25, 30, 38, 58

Zinacantan, 58-63, 67, 189

For Product Safety Concerns and Information please contact our EU representative GPSR@taylorandfrancis.com
Taylor & Francis Verlag GmbH, Kaufingerstraße 24, 80331 München, Germany

www.ingramcontent.com/pod-product-compliance
Lightning Source LLC
Chambersburg PA
CBHW071830300426
44116CB00009B/1497